DATE DUE

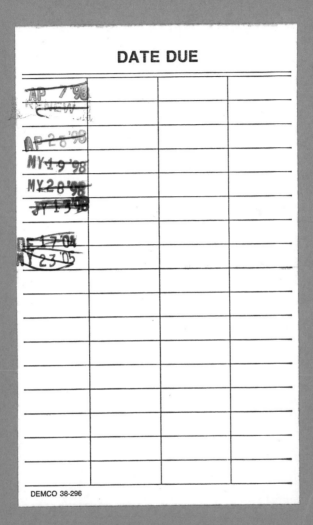

AP 7 '98 RENEW			
AP 28 '98			
MY 19 '98			
MY 28 '98			
JY 13 '98			
DE 17 04			
MY 23 05			

DEMCO 38-296

D. Keith Denton

ENVIRO-MANAGEMENT

HOW SMART COMPANIES TURN ENVIRONMENTAL COSTS INTO PROFITS

PRENTICE HALL
Englewood Cliffs, New Jersey 07632

K) Limited, London
. Limited, Sydney
ɔronto
Prentice-Hall Hispanoamericana, S.A., Mexico
Prentice-Hall of India Private Limited, New Delhi
Prentice-Hall of Japan, Inc., London
Simon & Schuster Asia Pte. Ltd., Singapore
Editora Prentice-Hall do Brasil, Ltda., Rio de Janerio

10 9 8 7 6 5 4 3 2 1

Library of Congress Cataloging-in-Publication Data

Denton, D. Keith
    Enviro-management: how smart companies turn environmental costs into profits / D.
Keith Denton
        p.   cm.
    Includes index.
    ISBN 0-13-073503-5
    1. Industrial management—Environmental aspects—Cost
effectiveness. 2. Environmental protection—Cost effectiveness.
3. Corporate profits. I. Title.
HD69.P6D46   1994
658.4'08—dc20   94-12332
                                                                    CIP

ISBN 0-13-073503-5

PRENTICE HALL
CAREER & PERSONAL DEVELOPMENT
A division of Simon & Schuster
Englewood Cliffs, New Jersey 07632

Printed in the United States of America

ABOUT THE BOOK

Some people believe environment issues are a curse on business. Some people believe that when it comes to the environment, it simply is the right thing to do. Both are wrong! *Enviromanagement: How Smart Companies Turn Environmental Costs Into Profits* shows that the environment is not a cost—it can be an asset. In the 1990s environment management is not something that we should do. It is not the ethical thing to do. It is the *only* thing to do if we are to maintain a competitive advantage. Environmental issues are no more a fad than quality was in the 1980s. It is a strategic advantage; it is a series of operational initiatives that enhance competitiveness.

This book is no theory; it is not speculation—it is fact. It documents how some of the most innovative and far-sighted companies in the world are turning environmental considerations into a competitive edge. This is not a book about possibilities, it is about certainties. Unless we incorporate environmental decision-making into routine managerial and employee activities, we are likely to lose perhaps the last competitive battleground. Signs of an ever-quickening recognition of the strategic advantages of good environmental management are everywhere.

According to conservative estimates, American companies are producing five times as much waste per dollar of revenue as their Japanese counterparts, and double the level of Germany. The book notes other cases where it appears American companies may be behind the competitive curve, but it does not have to be that way. There are notable American exceptions including 3M's Pollution Prevention Pays (3P) program that has saved the company over $400 million since its inception in 1975.

We will examine how others are also seizing the opportunity. It documents how Dow Chemical, Allied-Signal, Chrysler, UpJohn, Quad/Graphics, ARCO and others are on the cutting edge of being able to turn the environment into something more than simply a marketing strategy.

The book focuses on both strategic issues and how-to-do-it, by first showing why the environment should be thought of as a profit center. We will then look at sources of these environment profits including going from pollution control, to pollution prevention, and finally to pollution management. We will examine how to do environmental auditing, energy conservation, waste management and much more.

The last section of the book develops a more integrated system for better environmental management. This includes the need to develop a new Systematic Environmental Management (SEM). Through the "Pollution Wheel" we will look at how to turn piecemeal pollution management into a comprehensive and competitive approach. It will show you what is required to turn pollution management into profits and give you a way of discovering where you are at in your pollution efforts and highlight what is needed to go from compliance to competitive costing to profit making. The book also contains a self administered questionnaire that allows you the chance to plot a pollution wheel for your company. When you do it, you then will know what pieces are needed to turn your pollution efforts around and go from cost control to profit making.

ACKNOWLEDGMENTS

Writing a book is always a team effort, but some deserve special recognition. The book would not have been possible without Lynn Grable's word processing and patience. I am also indebted to Becky Niehoff for her copyediting and suggestions. Both greatly improved the quality of the book. Finally, I appreciate Tom Power's support and faith in the project.

Dedicated to my son, Shane

CONTENTS

PROFITING FROM BETTER POLLUTION MANAGEMENT *1*

THE ENVIRONMENT AS A COMPETITIVE WEAPON *11*

ENVIRONMENTAL COSTING: REDEFINING THE RULES *19*

MEET YOUR "GREEN" CUSTOMERS *33*

Your Customers' Environmental Desires/34   Profit Potential of Pollution Control/36   The Environmental Factor/38   The Power of Green Marketing/39   Unethical Marketing Claims/45 Certifying Ethical Claims/46   Think Global, Think Green!/47 Closing Thoughts/49

CONDUCTING AN ENVIRONMENTAL ASSURANCE SURVEY *53*

Environmental Assurance/54   Elements of a Successful Program/54 Preassurance Activities/55   Assurance Activities/56   Postassurance Activities/57   Closing Thoughts/58

USING WASTE REDUCTION AS A COMPETITIVE ADVANTAGE *59*

Dow Chemical's WRAP/59 Developing a Language of Measurement/60   Success Stories/62   The Role of Technology/63 The Role of People/63   Corporate Environmentalism/64   Closing Thoughts/65

GUIDELINES FOR PREVENTING POLLUTION *67*

THE ENERGY FACTOR *87*

A MONEY-MAKING MODEL—SEM *97*

MOVING TO EMPOWERED POLLUTION MANAGEMENT *129*

MAKING SURE ENVIRONMENTAL POLICIES MEASURE UP! *145*

THE POWER OF EMPLOYEE INVOLVEMENT *153*

PROBLEM-SOLVING TOOLS FOR CONTINUAL IMPROVEMENT *165*

How to Do It/168   Benchmarking/168   Cause-and-Effect Diagram /169   Check Sheet/170   Flip Chart/171   Histogram/171   Pareto Chart/172   Run Chart/Control Chart/174   Scatter Diagram/175 Flow Chart/175   Closing Thoughts/175

WHERE DO WE GO FROM HERE? *179*

Legal Risks/180   Source Reduction Ideas/181   Eliminating the Source of Pollution/182   Creating the Need for Change/184 Accounting for Internal Cost/185   Developing a Comprehensive Financial Analysis/186   Prioritizing Pollution Efforts/188   Allocating Costs and Benefits Stages/189   Assessing True Cost/191   An Alternative Approach to Pollution Costing/191   Closing Thoughts/194

Appendix A

SUMMARY OF FTC ENVIRONMENTAL MARKETING GUIDELINES *197*

Background/197   General Concerns/198   Guides for the Use of Environmental Marketing Claims/201   Table of Contents/202 Statement of Purpose/203   Scope of Guides/203   Structure of the Guides/203   Review Procedure/204   Interpretation and Substantiation of Environmental Marketing Claims/204   General Principles/205 Environmental Marketing Claims/207

Appendix B

EPA GREEN LIGHTS PROGRAM *219*

1

PROFITING FROM BETTER POLLUTION MANAGEMENT

Recently when I was making a presentation overseas I remarked to the seminar organizer that I was working on a new book, *Enviro-Management*. Her response was a subdued, "Oh, well—we've already done that." She went on to point out, "Everyone's already done that! They've already got their Environmental Managers." She felt, as a so called "hot button," environmental management's time had passed because everyone (i.e., potential clients) had already made the changes they were going to make, such as hiring an Environmental Manager to oversee corporate concerns, for instance. She then asked if I was doing anything on learning organizations or entrepreneurship.

What I did not tell her was that she had missed the point. To truly turn environmental green into monetary green you've got to do more than hire environmental managers. The process cannot occur by simply creating a new job title for someone, nor by publicizing the new corporate recycling program. The best bet is that this attitude will create a lot of heat but little change.

Let me make one point very clear. This book will show you how to be more competitive using better environmental management. It is not a "cookbook" of the 10 best waste reducing ideas, or the seven best energy conservation approaches. It will show you how to make money through better pollution management. Do not assume pollution control is an overhead liability; you can use it as a means to create a more effective organization. Pollution management can be profitable, but it cannot occur if it's approached in a piecemeal manner. Any new procedure demands coordination. When there is no theory, or structure, there can be no change, only movement. This book provides a three-stage process for going from compliance to cost reduction to finally using pollution management as a revenue generator.

All too often as managers we are interested in what is different. We all seem to want something new and bright. Looking for the "magic bullet" is the hope of anyone who's feeling the pressure and wants a cure for what ails the organization. At least we managers are not alone; everyone, it seems, wants to hear something different.

In doing research for the book, one specialist involved in the environmental information dispensing area noted, "Don't talk about those companies whose efforts (environmental) are well-documented." Companies like DuPont, 3M, and Dow Chemical were on his lips. His point was that his specialist friends, involved in the environmental movement, would be bored if I documented the same old stories well known by him and his colleagues. He assumed that if he knew of something, it must be common knowledge. No, I thought. I knew I was a regular guy, not one of this group of intelligent, somewhat detached, specialists who doesn't understand the managerial "mindset." So he didn't "get it." I also knew as a teacher that it is not so much what you say, but how you say it that is important.

WHY CARE ABOUT ENVIRONMENTAL MANAGEMENT?

The previous comments, the one about the seminar and the other by the specialist, for me galvanized the reason for writing this book. It would be a serious mistake to think that just because you have assigned responsibility and created programs that somehow "environmental concerns" have been addressed. It would also be just as serious a mistake to think that once you've heard of a company's success, that somehow, it is enough. Most new techniques and approaches fail to achieve what is expected because they are not properly implemented or understood.

This book is written for people with managerial responsibilities. It is for those who couldn't (up to now) care less about environmental management. Oh, they know they should recycle. Their kids, the TV, and most everyone else seems to be into the environmental movement. The trouble is, environmental management does not pay corporate bills. When promotions occur, when budgets are drawn up, and when the board of directors wants to know about dividends and when push comes to shove, who's really thinking about the environment? The answer is no one, but here's the key point of the book: *they had better be if they want to capture market share and profits.* In fact, if they don't care they will probably miss *the* competitive advantage of the 90s and beyond.

Environmental management can even be the key corporate unifying factor, not profits, not quality, and not the customer, because it is a bigger concept. It can hold the power to draw people together, to unify them. It can also make you a lot of money if it's integrated properly.

Knowledge Is Useless

Environmental management needs to be a key concept for any competitive strategy, but it isn't, in part because of environmental engineers and specialists. You see, they share part of the blame because what many do not understand is that information without access is useless.

People who are always looking for the next hot button must also share some of the responsibility. They, as well as the specialists, do not seem to appreciate that there is value in "old" information, especially if someone has not heard it. There is a great deal of new information in this book so the specialist and hot-button types will enjoy it. But the real focus is on teaching. What we need are teachers of old information, as well as researchers, expanding new information. If facts are not explained in an interesting way, we lose interest. I think the nonexpert will find this book both informative and enjoyable.

This book is written for managers, owners, shareholders, and in this age of team management, any who have managerial responsibilities. It is not about saving the whales, it's about saving the bottom line through more effective environmental management. It's about how to do it, not should we do it. It's not about recycling or about the need to hire environmental managers—though they have their place.

The book is about using an environmental focus to reshape the way to do business. It's about getting rid of wrong, wasteful, and even dangerous assumptions about the environment, and its impact on business. One of the wrong assumptions is that environmental concerns are a cost burden or that it's the price of doing business in the 90s. Waste can be a resource and you can enhance not only your reputation, but your competitive position through more efficient management of environmental resources.

When you challenge your assumptions, remarkable things can occur. One company, Unocal, proves this point. The Los Angeles based company executives were frustrated with the high cost of pollution and the so called "non-point" cause of much of it. To prove that there were other options they went out and spent six million dollars to buy and then junk 8,376 pre-1971 autos for about $5,700 each. Each of the cars was made before the advent of emission control and on average belched out 60 times the pollution of new autos.

Unocal efforts saved the L.A. basin from an annual 10.7 million pounds of smog-forming hydrocarbons and nitrous oxides, not to mention carbon monoxide. The company figures that to create the same pollution savings at its local refinery, which already has pollution controls, they would have to eliminate virtually all emissions at a cost of about $160 million.[1]

In another case, furniture maker Herman Miller knows all about assumptions. While some less innovative companies might assume all his company does is make new furniture, that is not the case for Miller. By challenging assumptions the company has taken others' waste and turned it into a profitable business. The thriving business is a secondhand furniture business, in which it buys back old furniture, refurbishes it and resells it. Thinking like this is one of the reasons why the company was able to reduce waste by 80% in 1993.[2]

CHALLENGING ENVIRONMENTAL ASSUMPTIONS

The book has three parts. First, we will look at *why* you need to start incorporating environmental factors into your day-to-day decisions. Some of this may be obvious, like the fact that our customers are demanding it. Other reasons may not be quite as obvious, such as the fact that environmental inefficiencies are creating competitive disadvantages similar to the ones that occur because of poorer quality products.

The 90s have seen continuing efforts to better define customer expectations and perceptions. First, it was cost, then quality became the issue of the 80s. Increasingly, our customers want the environment to play a major role in our offerings. In order to understand this "green factor" we need to continue to upgrade our understanding of our customers' needs. In chapter four we will document some of their attitudes toward green products. This same concerned attitude seems to be present when business deals with business.

A 1989 survey of 2,500 European business representatives found that 20% said the *most important* attribute they look for in a supplier is, "Care for the quality of the environment." If the percentage does not sound very impressive, consider the fact that environmental concerns ranked even higher than "value for money" which was cited by 17 percent as their first concern![3]

We will also identify our long-term as well as short-term customers. Short-term customers are the ones who buy our products and services. Long-term customers are an often overlooked resource, comprised of the community at large. Companies like Monsanto are redefining their understanding of who their customer is and using this knowledge to a competitive advantage.

Defining exactly why you should control pollution eventually comes down to a number. Throughout the book we will show how companies have turned environmental concerns into profitable ventures. Costing out true environmental cost is still an emerging science, but we will look at what we know about those costs and examine how you can get a better handle on what your true environmental costs are. The reason for this is simple. In business, if something does not have a number, it has no value. Through techniques like eco-balance sheets we will attempt to better define those numbers.

A PIECEMEAL APPROACH

The second section of the book shows what's involved in modern pollution control and management, and cites some famous, and not so famous, examples of what was once thought to be a problem. Many citations support pollution control as a profitable venture if the pieces of the pollution puzzle can be used to create opportunities.

The process for eliminating and reducing pollution are reviewed in the second section of the book. We will examine many operational procedures, processes and techniques that have proven to be effective ways to eliminate waste and conserve energy.

The book will also show you how companies are making money and reducing cost through better pollution management. Be careful, though, because without a plan it is a piecemeal affair. It *is* possible to make money, reduce cost, and increase competitiveness by better managing your environmental resources, but this does not always happen by simply hiring an environmental manager and starting a recycling program. If you use the waste reduction process described in this book you can go far beyond a "cookbook" approach and create a truly competitive advantage.

The Plan

The environmental techniques described in the middle section can be quite sexy, but don't be fooled. They cannot stand alone. They must be incorporated within some framework, some plan, or they cannot satisfy the bottom line. Total Quality Management (TQM), and quality tools, like Statistic Process Control (SPC), customer service, and inventory tools such as Just-In-Time (JIT) all share one common history. It is relatively easy to go to a seminar about some new "hot button" and get all excited. The trouble is, passion is not enough. When a disappointed and indistinct approach is used, trouble is sure to follow.

A survey of 200 CEOs showed the results of ill-planned changes. In the survey, 79 percent said their companies had a quality improvement program in place for more than a year. Of these respondents, 39 percent said they had seen little bottom line improvements, and 57 percent also felt money spent on seminars and classes yielded no direct financial results.[4]

It's a typical story because it is just as typical that about half to as much as 80 percent of new techniques do not live up to expectations of improved financial performance. It does not matter whether it has to do with employee involvement, team management, or even environmental management. The story is the same. If the techniques are not connected together, all the training in the world will not help.

A survey of over 100 managers from *Fortune* 500 companies highlights this problem. The survey noted that even simple techniques such as customer service can be important. The consulting firm of Roth and Strong, for example, found that 87 percent of their respondents believe delivering value to their customers is critical to their survival. More astonishing, though, was the fact that 70 percent said their corporate performance was driven more by *internal operating measures* than by key external customer service measures. Moreover, it was reported that a whopping 80 percent of all compensation for employees is not tied to customer satisfaction.[5] Is it any wonder we do not achieve what we hope we can?

That is why the last section of the book is designed to provide you with a roadmap to change. Changing your definition of who your customer is helps. Improving operational and design efficiency also helps. But that will not be enough unless you can engage the entire organization.

The book lays out a three-stage plan by first looking at each component or pieces, then ties them all together with a unifying factor so you can create not just passion, but performance.

POLLUTION MANAGEMENT

The days of dramatic leaps are gone. We live in an age where continuous improvement means incremental changes. A manager once asked me with some degree of frustration if this concept of continuous improvement would ever end. The answer is *no*! If you are going to compete you must be better than your competition at squeezing out tiny improvements—small, some would say insignificant improvements.

At one time we would never have worried about how good our products were. We would never have catered to the customer like many do today. We certainly would not be worried about an almost obsessive focus on, "good, better, best, never let it rest till your good is better and your better is best." If you let up on trying to maximize your resources, your competitors will run straight up your back.

You need only to improve continually in order to prosper. We will look at many ways to do just that. Focusing on operational inefficiencies will help. Changing your definition of who your customer really is can also make a difference. Certainly, challenging your assumptions about environmental management and its role in business success can be of value but it takes more than just this understanding. Innovative approaches, like the ones we will look at, would never have occurred unless individuals and companies had not challenged worn-out, rigid thinking. Simply, you must have a plan in order to be successful.

Success requires a systematic and integrated effort aimed, like a laser beam, at improving managerial practices. "Do it right the first time" is not just an old quality proverb, it is a call to arms for managing pollution. For example, one outcome of pollution prevention is often the realization that raw materials are being squandered unnecessarily. In 1988, Richard Mahoney, chief executive of Monsanto, committed the company to reducing air emissions of toxic chemicals from Monsanto plants worldwide by 90 percent by the end of 1992. At the time he calculated that about $150 million worth of energy and raw materials annually do not end up in products, but is rather vented or discharged as waste. When executives at the company asked their chemists to reduce the volume of waste left over from the manufacture of its herbicide called Roundup™, scientists stumbled on a new formula that saved millions in raw materials. The new process also cut pollution by 80 percent while reducing cost 22 percent.[6] To maximize your resources you must have a clear perception of your customers' needs, understand how to meet them, and just as importantly not make *any* major mistakes along the way. It's not easy, but it can be done if you're logical about your approach.

A dysfunctional organization pollutes because its component areas are not connected in a logical manner. The result is we produce poor products, undervalued services, and untold operational inefficiencies. Highly efficient organizations have little or no waste. They understand their customers' needs and have close links between functions.

Poorly organized operations waste energy and resources. We know they create both physical and psychological waste. Different levels, different functions within an organization need to be on the same wavelength to be produceable, profitable, and to prevent pollution. Environmental management can provide the most comprehensive yardstick to date on measuring this efficiency or lack thereof.

In the last section we will show why it is a mistake to separate environmental concerns from organizational concerns. It is a new field, one I have named organizational design and pollution. It is truly new, and hot-button types will love it. The concept behind the name is that production people, accountants, marketers, designers and even environmental managers are only *part* of the pollution solution if their efforts are not integrated.

Turning pollution into profits is not an unduly complex or difficult undertaking, but it does require a multiperspective, multiexperience, and multiknowledge approach. Cross-training will be a big part of pollution-into-profits management.

IT TAKES MORE THAN RECYCLING

We will show that the key to turning pollution management into a profitable venture rests not with complying with environmental regulations, getting people to recycle, or simply reducing waste. It depends on a company's ability to restructure its decision making. Pollution management for profits must eventually involve a redesign not of products, but of decisions, so that psychological as well as physical waste and inefficiencies are eliminated.

It makes sense. The more disconnected and inefficient the decision-making, the greater the risk of errors, mistakes, and waste. Waste is more likely when there is layer upon layer of disjointed management. The more functional areas are isolated from the key decision process, the greater the risk of pollution. An environmental system includes managing all the pieces and includes your equipment, processes, procedures, and the employees who must work together.

Product and process development was challenging enough before we had to be concerned about the environment. There will still be a need for speed and competence, but now decision making needs to be more inclusive. Members of production and design teams will need to include environmental representatives. It would be even better if each department was truly knowledgeable about environmental concerns.

A big part of the pollution solution is to change the decision-making systems we use so that we can structurally empower people to prevent pollution. One example of changing decision making would be the use of the inventory control technique called Just-In-Time (JIT). In principle, JIT is supposed to "pull" inventory through the production system rather than "pushing" it as with traditional inventory systems such as (Economic Order Quantity). When a business uses JIT it helps reduce excess waste and inventory because the person upstream controls how much inventory is needed. Using these "internal customers" to control inventory is better because it is very difficult to ship the exact amount of materials if you push inventory. When you push inventory you are out of touch with your internal customers and it is difficult to know exactly what is needed. On the other hand, as a puller of inventory (JIT) it is you, the internal customer who decides exactly how much you need, not someone downstream pushing it on you. With little understanding of exactly what is needed, we are likely to order too much, order the wrong amounts, or otherwise mismatch production to inventory. Pollution to profits begins at the bottom and it begins with our internal customers.

There would be very little pollution or waste if we could turn 100 percent of our raw materials into 100 percent good products. If there are no extra raw materials, work-in-process, or useless finished goods and suppliers, then no production waste would be generated. Improved design and closing the loop on production are critical to a total elimination of pollution. Even small improvements help. If the techniques sound too difficult, remember, they do not all have to be implemented at once.

A good story of how a little inventory coordination and packaging can go a long way involved a hospital. A team project at this particular hospital included surgeons and nurses. One scrub nurse pointed out that many surgeons would only use one suture out of a package that contained six or more. The rest were discarded. This incidental point was not insignificant. There was substantial waste at the hospital since several types of sutures were used during surgical procedures. Because of the comment, surgeons changed the way they used sutures, and the purchasing department changed the way they bought them. Better procedures and inventory control of this one item saved the hospital $40,000 in one year alone.[7]

Good inventory control can be pollution control, but like other operational techniques, people must be trained to personally manage and assume responsibility for it. Like the surgeons and purchasing department in the above example, managers must be able to recognize when waste problems are occurring and solve them. Everyone must be responsible for inventory and pollution control. Employees, as well as managers, must assume ownership for pollution problems.

CLOSING THOUGHTS

You can make money from pollution efforts if, and only if, you integrate, and not procrastinate. As we will see, this begins by redefining the problem —once redefined, it is half-solved. You can make money if you change your assumptions, but it is going to take some rethinking about how your business is organized. For example, do you think it's possible to reorganize your company around pollution management rather than profits? We will examine how this can happen and, in some cases, is already happening.

The journey begins by looking at why you should bother with controlling pollution. Later on we will look at the various points of a solution. These "who's," "what's" and "where" it is occurring will be followed by the last section of the book that defends a strategy for doing it. We call this three-stage process *Systematic Environmental Management* (SEM). It's an approach that can be used to stay ahead of the competition to create a logical and integrated approach to empowering people and pollution control. There is even a test to find out how far along you are and what is needed to turn pollution management into your competitive advantage.

ENDNOTES

1. Boroughs, Don L., Betsy Carpenter, "Cleaning Up the Environment," *U.S. News and World Report*, March 25, 1991, p. 55.

2. Rice, Faye, "Who Scores the Best on the Environment," *Fortune*, Vol. 28, No. 2, July 26, 1993, p. 116.

3. Taravella, Steve, "Employee's Ideas and Efforts Can Make Hospital Environmental Programs Thrive," *Modern Healthcare*, February 24, 1992, p. 28.

4. "Lack of Confidence in Financial Benefits of Quality Programs," *Industrial Engineering*, Vol. 25, No. 6, June 1993, p. 12.

5. "Is the Customer King? Well, Yes in a Way," APICS—*The Performance Advantage*, Vol. 3, No. 6, June 1993, p. 15.

6. Boroughs, Don L., Betsy Carpenter, "Cleaning Up the Environment," *U.S. News and World Report*, March 25, 1991, p. 49.

7. Gardner, Elizabeth, "Teams Can Solve Environmental Quandaries," *Modern Healthcare*, February 24, 1992, p. 29.

2

THE ENVIRONMENT AS A COMPETITIVE WEAPON

If I told you that American business and the United States are suffering from a competitive disadvantage, you probably would not have any difficulty believing that environmental worries are a major cost burden. Perhaps you would believe that environmental protection is simply a major cost of doing business today and must be shouldered in order to set a good corporate standard.

The truth is that the environmental "problem" is a major disadvantage only if business sees it in terms of a cost issue rather than a competitive opportunity. The solution to a problem begins and ends with the definition of the problem. It is only the most innovative of companies that have recognized the relationship between the environment and profits.

False assumptions and poor definitions have created a perception that enhancing the environmental friendliness of a company's products and services will somehow be an overhead burden, like health care. Just as bad are those companies who will tell you that they are environmentally conscious because "it is the right thing to do." It is the profitable and competitive thing to do!

It is a story that has been repeated before; most recently in the area of quality. At one time people thought that there was a trade off between higher quality and lower costs. Today with TQM and a "focus on continuous improvement" we know these two concepts of quality and cost are not mutually exclusive.

Most companies will tell you of their high ethical standards when it comes to the environment. They will tell you of pollution control measures, but few understand or define the environment in terms of pollution prevention, and that is a mistake. Fewer still see the opportunities of revenue generation by better pollution management. In order to be competitive in the 1990s and beyond, we must begin to define the environment in terms of profit opportunity. It is not the kind of opportunity where we gouge the consumer, but one that comes from better managing the bottom line research and development and the corporation as a whole. When you better manage environmental issues, like quality, you enhance your competitive position. For most companies this remains an untapped concept—the environment as a cost advantage.

THE COMPETITIVE ADVANTAGE

One example of business' general lack of awareness of the enormous profit potential of environmental concerns involves energy efficiency. Currently, the United States consumes twice as much energy to produce a unit of GNP as Japan and Germany. Think about that—twice as much! As a result, American businesses are less competitive in the world marketplace. Some experts say more efficient use of energy gives Japanese and German products a five percent cost advantage over their American counterparts. In fact, the United States Environmental Protection Agency (EPA) points out that, when compared to Japan, the United States consumes roughly 60 percent more energy per dollar of national income.[1] Clearly, in energy consumption alone, there are environmental competitive advantages.

According to Worldwatch Institute, improved energy efficiency has the immediate potential to cut fossil fuel use at a rate of two percent annually in industrial countries. More importantly, this means a corresponding reduction in carbon dioxide.[2] While helping reduce carbon dioxide emissions may be the ethically correct thing to do to reduce greenhouse warnings, this may not impress those in the corporate board room. What would impress any stockholder is the means of making a business more profitable, and that is exactly what improved energy efficiency, along with other environmental solutions, can do.

For a start, this means focusing on pollution prevention and management rather than pollution control. Improving environmental effectiveness by preventing energy inefficiencies is as good a place to start as any. A business can begin by improving and purchasing devices that use electricity efficiently. These would include a host of electrical appliances and lighting devices as well as the building itself. In fact according to the EPA, with current technologies, electric motors can be made at least 40 percent more efficient, and items like refrigerators can be made over 75 percent more efficient.[1]

The transportation of goods and services is another area of opportunity. The EPA says that transportation emissions worldwide annually add more than 700 million tons of carbon to the atmosphere. Increasing the fuel efficiency of cars would not only lower carbon dioxide emissions, it would also lower fuel bills. In one study by the EPA, it was noted that if car fuel efficiency were doubled to 50 miles per gallon, this would not only reduce carbon dioxide emissions by half but, just as importantly, lower the annual gasoline fuel cost by almost $400. Such a savings would be of enormous competitive advantage for any business with significant transportation and fuel overhead costs.

POLLUTION PREVENTION PAYS

If this discussion sounds familiar so far, it might be because that is what others have told us to do about how we can improve quality—by looking through the eyes of our customers. The difference is that this time we are saying if you want to make the environment *pay off* for you, like quality has done for some companies and countries, then begin by finding out your customers' needs. Solve their environmental problems and you create your own environmental profits and opportunities.

One opportunity near and dear to many customers and one that many competitive companies are seizing upon is waste reduction. Corporations currently spend about $115 billion annually just to comply with federal regulations. If that is all the business does, then it is a cost. However, it would seem reasonable to believe that it would cost less to prevent pollution rather than clean up after it. As in other areas, prevention pays. One of the first companies to focus on prevention instead of control was 3M. They started the cutting-edge 3P (Pollution Prevention Pays) in 1975. Voluntary waste reduction has saved the company an estimated one-half billion dollars.

Compaq, too, has been able to make prevention pay even in their white collar areas. When their purchasing department went to a paperless order system, they were able to save several pages of paper for each transaction (e.g., purchase orders, no-production requisitions and change orders). With over 90,000 transactions per year there is a potential paper savings of over 4,000 pounds per year. They also developed a paperless work request system. In Houston, their facilities team receives over 17,000 work requests per year. Before their current system, this meant each request generated 9 pages of paper or approximately 2,000 pounds of paper per year.[3]

Eliminating waste, any waste, can be a competitive advantage. Even small improvements can have a dramatic impact on the bottom line. Kraft General Foods found this out when they narrowed the inner trays of their Oscar Meyer Lunchables® by *two-thousands* of an inch. That minor change resulted in savings of hundreds of thousands of pounds of material annually.[4] This change, along with other material reductions, has helped them prevent more than one billion pounds of packaging from becoming waste. Obviously, management's foresight meant it was also able to save money as well as materials. Using the least amount of materials to make and package products makes very good business sense, but it's not the only way to make money. Reynolds Metals replaced a solvent-based ink with water-based inks in their packaging plants. It not only cut harmful emissions by 65 percent, but also eliminated the need to spend $30 million for pollution control.

Good pollution does not simply have to be a cost container, it can even be a revenue generator. Polaroid stopped using mercury in its batteries because they could not be recycled. In the process they not only eliminated dangerous chemicals, but created the recyclable battery![5]

WASTE IS AN USUSUAL RESOURCE

For companies in the know, waste is not scrap, it is an unused resource. Today, chemical companies are under enormous pressures to change the way they are doing business. One chemical company that has had tremendous success at seeing waste as a resource is DuPont. As we will see, it owes a great deal of credit to being able to change its *definition* of what is meant by waste. As a result, it has waste-reduction teams that make a difference. From 1985 through the early 1990s DuPont estimates it produced *one billion pounds* less waste. This means DuPont is saving $50,000,000 per year because of waste reduction activities.[6] Is there any doubt that DuPont might be changing its definition of waste?

DuPont notes that, just as a weed can be described as a plant out of place, waste manufacturing may be a product looking for a market.[6] Several examples of using this approach were cited by DuPont including where it was able to convert a waste by-product (methylglutaronitrite) from a nylon manufacturing process into a new chemical commodity. The new product is now sold by the DuPont Nylon Strategic business unit. What was once a waste by-product is now used for epoxy coatings for concrete and construction use. It is also a highly effective epoxy adhesive used to bond metal to plastic.

DuPont states that what it once thought of as a waste is now a new product. The change has been dramatic; in 1991 alone this created a waste reduction of approximately two million pounds.

While the research and development to convert waste into products may not be simple, the logic is clear. It says it simply makes more sense to sell by-products than pay to dispose of them. Nothing succeeds like a little success, to the point that the company is continuing to expand product use from this process. DuPont now claims that *all* of the waste in this particular process will be consumed in this manner. That would amount to 50 to 60 million pounds per year.[5]

Paul Tebo, Vice President of Safety, Health, Environment says that environmental solutions don't have to be cost prohibitive. They can add to the bottom line, making a company better able to meet the needs of consumers and society while remaining profitable.[8] To drive home this point he cites the experience of the chemical industry. In any chemical production process, about 80 to 90 percent of it is unintended by-product. In the past, chemical companies treated this by-product as waste, but the definition of waste began to change with the oil crises of the early 1970s.

DuPont felt the key was to match product value to consumer need. One of its first applications of this idea was when it was able to collect and market a chemical referred to as Di Basic Acid (DBA). The chemical is a *by-product* (no longer waste!) of their nylon manufacturing process.

This is one of the best examples of being able to convert what was once a waste into something that is a true resource. Today, DBA helps clean the environment. It is added to limestone scrubbers at coal-fired power stations in order to reduce acid rain emissions by making those scrubbers more efficient.

The story of DBA does not end here. Since these initial efforts, DuPont has been converting it into another chemical that was first sold to customers in the coating industry. Now it is a preferred solvent in many industries, replacing such environmental and safety hazards as acetone and methylene chloride.

The company's approach of converting "waste" into desirable consumer products has created a thriving enterprise. The company has developed many businesses from the "waste" or by-products of other manufacturing processes as well. DuPont notes that as of 1991, had it not pursued these businesses, disposal costs alone for what was once defined incorrectly as "waste" would have exceeded a projected $100 million each year by the turn of the century.

ENVIRONMENTALISM AS VALUE ADDED

Tebo of DuPont stresses that finding an alternative use for waste chemicals is not new, but what *is* new is that they are no longer viewing waste materials as an environmental problem but rather as a *business opportunity*.[8] Another individual who recognizes the environment as a business opportunity is Richard J. Mahoney, Chairman and CEO of Monsanto Company. He sees the potential for turning environmental leadership from a cost to opportunity. In a no-nonsense attitude, he goes on to say that you can gain a competitive advantage because environmental leadership can add "measurable value to the corporation."

To demonstrate the measurable value of environmental leadership, he provides an example. Assume you have a product that "costs 10 cents a gallon to make and brought solid value at $1 a gallon to the farmer." The quiz is, what should we charge? He says some say 11 cents, and he says, "Thank you very much!" Some say it should probably range from 20 to 40 cents, and he says, "We both need to think about it." A few say we ought to charge a dollar if it's worth it and he says, "Report to work tomorrow."[9] The point is that it is the few that would charge a dollar that recognize the premium of *added value*. It means getting paid when you add real value and not getting paid when you do not add value.

So what is the value of environmentalism? Monsanto's CEO believes that the environment should be, and will mean, added value. He notes that often when he talks to people about the environment and added value he gets blank stares, skepticism and comments that the environment is simply a cost of doing business and always will be.[9]

Mahoney believes that most people perceive environmental concerns as a cost. He stresses that it is few leaders who instinctively know that they can find a way to add value and gain a competitive advantage through environmental management. These few understand that the environment must not merely be thought of as a cost of doing business, but rather a cost to be managed and a competitive advantage to be won.[9] Citing the work of his own company, it is these types of people who convert waste products into useful chemical products, and who create environmental training programs that their dealers want.

Specific examples of value-added people at Monsanto include those in its Chemical Group that created a partnership with its customers to reduce the potential threat from the transportation of the chemical P_2S_5 (phosphorus pentasulfide). Value-added people were the ones who supplied a system to eliminate vapor emissions for their customers and got paid for it. This business was sold by Monsanto in 1991. Still another group was able to recycle used values from some of their customers' plants. Value-added people were also the ones at Monsanto's NutraSweet® plant in Georgia who implemented a *cogeneration* (more about that in a later chapter), thereby saving energy and millions of dollars in manufacturing costs.

Mahoney says it is these people who do not give him blank stares. There is no skepticism, no comment about the environment being a cost for doing business. Rather, these value-added people have a desire to add value, to integrate the environment into their business and jobs in order to gain an advantage by doing the right thing.[9]

Creating a Desire for Change

In order to encourage Monsanto personnel to rethink their attitude toward environmental issues, Mahoney gave his people some things to consider. The first was cost. As noted earlier, he cited Monsanto's own raw material challenge where it threw away $150,000,000 in raw material and energy. He wonders how much could be saved by redesign and by reducing the cost of storing and disposing. Emphasizing his new definition, he says each cost should be thought of as a potential competitive advantage. In other words, don't make waste in the first place—instead, focus on pollution prevention.

The second consideration was the need to find out what the competition is doing in the area of the environment. Key questions to consider are, "What are their environmental problems and issues?" "What are the problems of their customers?" Environmentally, benchmark your competitors' environmental programs. If you know what your customers' environmental problems are, and if you know what your competition is doing, then you know how to position your products and services, thereby gaining a competitive advantage.

HOW TO CHANGE

In the next few chapters we will look at some sources of environmental profits. Later we will identify a managerial system for creating profits from environmental factors. Speeches are fine, but change requires not only a new definition but also requires new training and the creation of new communication networks. One good overview for how we can begin to change the environment from a cost center to one of a profit center has been provided by DuPont. In order to do that it believes we need to:

- identify all waste in a systematic manner
- establish goals and priorities
- create and implement action plans
- establish systems for tracking generated waste
- measure our progress at eliminating it

From its own viewpoint the company found that they were able to make major reductions by:

- changing operating conditions
- modifying production process
- tightening process control
- improving operating and maintenance procedures
- recovering, recycling, and revising process materials and coproducts[6]

Later we will look at many examples of how these activities lead to profitable management. Once we've examined how some companies are increasing competitiveness and profits, it will be necessary to lay out a comprehensive roadmap for change.

First, though, let's look at two big reasons for change, namely cost and the customer.

ENDNOTES

1. U.S. General Accounting Office, *Global Warming: Emission Reductions Possible as Scientific Uncertainties Are Resolved* (GAO/RCED 90–58) Report to the Chairman, Environment, Energy, and Natural Resources Subcommittee, Committee on Government Operations, House of Representatives, September 1990, p. 48–49.

2. Buzzelli, David T., *Remarks to WESTEC Meeting* (in-house publication of Dow Chemical), November 1, 1990, p. 5–6.

3. *Application for Spirit of Texas Environmental Quality Award* (internal document for Compaq Computer Company).

4. Quality Food Quality Environment (Kraft General Foods in-house publication).

5. Sinclair, Lani, "Corporate Environmentalism Makes Good Business 'Cents'," *Safety & Health*, July 1992, p. 75.

6. *Resource: The DuPont Program for Waste and Emissions Reduction* (DuPont in-house publication), p. 2–3.

7. *1991 Environmental Report Awards* pamphlet (in-house publication by DuPont), 1992, p. 2.

8. "The Value of Waste," *DuPont Magazine*, September/October 1991, p. 19.

9. Mahoney, Richard J., "Our Policy Is Greatness," *Remarks at Worldwide Environmental Conference*, St. Louis, MO, May 21–22, 1992, p. 9–11.

3

ENVIRONMENTAL COSTING: REDEFINING THE RULES

There is a lot of discussion going on about landfills, garbage, environmental regulations and cost, but that is not the real problem we should be discussing. What we have is an economic problem, not a landfill problem or a garbage problem. Until recently, it was cheaper to bury old magazines, cardboard, and plastic than to eliminate or recycle them. However, things are changing rapidly and our definition of the environmental problem should also change. In Germany and Japan landfill costs are considerably higher than in the U.S. and their costs are continuing to rise. Even in the U.S. landfill space is diminishing rapidly. That is why defining environmental problems as one of garbage, landfills, regulations, and hazardous material is becoming outdated. In the 1990s environmental management will be defined increasingly as an *economic problem*. Redefining as such allows you to find opportunities to enhance the bottom line. Defining environmental management in economic terms means a greater reliance on assessing economic alternatives.

According to Dow's recent statements, being able to analyze the entire product life cycle makes good business sense. It means truly understanding how a product is made, as well as its final fate. The company emphasizes there is no one-way trip and that there is no such thing as a free lunch. Short-sighted business managers might only see costs, but there are environmental costs and *benefits* for each product.

To fully understand these benefits, Dow for one, tries to look at the environmental impact of a product and its raw materials, energy use, and product emissions. It encourages its people to look at what happens to its product when it leaves the plant. The company's focus is to try to become a preferred supplier for a customer's products and services. It is an effort to develop a more comprehensive understanding of the true cost and opportunities for products and services. It is what is increasingly becoming known as a *life-cycle approach* to pollution management.

LIFE-CYCLE COSTING

In the new journal *Pollution Prevention Review* was an article on a concept called "life-cycle costing." It described how this applies to pollution prevention. As the name implies, it is a cradle-to-grave product accounting. It has only been recently adapted to ecological problems. The object of life-cycle costing is to assign some monetary figure to every effect of a product. The list is expanding, and would include such things as landfill costs, potential legal penalties, degradation of air quality, and so forth.[1] When all these costs are factored in, it helps you project true future product costs much like cash flow analysis does. From a pollution point of view, you can compare two or more products or services and packaging alternatives to see which hold the best business potential. Life-cycle costs include the purchase price and their operations and maintenance cost expressed in constant dollars over the *lifetime* of the appliance, less scrap value at the end of its lifetime. For instance, one type of package might at first appear to be easier to recycle than another, but it might also require more energy, manufacturing, and transportation costs. In order to know, you have to track the item through its entire life-cycle.

The concept of life-cycle costing began in April of 1965 when the Logistics Management Institute in Washington, D.C. prepared a report for the Assistant Secretary of Defense for Installations and Logistics titled, "Life Costing in Equipment Purchase."[2] It was eventually used for procurement of major defense systems and equipment using mathematical tools taught in the nation's business schools. For the first time there was recognition that operation and maintenance cost (O&M) were a significant part of the total cost of owning equipment and systems. An early revelation was that life-cycle costing often showed that ownership cost far exceeded procurement cost.

Life-cycle costing could show that a product with a relatively low purchase price was not always the best deal. A product could have a high life-cycle cost, and might also have a relatively high operations cost because of waste byproducts or energy inefficiencies. A high maintenance cost might also exist because it would break down easily. If you factored in all these cost components over the life-cycle of a product or system, you could make more realistic comparisons.

The next result of initial life-cycle costing is more emphasis being placed on operation and maintenance cost. This in turn means a greater emphasis on designing systems and products that reduced these costs. Today there are many trends that continue to increase the O&M component of this equation. Increases in labor cost, more complex and less reliable equipment, and rapidly increasing energy expenditures are but a few of these costs. As these ownership costs rise, so does the interest in life-cycle costing.

Life-cycle cost analysis is an ideal way of assessing the energy requirements of buildings, equipment, and other systems. Such requirements are easy to predict and easy to calculate. You can look at the energy requirements, examine potential energy conservation measures like special lighting or additional insulation, and determine payback and Return-On-Investment (ROI). In the past, life-cycle cost analysis has been used on computers, heavy industrial equipment, automobiles and tires, lighting, heating and cooling, and appliance purchases. It has also been used to assess hospital facilities, medical equipment, buildings, office equipment, and energy systems.

When you use life-cycle costing, products or purchases that last longer have an advantage. Vehicles that get more miles per gallon can offset higher initial purchase price. Something that has easier maintenance, based on how many hours needed for upkeep, could have an advantage. If a purchase has greater reliability, and lower repair cost because of fewer breakdowns or less severe ones, then the life-cycle analysis would show it. By reducing all of these elements to a monetary number, buyers can assess potential trade-offs like shorter life-span versus higher reliability. It is possible to do such analysis because everything is translated into dollars.

COST FACTORS

Life-cycle costing requires that you think through the key purchasing cost factors for the lifetime of each purchase. From acquisition to eventual disposal each item should be costed in dollars for the year, or years, that cost will be incurred. Existing costs have to be collected and future costs projected. These same costs are then "discounted" to present day dollars, so you can compare those costs to a competing goods cost.

There are many mathematical formulas used in the process. Key variables in this analysis include procurement cost, delivery and installation cost, operation cost (energy, labor, materials, insurance), maintenance cost, taxes, and disposal cost. Obviously, there will always be some uncertainty with such future costing.

Some of this discussion should sound familiar to those with capital investment knowledge. All the life-cycle cost factors are the same ones that business people use to project potential ROI. These capital investment decisions resemble procurement decisions because in both cases, several projects compete for funds. One difference is that capital investment decisions also apply to individual projects where you look at ROI and payback period. Life-cycle costing is most frequently thought of as a tool for helping you choose between competing expenditures.

Limitations?

Life-cycle costing is a tool for analyzing *comparable* items. It would not be appropriate to use it to compare dissimilar items like planes and automobiles. Each has a different *goal*. If you wanted to, you could compare paper versus plastic packaging, but not, say, paper packaging versus styrofoam cups—it does not compute; it's like comparing apples and oranges.

Life-cycle costing is not without its drawbacks. Maybe the biggest limitation is its inability to identify *all* your potential cost. This is an important point. If there are costs for an item, but you do not calculate them, then you cannot expect an accurate analysis. One of the values of life-cycling is that it is trying to put a number on cost concerns that, in the past, have been ignored. But one drawback is that you cannot put a number on something that involves aesthetics or other subjective concerns. It would not be wise to purchase items, say for instance in retail, strictly on life-cycle cost because your customer may care about *how it looks* as well as how it performs. Consumer behavior is marketing's job. It should work closely with whomever is doing life-cycle choices, whenever subjective customer preferences are a significant factor. Life-cycle costing focuses on maintenance, operations, and procurement cost, but sometimes social cost is also an important factor. In such a case, judgment is of critical importance.

FULL-COST ACCOUNTING

Life-cycle costing can make decision making easier and more rational. Reformulating products, making substitutions of less polluting material, and making modifications to reduce pollution could be fertile ground for such costing. All these approaches look to reduce waste and can be costed.

Like anything else, you must choose your battlegrounds carefully. Life-cycle costing takes time and some types of analyses are not useful. For example, trying to use this type of costing would be wasteful for analyzing a company's paper and plastic packaging because of these products' short life and technical simplicity. Normally, this type of packaging is not around long enough, nor complex enough to generate much maintenance or repair costs. Therefore from the life-cycling point of view, it's a toss up.

Things are changing now because of something called *full-cost accounting,* which attempts to reconcile some of the weaknesses of life-cycle costing. A summary of this approach can be found in the EPA's *Pollution Prevention Benefits Manual.* The manual helps you identify the costs involved with hazardous materials and hazardous waste management. It also helps you determine net present value, internal rate of return, and annualized cost savings of pollution prevention projects.

The manual identifies *four levels* or types of cost. These are the *usual costs* like equipment, materials, or labor. Then there are the *hidden costs,* which include monitoring paperwork, permit requirements, and so forth. The third type are *liability costs,* including future liabilities penalties and fines. The fourth are *less tangible costs.* Included in these are your corporate image, community relations, and consumer response.

The full manual also contains worksheets and information to assist in doing the cost estimation. An example is provided in the form of a hypothetical firm that is involved in electroplating gold. A key point is made that unless liability costs and less tangible benefits are considered, it is doubtful that the economic justification for avoiding such hazardous waste by substituting it with a mechonizid aqueous cleaner, could have been made.

Despite this fact, most research on life-cycle costing does not factor into this important consideration. It is nevertheless very important. As a testimony to this is the fact that General Electric has already developed its own model that includes liability exposure. GE is not the only one that is learning the true cost of pollution.

LEGAL COST OF POLLUTING

Occasionally, out of adversity comes insight. That was the case for Werner and Mertz, a medium-sized German chemical company. Consumers had claimed some of its products caused asphyxiation and they took the company to court. When the company did go to court, it eventually lost. In the process they reexamined their business. What they discovered was that customers were not judging products solely on their ability to do their job. A large segment was willing to sacrifice some performance for more environmentally friendlier products.

As a result of this discovery the company introduced a new line of biologically degradable cleaning products. They had no sales in 1986, but by 1991, sales were $200 million. Now about 45 percent of all the company's revenue comes from these environmental friendly products.[3]

Such a far-sighted approach may not be for everyone, but every organization should be increasingly aware of legal environmental challenges. One of these involves the United Nations Conference on Environment and Development (UNCED) that was held in Rio in June of 1992. UNCED was created as a way of mobilizing the world's nations to take concrete actions to address worldwide environmental economic imbalances.

One of UNCED's actions was *Agenda 21*, which calls on governments to monitor inventory and assess the hazards of sea- and land-based pollution sources. Furthermore, there are plans to set up regulatory and legally-binding agreements. Businesses can expect liability and compensation regimes covering pollution damage. As global concerns for pollution grow, expect tougher industry regulations. The pressure is on for legal action. In a recent survey in the U.S., 84 percent of respondents said that they felt industrial pollution to be the worst business offense. Moreover, three out of four believe senior executives should be held *criminally* liable when pollution occurs.[3] If you want to hear one more scary fact concerning criminal liability, environmental law is the fastest growing specialty for lawyers, which is estimated at 20,000 lawyers now compared to 2,000 a decade ago.[4] Perhaps just as surprising is that 83 percent of executives believe environmental damage is a serious crime and 49 percent believe *they* should be held personally liable for such offenses![5]

The true liability for waste is just starting to be understood. It is a fact that if your waste is mishandled, your company and other customers of the waste disposal company could be blamed and sued right along with the operator. At employee-owned companies, the prospects of steep expenses down the road should give employees a real incentive.

Still, many do not appreciate the risk. For example, hospitals for one are generally unaware of the potential liability risk they face because of waste products. Liability specialists note that any hospital that generates waste is exposed to liability. There are direct and indirect liabilities involved. Direct liability applies to waste a hospital or any other business disposes of itself. Indirect liability is the result of contracts signed with outside firms to dispose of infectious, radioactive, or otherwise dangerous waste. As the previous paragraph notes, one's liability does not end because of the contract. That's a point many do not comprehend. When waste gets into the environment, one is held responsible for paying for cost of the cleanup, fines, and penalties. Personal liability also occurs when people are injured as a result of improper disposal.

While the case for criminal liability is still emerging, one thing is certain. Almost daily, there is worldwide legislation aimed at making owners of companies liable for both clean-up costs and damage caused from the improper handling of environmental waste from all previous owners!

Worldwide Liability

Liability for pollution extends beyond personal liability. Just as serious is rising worldwide expectations. For instance, a new recycling law in Germany will probably become a model for other countries' efforts to reduce waste from product packaging. The first step of the three-step law took place in 1991 and required manufacturers and distributors to take back the cartons and crates that they used to ship their products to retailers. The second step in 1992 requires recycling of product packaging. It allows customers the option of leaving the outer packages such as cardboard boxes behind in the store. In 1993, the last stage of the law went into effect that even a tube of toothpaste could be left at a store for recycling. The goal of the law is to reduce the amount of waste sent to landfills.[6] In the future, Germany is also likely to pass, in some form, a law that requires manufacturers to accept old products from their customers.

EXTERNAL ENVIRONMENTAL COST

Despite much work, most costing still does not produce a true picture of environmental cost. Most economists recognize that the real cost of solid waste, air, and water emissions are not always seen on the balance sheet nor are their full costs known to society. The term *external cost* means that some prices of goods and services do not reflect their full cost to society. This being the case, it is likely that the free market will encourage more use of goods and services that produce more pollution.

The external costs are such potential liabilities as the risk of cleanup and the more subtle concerns of your customers, including damage to natural resources or damages to people and property. Other costs include social cost not recoverable in liabilities. Until we refine these costs, it will be impossible to make good decisions concerning pollution management.

At present, it is difficult to measure the time cost to society for things like degradation of our quality of life due to air pollution. But, it is easier to measure production losses, or cost incurred by taxpayers, to support pollution activities (inspectors, bureaucracy, and so forth). One tool being used to develop environmental protection standards is *risk substitutions*. The purpose of this tool is to identify all risks posing a problem during the complete life-cycle. Baseline risks are determined for your current practices involving production, waste handling, and management. Along with this process, alternative management practices are assessed. Usually, these later risks are lower than current practices.

Risk assessment has been around for over 15 years. During this time, there have been ongoing efforts to link the various aspects of risk assessment to life-cycle costing, but much work remains. Some ongoing efforts are worth noting. In 1989, efforts were made for the National Association for Plastic Container Recovery to assess the total energy and environmental impacts of soft drink packaging. The life-cycle of energy consumption from extracting raw materials through production, its use and final disposal were assessed. The study concluded that polyethylene terephthalate (PET) containers were more energy efficient when compared to aluminum or glass. The study also noted that PET containers contributed the smallest amount of solid waste by weight. Since the study was done by the "plastics association," all assumptions, data, and methodologies would need to be carefully examined in order to remain objective.[2]

Another study completed for a plastics trade group said plastic bags were superior to paper because they produced less solid waste and less atmospheric emissions and waterborne waste. At first glance, such studies appear to be self-servicing, but they do show the potential for such assessment when it is unbiased.

One such unbiased assessment involves the nonprofit research group based in Boston cased The Tellus Institute. They were contracted by the New Jersey Department of Environmental Protection (NJDEP) to conduct a life-cycle analysis of the environmental impacts of producing, as well as disposing of, packaging material. Currently, they are in the process of analyzing specific pollutants being released. The focus of the Tellus Study was to analyze the impacts of pollutants on human health. In the last chapter, we will look at some outstanding research that has come out of their efforts and show how it affects your business.

ECO-BALANCE SHEET

In order for any reasonable manager to invest in better environmental management, one question comes immediately to mind and that is "What is my return-on-environmental-investment?" We know there are certain costs associated with pollution. We know there are legal costs for pollution and there are liability concerns. Consumer preferences and expectations also have their place but they can remain somewhat intangible and, as the saying goes in business, unless it has a financial number, it has no value. That is why today there is a great deal of effort going into the *eco-balance sheet.*

The American and British Accounting Boards are trying to deal with the environment and bottom line. The idea of the eco-balance sheet is that in order for something to be valued it must be measured. Initial experimentation is only ten years old so the concept is still being defined and changed. The hope is that it can become an indispensable tool of business. Once it is totally developed it should be a way to integrate environmental concerns into day-to-day decision making. When it is fully developed, for instance, it may be possible to trade environmental impact units with other product managers. It also will make it possible to tie rewards to environmental performance.[3]

Migros is a U.S. retailer whose Switzerland operation is interested in the environmental impact of what it sells. Included in this is its energy, emission and waste. By getting detailed knowledge of these and other environmental costs it is able to set environmental goals for products and services. For instance, one goal was to reduce heating oil per square of sales area to 21 liters by 1995.[3]

Redefining the environment so that you can focus on profit potential and better defining what the true life-cycle costs are opens up a lot of competitive advantages. Once environmental costs are known and assigned to individual stores and products, it is easy to determine their return-on-their-environmental-investment. Migros is still in the process of developing an understanding of the eco-balance sheet. The first step occurred in 1975 when it issued a report describing the systematic environmental actions and initiatives the company was undertaking. Later they created an *environmental management balance sheet* where investments and returns were quantified. The key question to ask during this stage is "What is it worth?"

It's third level of environmental financial sophistication involves *product line analysis.* The company sells tens of thousands of products but they look at each and do a complete evaluation of a product's environmental impact. At this stage, Migros can only evaluate selected aspects of a product's environmental impact. The hope is to continually improve this evaluation process so it can determine a more comprehensive assessment of a product's environmental impact.

When it was fairly cheap for business to produce and pollute, you could define the environment cost in terms of minimizing cost of compliance and avoiding obvious legal risk. In today's changing world, the obvious and hidden cost of polluting is continuing to rise. By redefining the environment from cost avoidance to *environmental profitability* you position yourself for long-term success. It helps you assess your true cost and choose products and services that maximize long-term return on investment.

IS COST CUTTING REALLY WORTH IT?

Throughout this book, you will see challenges to basic tenants. Challenging assumptions helps us think creatively. It produces new and better solutions. At other times it just shakes our thinking up a bit so we can get just a little bit of improvement. One of the assumptions that we should challenge is the relative usefulness of leaving accountants in charge of the business even for something as comprehensive as life-cycle costing. All too often today, if it does not have a "number" it has no value. The problem with this type of bottom-line thinking is that a lot of things get left out of the equation.

In tight times, in times of financial crises, the first reaction of business to downturns is a round of cost cutting, but does this do any good? A survey of 271 top executives by the consulting firm Kepner-Tregoe shows that only 50 percent of those companies making corporate cost measures saw improvements in quality. More striking was the fact that fewer than two out of five said their cost-cutting actions had a positive effect on their financial information or other systems![4] The consulting firm concluded that far too many corporations concentrate on the cost side of the equation, but neglect business development and growth. Nearly 75 percent of the CEOs in the survey said cost cutting or improved profitability were major objectives of the corporations, but very few mentioned *increased revenue* as a goal.

This seems especially relevant to pollution management. Pollution to most executives means pollution control, and pollution control means cost control. Some managers see their objective as minimizing the cost of complying with environmental regulations. The idea is to avoid sinking any more money, capital, or time into pollution control than is necessary. It is seen as a necessary evil, or an overhead that makes it harder to do business. Often, these managers are reactive in nature because outside agents are viewed as "nit picking" their business to death. At their best, *minimum-cost managers* believe their role is one of compliance with accepted standards.

COMPETITIVE COSTING MANAGERS

Later, we will look at another group of managers and companies that see cost differently. Oh, they still see environmental issues as a cost, but not a negative one; rather, they see potential for their business. Their thinking goes, if it is a cost for you (my competitor) and is a cost for me, then I can use it. If I find a way to lower my *long-term* cost, I will be in a better position to win. The focal point for the two differing cost views is a matter of perspective. Rather than seeing their objective as minimizing cost of compliance, these managers are in it for the competitive advantage. They seek ways to eliminate or *avoid those costs* by investing in new technology, training and incentives to encourage cost reduction, so they will lower their overhead and beat their competition. It is these types of *competitive costing* managers who would be especially interested in something like life-cycle costing because it is a more comprehensive and true assessment of pollution cost, therefore, it gives them a competitive advantage.

Pollution overhead, due to poor energy and waste management, is higher for U.S. firms than for typical Japanese and German firms. These "cost avoidance" or competitive costing managers immediately recognize that, like high labor cost or poor quality, they had better do something so they do not put themselves at a greater disadvantage. For these managers, product and process redesign, more emphasis on employee involvement and management attention to environmental concerns are certainly worth the time.

Still more rare is the manager who does not focus on cost, but rather chooses to concentrate on revenue generation. They recognize that excellent pollution management is an absolute necessity, as we will see in succeeding pages, for long-term market viability and *growth*. It is this type of manager that shuns short-term ROI schemes in favor of long-term profitability.

More managers than you might suspect are questioning the sanity of measuring success based on ROI. Still today, it dominates internal capital budget decisions. It certainly is the most important driver of financial investment decisions.[5] Authors Hayes and Abernathy note in the *Harvard Business Review* that maximum short-term financial returns have become the overriding criteria for many companies.[6] It is the thing that links investors' decisions with managers' actions. For 30 years, ROI has been the most important performance measure in the business world. But many question whether or not a focus of ROI has brought better performance. It certainly has not for many American firms.

Numbers are powerful things; they make decisions cold and impersonal. Add this, subtract that, divide here and presto—you have a decision. Trouble is, it is a decision made by a "bean counter" and a smart one at that. Who could question his or her figures? It's right there in black and white. If you doubt it, they pull out their calculators and show you what to do. It is these financial types that hold the ear of the cost-minimization managers, and chances are good that these managers were one of the "bean counters" before they became the boss. Even cost-avoidance managers weigh investment decisions on which way to go, which is the greatest ROI.

POLLUTION MANAGEMENT AS A REVENUE GENERATOR

It is the revenue-growth manager who has his or her sites set farther out. He wonders where the customer fits in. Maybe this revenue growth manager is not a revenue-growth manager at all. Perhaps we could call her a customer-focused manager. Maybe some are even market-share managers. In any case, the revenue-growth, the customer-focused, and the market-share managers all share one thing in common: they are not worried so much so on short-term as they are about the *long-term*. It is these types of managers who see the potential for turning pollution control to pollution management. Rather than thinking of concentrating on controlling the cost of pollution, they are trying to figure out how to manage it, and how to increase market share and long-term revenue.

At best, a cost manager tries to prevent pollution whereas long-term managers know planning, organizing, directing, staffing, and control are needed to run a business. They plan to eliminate it, to organize coordinated efforts and reduce the risk. They know they have to find the right people and lead attempts to rethink how they do business. That is exactly what Herman Miller, the furniture maker, did. The company has found ways to recycle or reuse nearly all the waste from its manufacturing process. Fabric scraps are sold to the auto industry to reuse as lining for cars and luggage makers buy leather trim for attaché cases. Stereo and auto manufacturers use the company's vinyl for sound-deadening materials.[7]

True, long-term resource managers know that if they are able to integrate pollution considerations into day-to-day, as well as long-term decisions, then they can have a more efficient, less wasteful, more competitive organization. The focus is not on generating quarterly earnings so they will support a high stock price. Such an approach creates underinvestment, and big dividends. The long-term manager concentrates on market share and long-term revenue growth—and avoids short-term thinking.

Is such a long-term manager a fool? Everyone talks today about the need for continuous improvement, but ROI does not "fit" very well with continuous improvement. ROI also looks inward, ignoring the market and any short- or long-term customers. Bill Parks, a business professor, makes the point that sales dollars also are a poor measure to use because no indicator exists of a firm's performance versus the industry in which it competes.[5] He goes on to point out that market share increases not only measure long-term performance, but also identifies the firm's relative effectiveness. It improves the company's chances for long-term survival. Gains in market share will ultimately result in improved performance. Losses in market share will, over time, result in failure.

Are there any case studies to support this long-term perspective? Japan provides many examples where high-growth conditions have existed, but studies concentrated on market share rather than profitability. Abegglen and Stalk point out that Japan had a preoccupation with market share and competitive positioning in contrast to western firms ROI.[8] Michelin, the tire company, provides another example. Since 1946, it has consistently sacrificed short-term concerns for two things—quality and market share. François Michelin, the founder, believes he succeeded by using the American firm's concern for quarterly profit increases against them. The company puts out five percent of sales for research and development in good and bad times. If Michelin succeeds in its planned takeover of Uniroyal in the mid-1990s it will become the world's largest tire maker, despite having been a poor performer on the Paris Stock Exchange historically.[9]

CLOSING THOUGHTS

This chapter has examined perspectives on cost and the environment. Clearly, environment cost and "putting a number to it" is not an easy task. Unfortunately, this has led to apathy and ignorance. Companies that do not begin to asses the true cost of their environmental decisions are living in a fantasy world. A reality check may be painful, but at least it gets managers to deal with facts, not fiction.

The fact is that life-cycle costing, full-cost accounting, risk assessment, and environmental value analysis can bring a sense of reality to managerial decision making. No one person can do this alone, but management has always been interdependent. To get a true picture of an organization's cost will require the efforts of specialists and managers. Accountants and consultants may be needed to do major cycle costing. Some decisions can be made by managers, but they must draw on engineers and others to use value analysis to improve the design of the production process.

Life-cycle costing is not a science, but increasing its use may become necessary. This type of costing consumes time and resources and some of its mathematical analysis can require specialists to verify conclusions. In this case, it is management's job to identify the key risks, then provide the resources so that they can be solved.

As we will see in the next chapter, perhaps it is time to reconsider the place pollution has in management's thinking. If you are in it for the long haul, you may be surprised about what customers are saying here and abroad. The "environmental thing" is here to stay. It is only those who are behind the competitive curve who will miss this one.

Whether you see environmental concerns as a cost or a potential new way to capture additional revenue and market share, it is not as important as what your competitors are doing. We will look at how to use both reduced cost and increased revenue due to better pollution management. We will look at what your customers are asking for, and we will look at some of the pieces of the pollution solution. Later, we will pull all of them together so you have a chance to decide what it is you want to do so you have a united attack. You will better understand where you're going, and, most importantly, how to get there.

ENDNOTES

1. Kleiner, Art, "What Does It Mean to Be Green?" *Harvard Business Review*, July–August 1991, Vol. 69, No. 4, p. 40.

2. Bailey, Paul E., "Life-cycle Costing and Pollution Prevention," *Pollution Prevention Review*, Winter 1990–91, p. 27.

3. Williams, Jan Olaf, Ulrich Golüke, *From Ideas: To Action Business and Sustainable Development*, International Chamber of Commerce (Ad Notam Gyldendal Publishing), 1992, pp. 56–110, 144.

4. "Cost Management Is Better Than Cost Cutting," *APICS—The Performance Advantage*, July 1993, p. 18.

5. Parks, Bill, "Rate of Return—The Poison Apple?" *Business Horizons*, Vol. 36, No. 3, May–June 1993, p. 55.

6. Hayes, Robert H., William J. Abernathy, "Managing Our Way to Economic Decline," *Harvard Business Review*, July–August 1980, pp. 67–77.

7. Rice, Faye, "Who Scores Best on the Environment," *Fortune*, Vol. 28, No. 2, July 26, 1993, p. 115.

8. Abegglen, James C., George Stalk, Jr. *Kaisha, The Japanese Corporation* (New York: Basic Books, 1985).

9. Gitman, Lawrence J., *Principles of Managerial Finance*, 6th Edition (New York: Harper Collins, 1991).

4

MEET YOUR "GREEN" CUSTOMERS

In the previous chapter we mentioned a journey. Well, the first stop on this journey has to be our customers. Earlier, we discussed tools to help assess the true cost of decisions that create pollution. The concepts of cost and our customers are inseparable. Customers *will* pay for more environmentally friendly products, and companies that do not pay attention to their customers' environmental needs will lose business. Many managers would agree, but just as many managers do not truly understand the relationship between cost and their long-term customers. Some managers do not think of groups like the community at large, governmental regulators, or environmental groups as customers, but they are and their decisions can have a dramatic affect on your business. If we viewed them as customers, just like any others, we would more likely be proactive rather than reactive. Good customer service can only occur when the customer does not have to ask for it.

If you do not think of these groups as your customer, you may be stunned by their actions. That is usually the way we feel when we do not listen and suddenly we are in the middle of crisis management. The New Jersey EPA (NJDEP) group, mentioned in the last chapter, should be someone's customer. They have already begun using life-cycle studies to determine which products are environmentally superior. One project they are working on involves analyzing predisposal fees for packages and for future products. Many of your external customers are coming to the conclusion that external factors like these are needed to "level the playing field." Such action may also be supported increasingly by citizens (another external customer) who are paying higher and higher landfill and other "after the fact" pollution costs. These front-end fees are most likely a thing of the future. Companies that do not focus attention on long-term customer needs will end up fighting fires, trying to figure out how to react to "sudden" shifts in public opinion.

External customers are everywhere, and it takes constant attention to keep abreast of their needs. The State of California is in the process of developing recommendations (and/or legislation) for a disposal cost fee system so those that generate the waste will pay the *full* cost of waste management, including environmental degradation and state and local waste management programs. It seems only a matter of time until most of our external customers realize that those who initially produce waste *should* foot the entire bill. As landfills close, publicity continues and expectations rise, and more and more citizens/customers will come to resent the fact that they are paying for waste created by those corporations.

In the last chapter, we noted the U.S. customers' opinion about criminal liability. The concern for the environment has been noted in Germany's approach to new packaging laws. It seems to be a worldwide movement. Even in Britain, long noted for lax pollution control and a sluggish economy, there is movement. In one survey, 75 percent of respondents believe that Britain should emphasize protection of the environment at the expense of economic growth, and only *12 percent* believe that Britain should emphasize economic growth at the expense of the environment.[1]

YOUR CUSTOMERS' ENVIRONMENTAL DESIRES

The point is that if business is supposed to be market driven, guess who the driver is? Today, it is a customer with a decidedly environmental temperament. Eighty percent of Americans say protecting the environment is more important than keeping prices down. Polls tell us that most Americans place a high value on the quality of the environment and the environment that their children will inherit. Several recent polls by *Newsweek, The New York Times* and *USA Today* show that over 80 percent of Americans are concerned about environmental problems. An impressive 57 percent to 75 percent said they would be willing to pay more for products and services made more expensive by environmental regulations.[2] Surveys by Gallup also suggest that about half (52%) of their respondents in a 1990 poll stopped buying particular products because of the poor environmental image of the manufacturing company.[2] The message is clear. Companies producing products need to make consumers' environmental concerns a top priority because consumers report that the environmental attributes of a product or service play a significant role in which products they buy and which products they avoid.

The depth of consumers' desire for environmentally friendly products and *companies* should not be underestimated. According to a Roper Poll, when Americans were asked what they believed to be important in the 1990s, 85 percent of them said the environment was *the most important issue*. The concern for the environment was followed by a concern for patriotism and safe sex.[3] Think about that, it is pretty important when more people think the environment is more important than either patriotism or safe sex!

It is encouraging to note that Americans are increasingly willing to translate their concern for the environment into action. Most Americans say they would replace 8 of 17 types of product packaging for the sake of the environment.[4] In a related 1990 study, it was found that consumers now say packaging recyclability "often or sometimes" affected their decision to buy a product. This was a 15% increase from the previous year. Consumers also said they would be willing to pay 7 to 10 cents more for a product contained in an easy-to-recycle package.[2]

The fact that consumers are willing to pay for environmentally friendly products is the "up" side for business people, but, there is a down side as well. In the area of accountability about 83 percent of surveyed corporate executives believe that causing damage to the environment is a *serious* crime, but only 49 percent of them felt they should be held personally responsible for such an offense. Their customers see this accountability differently! Although 83 percent of both the public and corporate executives believe damage to the environment is a serious crime, each group differs dramatically with regard to accountability. As already noted, only 49% of corporate executives said they should be held personally accountable, but the vast majority of the American public thinks corporate executives need to be held *directly* accountable.

Most business managers are aware that the degree to which they understand their customers is critical to their success. Japanese and German penetration into the American automobile market could not have been so successful if American manufacturers had not misunderstood their consumers' need for fuel economy and greater quality. Hopefully, most businesses will not look past their customers this time.

Increasingly, customers are asking for products and services that do not produce by-products or waste. One reason for this attitude is that many customers, from private to commercial, are faced with the cost and responsibilities of handling and then cleaning up pollutants. As landfill space diminishes, business will have to come up with *cleaner* products, if they hope to stay in business. The good news is, at least some consumers understand they will need to pay more short-term cost to reduce long-term cost. Consumers in Europe are already paying a premium for goods that are recycled, recyclable, or nondamaging to the environment. Those willing to pay this premium range from 50 percent in France to 80 percent in Germany, according to current statistics.

Making Money

It should be clear to everyone that consumers have mandated greater environmental responsibility. Business is recognizing that this will be a major challenge. Many businesses that recognize environmental issues believe the challenge will be to stay in business under the weight of more environmental regulation. This is a legitimate concern. The EPA, for example, estimates that by the year 2000 we will spend $160 billion or nearly three percent of the nation's GNP on pollution control.[5]

PROFIT POTENTIAL OF POLLUTION CONTROL

Figures like the ones just mentioned often seem to support many business leaders who worry about environmental costs. However, it is unfortunate that too many businesses assume the environment is a *cost*—just like they once assumed quality was a cost. The environment, like quality, may entail some short-term costs, but in the long-term factoring in, environmental issues are not a potential cost, but potential *profit*. Probably one of the most famous examples of profit potential is 3M's approach. The environmental goal of 3M is to lower releases to air, water, and land by 90% and to reduce the generation of waste by 50% by the year 2000. If successful, 3M expects substantial cost savings and improved products to result from achieving the goal. Similar savings should be available for many companies. According to conservative estimates, American companies are producing five times as much waste per dollar of revenue as their Japanese counterparts and double the level of German companies.

While 3M's pollution-prevention savings are still subject to conjecture, profit potential from good environmental decision making is a fact. Several of the hundreds of cases where good environmental decision making produced profits are slowly coming to light and these potential profits are in almost all areas of business.

Consider the case of Melitta, Inc. that introduced a line of unbleached coffee filters to their U.S. markets in July of 1985. After just ten months, unbleached filters accounted for 15 percent to 20 percent of Melitta's consumer sales in the U.S. and as much as 50 percent in some West Coast markets.[2]

Proctor and Gamble packages a fabric softener in a 21.5-ounce carton container. The fabric softener is intended to be mixed with water. The fabric softener previously used a 64-ounce rigid plastic bottle. These containers say "Better for the environment—less packaging to throw away," and do contain 75 percent less material and *costs approximately 10 percent less* than the company's regular size and formulation of fabric softener. The product's test marketing has been so successful (e.g., accounting for 20 percent of the company's sales test market) that as of October, 1990 it became available nationwide.[2]

Jim Liggett introduced a new shampoo bar in the U.S. market. The product is made entirely from natural oil and is one of the few shampoos sold without a rigid container. In two years of operation, sales have increased by more than 280 percent.

America, long noted by many as a "throw away" society, is starting to see some fundamental changes occurring. Schroeder Milk Company serves a regional market around Minneapolis/St. Paul. It offers milk customers returnable/refillable heavy-duty containers that can be reused 50 to 150 times. The wholesale price of milk in these containers is 10 to 14 cents less than milk in nonrefundable containers, but there is a 40- to 50-cent deposit per jug. In the two years since its introduction, the price of milk has not changed, but milk shipped in these reusable containers has *doubled*.[3]

Cloth diapers are another environmental profit success story. U.S. births between 1988 and 1989 have increased only *2 percent*, but the demand for cloth diapers, as measured by the number of customers, has increased by *56 percent*. In reality, there is some dispute over the relative benefit of cloth diapers versus disposable diapers. However, it is the customer who makes the difference and they cite a concern for reducing solid waste as an important reason for selecting cloth diapers.[2]

Speaking of cotton, Treekeepers makes 100 percent cotton, reusable canvas shopping bags sold through grocery store chains as an alternative to paper and plastic grocery bags. When introduced in California in 1989, consumers showed remarkable acceptance. In one year shipments grew dramatically from 500 units in January 1990 to 10,000 units per month and sales of $50,000 per month in March and April of 1990.

Reusable markets also extend to books. In fact, believe it or not, there is a growing market for reused books. Half Priced Books, the tenth largest used-book store chain, regularly advertises "Books should fill our minds, not our land." In two years, revenues from the 33-store chain doubled from $10 million to $20 million.[2]

THE ENVIRONMENTAL FACTOR

The rules for being successful are continuously being rewritten and that is true for the 1990s. In the last ten years, business priorities have had to shift due to changing consumer attitudes. One example of how these rules have changed comes from the Toro Company. The company first introduced a grass-mulching mower in the late 1970s, but then had to withdraw from the market in the early 1980s due to insufficient customer demand—but things change.

In the fall of 1989, Toro introduced an improved grass-mulching mower for their 1990 season. In its first year on the market their grass-mulching mower accounted for approximately one-quarter of Toro's lawn mower sales. Based on initial spring stocking sales, the grass-mulching model was expected to account for well over one-half of 1991 lawn mower sales.[2] In hindsight it makes sense; with diminishing landfill space, it becomes increasingly difficult for consumers to get rid of yard waste. Things change. Now mulching mowers make sense. Like so many other environmentally friendly products, it also makes *dollars* and cents.

While personal needs are also important to consumers, it would be a mistake to think that consumers make buying decisions strictly on their own personal needs. Often consumers buy products based as much on the company's reputation as anything else. For instance, Body Shop International began business in 1988. It sells naturally-based skin and hair care products which are advertised as being developed in an environmentally and socially responsible manner. Its cosmetics are not tested on animals and the containers can be recycled. (Most other countries allow refilling of containers, unlike the U. S. where refilling is prohibited by FDA regulations.)

The Body Shop also points out to prospective customers that its products are biodegradable. So what are the results? The company entered the U.S. market in late 1987 and by May of 1988 there were eight shops, all selling at higher than forecasted levels. As of February 1990, another 27 shops were opened.[2]

As you can see, environmentally conscious customers present opportunities for companies that are focused on generating revenue and market share. In order to carve out your niche, define your customers' environmental concerns. Nordstrom, the retailing giant, knew their customers had environmental concerns and wanted to tap that resource. That is why they sell Waterman fountain pens that are made to last a lifetime instead of being disposed of time after time. They also sell "once again" pins that are creative keepsakes to be worn and passed down from generation to generation. These "once again" pins are made by two sisters who go to estate sales and antique shops to collect materials for pins from days gone by. Nordstrom also sells something they call the "Incredible Paper Making Kit" that turns junk mail (or any other type of paper) into hand-crafted stationery in half an hour. The store's four strongest cosmetic lines emphasize environmentally friendly features as well. Sales have increased over 60 percent between 1991 and 1992 and the company continues to increase its in-house share.[7]

THE POWER OF GREEN MARKETING

Nordstrom and others have gotten on the green bandwagon. Many are making changes, recognizing the growing customer preference for green products and services. Few, though, have taken the concept of green marketing as far as The Home Depot. This retailer has been on the forefront of the consumer environmental movement.

As seen in *Figure 4–1*, the company has published and adopted a set of environmental principles that guides its managerial thinking. Its practice of supporting and selling products that are manufactured, packaged, and labeled in an environmentally friendly manner is especially noteworthy. It has an extensive process for determining the accuracy and informative nature of product labeling appearing on its shelves. In addition to verifying supplier claims, it is also trying to eliminate unnecessary packaging, encourage recycling, and train employees to understand environmental issues.

The Home Depot employs a full-time marketing/management staff and hires outside consultants to investigate its impact on Wetland sites, to see if the company might endanger animal species if a potential building site is proposed. When necessary, it hires outside environmental engineers to investigate any prior use of hazardous materials. While all of this is noteworthy, its most innovative approach involves a demonstration project.

OUR ENVIRONMENT:
THE ULTIMATE HOME IMPROVEMENT PROJECT

- We are committed to improving the environment by selling products that are manufactured, packaged, and labeled in a responsible manner, that take the environment into consideration, and that provide greater value to our customers.

- We will support efforts to provide accurate, informative product labeling of environmental marketing claims and impacts.

- We will strive to eliminate unnecessary packaging.

- We will recycle and encourage the use of materials and products with recycled content.

- We will conserve natural resources by using energy and water wisely and seek further opportunities to improve the resource efficiency of our stores.

- We comply with all environmental laws and will maintain programs and procedures to ensure compliance.

- We are committed to minimizing environmental, health, and safety risks for our employees and our customers.

- We will train employees to enhance understanding of environmental issues and policies and to promote excellence in job performance in all environmental matters.

- We will encourage our customers to become environmentally conscious shoppers.

THE HOME DEPOT/GREEN CROSS
ENVIRONMENTAL CLAIMS QUESTIONNAIRE

PRODUCT _____

PART 1

A. General Vendor Information
Vendor Company Name: _____

Address: _____

City: _____ State: _____ Zip: _____

Contact Name: _____ Title: _____

Phone: _____ Fax: _____

Subsidiary of (if applicable): _____

B. Product Information
Brand Name (as used on label): _____

UPC Code(s): _____

Product Number(s): _____

General Description of Product: _____

Home Depot SKU #(s) (if applicable): _____

Please attach a Material Safety Data Sheet (MSDS), product sample, and additional information or documentation to support claim(s) as needed. If your manufacturing facility has received a Toxic Release Inventory (TRI) rating, please include appropriate documentation.

PART 2

C. Environmental Claim Information for Product
(Complete this section ONLY if claim is for a product)

Vendor's Statement of Claim:

_____

_____

_____

_____

_____

Complete #1 - #5 where applicable to claim:

1) If the product claim is for "bio-degradability" or "photo-degradability," please list all product ingredients. Check those ingredients which are claimed to be bio- or photo-degradable.

Chemical Name	Common Name	CAS No.	% Weight	✔

If the product is a liquid or powdered formula, please list all ingredients regardless of claim made.

Under what conditions do the ingredients and/or product degrade: _____
_____

Other Properties (e.g., pH, water soluble): _____
_____

2) If the product claim is for energy efficiency, what is the basis of comparison for this claim? _____
_____
_____

3) If the product claim is "recyclable," is the product recyclable in whole, or in part:
Whole _____ Part _____
If part, please specify: _____
What is the current recycling rate for that product? _____
Do recycling facilities exist in all locations where this product is sold?
_____ Yes _____ No   If no, where do facilities exist? _____
_____

Material	% Recycled Content	Source*

4) If the product claim is not covered under #1-4, please justify claim below: (e.g., ozone-safe, landfill safe, safe for incineration, environmentally friendly): _

_____
_____
_____
_____
_____

PART 3

D. Environmental Claim Information for Packaging
(Complete this section ONLY if claim is for packaging)

Vendor's Statement of Claim	Does claim pertain to Inner or Outer Packaging:

General Properties of Packaging:
Include all components

Physical Dimensions: _____

Composition of Colorants, Pigments or Inks: _____
_____

Primary Packaging*

Materials	Weight	% wt. of total

Secondary Packaging*

Materials	Weight	% wt. of total

* Source: Post-Consumer/Pre-Consumer Waste/Industrial Scrap
See attached Standards

Tertiary Packaging*

Materials	Weight	% wt. of total

Note: "primary" refers to the inner packaging, closest to the product.

Are any of the packaging materials multi-layer, co-extrusion, wax or plastic coated, or do they contain wet-strength additives? If so, please specify: _____

_____

_____

Complete #1-4 where applicable to claim:

1) If the packaging claim is for "bio-degradability" or "photo-degradability," please list all packaging ingredients. Check those ingredients which are claimed to be bio- or photo-degradable.

Chemical Name	Common Name	CAS No.	% Weight	✔

Under what conditions does the packaging degrade? _____

_____

_____

2) If the claim is "recyclable," is the packaging recyclable in whole, or in part:
_____ Whole _____ Part

If part, please specify: _____

What is the current recycling rate for that material? _____

Do recycling facilities exist in all locations where this product is sold?
_____ Yes _____ No   If no, where do facilities exist: _____

_____

3) If the packaging claim is for "recycled content," complete the following information:

Material	% Recycled Content	Source*

* Source: Post-Consumer/Pre-Consumer Waste/Industrial Scrap
See attached Standards

4) If the packaging claim is not covered under #1-4, please justify claim below: (e.g., ozone-safe, landfill safe, safe for incineration, no heavy metals in inks): _____

Authorization

As an authorized representative of _____ ,
I declare that, to the best of my knowledge, the information provided herein is true and correct.
Vendor's Signature _____
Printed Name _____
Title _____
Date _____

Figure 4-1
(Courtesy of The Home Depot. Used with permission.)

In Atlanta, a buy-back center demonstration project where customers can recycle and be paid for home improvement and traditional household recyclables they drop off at the center. The Home Depot is the first retailer that has a voluntary take-back system similar to the mandated system that is the law in Germany.

The recycling center in Atlanta is a 50–50 joint venture with the recycler Mindis Recycling. Both companies hope it will be a money maker. They call their center the Recycling Depot and it is located adjacent to The Home Depot retail building supply store. The Recycling Depot is a 217-foot long drive, that works like a drive through the lumber yard. It accepts building materials like copper pipe, aluminum gutter, as well as more traditional consumer recyclables such as paper, glass, and plastic. As a customer brings the material to the Recycling Depot, it is weighed and the customer is given a ticket that can be exchanged for cash. The cash is based on the volume and grade of materials. Often after they are paid, many Recycling Depot customers run next door to The Home Depot store to buy more stuff.

The Recycling Depot began when The Home Depot hired Mark Eisen as their environmental marketing manager. He and Terry Kinskey, a district manager, became aware of Mindis Recycling Mart (a buy-back center that also sells environmentally related products) where customers are paid by the pound for loads of leftovers. The two saw the on-site Mindis Mart as an ideal way to marry the sale of building materials with the idea of keeping them out of landfills. As a result, the Recycling Depot was born, where builders were paid to bring in discarded home improvement materials (aluminum, copper wire) to be recycled and resold to a network of companies.

UNETHICAL MARKETING CLAIMS

The Home Depot, like others mentioned here, have recognized a consumer need and are generating revenue by designing products and services to fit those environmental desires. There are a multitude of opportunities for companies wanting to tap these environmental needs. Companies like The Home Depot make good business sense in trying to satisfy those desires.

There is money to be made in consumer environmentalism. Unfortunately, a few businesses are out for the quick buck and don't worry about a little dishonesty and fraud to satisfy their own desires. Unethical practices soon create their own pressure, as is the case with misleading and unethical marketing claims. For this reason, the Federal Trade Commission (FTC) defined the legal penalties and procedures for punishing those who make fraudulent claims. The FTC's definition of acceptable and unacceptable claims can be seen in Appendix A.

While some unscrupulous businesses may see an opportunity in using exaggerated claims, there is a bright side to this practice. As consumers become more knowledgeable, they will increasingly rely on sources of information they can trust. The organization that builds on that consumer trust, builds on their future.

The Home Depot, in order to safeguard their own environmental reputation, makes sure any supplier's environmental claims are properly documented. Its purpose is to provide guidance to its consumers whenever environmental claims appear on packages and products. For this reason, all vendors are required to participate in its Evaluation Program. The analysis includes all claims involving the packaging, labeling and products' environmental friendliness. One tool the company provides its customers with is an Environmental Report Card, seen in *Figure 4–2*, that provides a detailed accounting of each product's environmental burdens associated with packaging and production.

The Home Depot asks any vendors asserting an environmental claim to fill out an Environmental Marketing Claims Questionnaire, as seen in the Appendix. Vendors complete the questionnaire for as many products as they want, then submit the requested information (and a small claims processing fee) to Scientific Certification Systems (SCS), an independent environmental claims evaluation organization. SCS reviews the documentation provided by vendors to determine whether claims meet proper "green marketing" regulations and guidelines established by the Federal Trade Commission and specific states. This review also provides vendors with information about the appropriate types of claims for products.

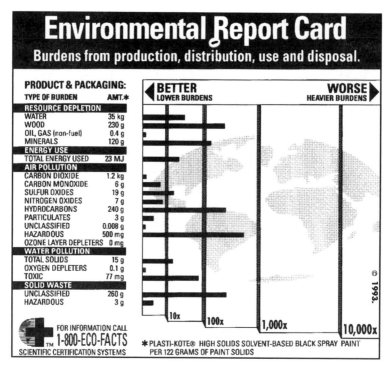

Figure 4–2

(Used with permission of Scientific Certification Systems)

CERTIFYING ETHICAL CLAIMS

In addition to examining vendor claims for The Home Depot and other retail chains, SCS provides a more comprehensive claims certification program. Under this program, SCS scientists conduct on-site inspections and audits to determine whether specific environmental claims, such as recycled content and biodegradability, can be substantiated. If the claim is documented, SCS issues a certificate and certification artwork that specifies the nature of the claim which has been verified. (See *Figure 4–3*.)

SCS also has developed a program to determine the overall environmental profile of products based on the science of "life-cycle inventory" assessment similar to that seen in Chapter 3. This evaluation considers the full range of resources depleted, energy used, air pollution, water pollution, and solid waste generated for the product and its packaging. These environmental "burdens" are tracked from the time raw materials are used, through manufacturing, product distribution, use, and final disposition.

Figure 4–3
(Used with permission of Scientific Certification Systems)

The results of the evaluation are listed on an "Environmental Report Card," such as that pictured in Figure 4–2. The report card provides a common frame of reference for comparing products within a specific category (e.g., spray paint to spray paint) as well as across categories (e.g., paper bags to plastic bags).

SCS, which was started in 1984, independently evaluates a product and its claim. This makes it possible for the products to be differentiated environmentally. The address for the organization is: **Scientific Certification Systems, 1611 Telegraph Avenue, Suite 1111, Oakland, CA 94617-2113, Phone: (510) 832-1415, FAX: (510) 832-0359.**

THINK GLOBAL, THINK GREEN!

The EPA as a competitive advantage may be a little hard for some business managers to accept; however, certifiers like SCS and others should be thought of as a competitive advantage for the U.S. rather than a nuisance because it allows you to benchmark yourself. Companies should recognize that it is a mistake to think that environmental issues are American issues. Often, environmental sentiment is stronger overseas than it is in the U.S. Up until recently, U.S. customers have not worried about pollution to the extent they have overseas. With its abundant resources and land, it simply was not recognized as a severe problem. Sometimes having too much makes you less competitive, just as expecting too little can reduce competitiveness. Japan was a fertile ground in which to sow quality seeds because it has very few natural resources. The country's lack of ample space, land, and raw materials made it more receptive to dollar-reducing and quality-increasing concepts like TQM and JIT. These techniques emphasize the need to be frugal and make the best possible use of all your resources. The focus is on process improvement and employee involvement. As a result, Japan and others less fortunate than us in terms of natural resources, were able to enhance their quality and lower costs.

The opposite is true of the United Kingdom (U.K.). In the U.K., environmental regulations are less restrictive than in some other 'developed' countries. As a result, potential export markets for U.K. companies are not available increasingly because the focus of the companies is on minimum domestic standards which can lead to noncompliance abroad.[7] In the U.K., at least, stronger environmental legislation could be helpful for developing international markets.

American manufacturers are embracing increasingly a set of international standards called ISO 9000 that encourages excellence in everything from design to quality control. Now the International Standards Organization has created new standards to promote environmentally sound manufacturing and products. Companies that meet these standards will be able to label their products "environmentally sound"—a very powerful marketing tool. John Donaldson, chief of standards and code and information at the National Institute of Standards & Technology believes U.S. companies already meet tougher environmental regulations than most foreign rivals and also believes that such standards may give them a competitive advantage.[6] Who would ever have thought that the EPA may turn out to be a competitive advantage. While many business people might have difficulty with believing the EPA could help create a competitive advantage, most would appreciate the value of benchmarking.

Environmental benchmarking against the best is critical for global industries. It might be worth noting that both German and Dutch companies believe their national legislation will continue to be tighter than the rest of Europe. Having higher standards can be a plus. Having lower standards is absolutely a minus, because you can't sell to other countries. If this sounds somewhat familiar, it ought to; it is a story that has already been told, only the last time you heard it it was quality, rather than the environment, that was the central character.

It is the opinion of many that what happened in the area of quality can easily happen with the environment. The ideal quality system would be to take 100 percent raw materials and to convert them into 100 finished goods with no waste and no inefficiencies. This same definition would be a good one for an environmental system as well. Improving operational and managerial efficiencies not only improves the quality of products and services, but also improves environmental competitiveness. In order to avoid being behind the competitive curve, you will need to benchmark against the environmental best. Do not wait for foreign companies to grasp the environmental initiative, as they did with quality issues.

Surely, most businesses today would recognize the potential of environmentally friendly products, and benchmark themselves against the best. Despite this recognition by many, most managers still fail to explore fully the enormous power of integrating environmentalism into corporate decision making. It's an opportunity that must not be missed.

It is an old story where some see problems and others see opportunities. One such individual is Ben Cohen of Ben and Jerry's Ice Cream. He has launched a new business focusing on concern for the Brazilian rain forest. One goal of the new company is to increase the demand for harvested rain forest products, rather than its lumber. It is trying to create a demand for forest products rather than slash and burn. At last report it was selling as much of a new ice cream with Brazil nuts as they could make.

Expect environmental opportunities to grow as consumer demand for better environmental decisions increases. Customers are increasingly putting their money where their convictions are. The Social Investment Forum represents 375 investment advisors and eight mutual funds that impose environmental screening on the companies in which they invest. The total assets of investment funds dedicated to sound environmental and social practices have risen from $40 billion in 1984 to $450 billion in 1990.[1]

There is enormous potential for profit where products and the companies that make them are seen as environmentally friendly, but as we will see, the potential for environmental profit extends far beyond your immediate customers' needs and desires. There are long-term customers who also play a role in your success.

CLOSING THOUGHTS

Change without direction is simply movement. Environmental change should only occur if you can decide where you want to go. As the adage goes "the customer is always right," so a business mission should be defined as to what the customer wants.

The problem in the past has been that far too many saw their customer in short terms. They only saw one aspect of their "customers," usually those who initially purchased their products or services. Little attention was paid to their *long-term customers*. In this chapter we looked at our short-term external customers' demands for more environmentally friendly products and services. These short-term customers are the ones buying your goods and services and it is true that their needs must be addressed—but they are not your only customers.

Long-term customers of a business include its regulators, legislators, the community in general and even national environmental pressure groups.

Long-term customers can also be the internal ones within a company, including all departments, functions, and managerial levels.

In the end, it will be the organizations that best satisfy both short- and long-term customer needs. Competing in the global workplace of the 1990s begins by changing the *definition of who is your customer*.

Monsanto was one of the first to perceive its customer as long-term. Monsanto's success at identifying environmental opportunities occurred because it was one of the first to broaden its definition of its customer base. Many organizations that deal with environmental cost see environmental regulators as their customer. Monsanto broadened its customer base to go beyond simply meeting environmental regulations and to redefining the customer as the general public. Changing its definition meant changing the way it managed environmental issues. In its case it meant adopting a TQM approach to the environment. The company's TQM approach required that environmental concerns be fully integrated into ongoing business programs and long-term business strategies. That's an issue we will look at later.

This also involves focus on all customers. While Monsanto still has environmental regulators in its customer base, other "customers" include local plant communities, environmental organizations, customers of its products and suppliers of its raw materials. To help focus on new customers, like local communities and environmental organizations, the company uses advisory groups, public outreach programs and environmental groups. For Monsanto, a key to this approach, as with any new customers, is identifying what its customers' concerns and needs are and incorporating those concerns into its operations. You cannot do that unless you know what you've got, environmentally speaking, and that is the subject of the next chapter.

ENDNOTES

1. Beaumont, John R., "Managing the Environment: Business Opportunity and Responsibility," *Futures*, Vol. 24, No. 3 (April 1992), pp. 16–197.

2. Kashmanian, Richard M., *Assessing the Environmental Consumer Market*. Office of Policy, Planning and Evaluation, United States Environmental Protection Agency. Washington, D.C. (April 1, 1991). pp. 3–11

3. Rosenberg, William G., "The New Clean Air Act of 1990: Winds of Environmental Change," *Business Horizons*. Vol. 35, No. 2 (March–April 1992) p. 34.

4. Schwartz, Joe, "Americans Annoyed by Wasteful Packaging," *American Demographics*. Vol. 14, No. 4, (April 1992) p. 13.

5. "Business Executives Differ on Business Practice Standards," *APICS— The Performance Advantage* (April 1992) pp. 13–21.

6. International Management, August 1990. Cited in Sanda Vandermerke, Michael D. Oliff, "Corporate Challenges for an Age of Reconsumption," *Columbia Journal of World Business*, Vol. XXVI, No. III (Fall 1991) p. 8.

7. "Environmental Efforts Company-wide," *Earth Focus*. In-house publication—Nordstrom Corporation. (March 1993), p. 6.

5

CONDUCTING AN
ENVIRONMENTAL
ASSURANCE SURVEY

Audits have always been a part of business. Financial audit procedures have been around since the beginning of modern business. These audits were the forerunner of environmental auditing, which got its start in the United States in the mid-1970s. Companies like General Motors, Allied-Signal, and ARCO, among others, developed programs independently to routinely evaluate health, safety, and environmental programs. These companies used the basic structure inherent in financial audit procedures and applied them to the environment area. Financial audits generally consist of a familiarization process where an auditor develops a basic understanding of the subject. Then there is a verification process where documents and physical aspects of the business are reviewed. Next comes an evaluation stage that reviews the financial status of a business, where oral and written reports are made as are follow-ups to make sure corrective action is taken. The same structure underlies environmental audits.

Internal environmental audits in theory are supposed to identify and then isolate environmental weaknesses. As with financial audits, environmental audits require that someone in the organization be independent and not involved in the problem or solution directly. All reviews should be detailed, comprehensive, and documented. Audits need to be limited to facts, be restricted to a certain period of time, and include formal corrective action procedures.

ENVIRONMENTAL ASSURANCE

Audits are usually done to make sure a company meets mandatory regulations and legal requirements. They are a good idea, and for many companies it is a good first step, but a better approach in the 1990s would be to recognize that simply meeting your environmental legal requirements will not ensure that you will remain competitive. To compete, we have to be *proactive,* not reactive. It is a matter of changing our *perception* from one that focuses on audits to one that focuses on customer assurance. Most of the procedures are the same, but with customer assurance rather than audits the focus is on improving environmental efficiency rather than on simply meeting environmental requirements or avoiding legal risk!

As with auditing, consumer assurance should be the responsibility of the companies themselves. Environmental Assurance (EA) should be designed to be a cost-effective way to assure that environmental consideration is integrated throughout corporate decision making. For this to occur there needs to be a *systematic* way to objectively and periodically examine a company's environmental performance. A systems approach would include determining how well, from an environmental standpoint, the organization as a whole, its people, and equipment are performing.

Performing an EA could have several practical advantages, not the least of which is identifying potential cost saving from waste elimination and minimization. It also lets you compare and exchange information between different operations, functions, and divisions within an organization. The assurance process helps you evaluate environmental training programs and provides data on how they might be improved. A by-product of this process is that employee awareness of environmental responsibilities is increased dramatically. The EA process gives management a chance to also give credit, recognition, and reward for good environmental performance. As with audit, EA also has the advantage of providing you with information you can use and to evaluate your emergency arrangements and insurance coverage needs.

ELEMENTS OF A SUCCESSFUL PROGRAM

One absolutely necessary ingredient in any successful change, including implementing EA, is *full management commitment* by upper management. In EA this commitment can be seen in many ways, including showing overt personal interest and concern about environmental issues. Setting high environmental standards, like zero waste, drives home the point that management takes environmental initiatives seriously. Of course, there comes a time when you have to "walk the walk" otherwise it is *just* talk. That means being willing to allocate the necessary human and technological resources. Later we will discuss some of the innovative energy-saving technologies now available. Unless someone makes the hard decision to invest in appropriate technology and training for personnel, you cannot expect to achieve anything close to zero waste. Management must also be willing to put in the time to actually follow-up on recommendations. Even employee involvement activities like sample suggestion programs will fail if there is infrequent feedback about the status of those suggestions.

Even though the assurance process occurs in-house, there is no reason why it should not be *objective*. It is mandatory that the team doing the assurance process be as detached and objective as possible. For this reason it would be wise to set up some mechanism, which we will look at in a moment, for assuring objectivity. Setting up systematic and well-thought-out procedures is important because you want to make sure each assurance activity covers what is relevant rather than what is easy to measure.

Expertise that is needed on EA teams includes knowledge of corporate policies, and operational expertise. That is why each member of an EA team needs to be there because of his or her competencies. Political connections don't hurt either. Competent people will find good solutions but they will only be useful solutions if they are implemented. Often that is why EA teams include some senior-level managers so that when solutions are developed they will not only be feasible technically, but also realistic politically.

Written EA reports should be documented properly. There should be no doubt about what you are recommending if there are sufficient factual and objective observations cited. The following Preassurance, Assurance, and Postassurance activities can help meet these conditions.

PREASSURANCE ACTIVITIES

Preparation is the key word. Before an EA review begins you want to make sure you have chosen the best site for the review and selected a team to do the EA. Time and resources are limited so you will have to maximize your efforts. EA plans will need to be drawn up that define the technical, geographic, and time scope. Background information must be obtained through the use of questionnaires or other means. Preparation minimizes time spent doing the EA. It also makes sure the EA team is ready.

At Allied-Signal, Inc., team leaders who are full-time surveillance professionals (because they do audits, not customer assurances) are responsible for confirming review dates and for organizing a team based on the scope of the review. The composition of the team can include members from the site being reviewed or not. Insiders have an advantage because they have knowledge of the specifics of a site. Using local employees also makes it appear to be more of an assistance process rather than an audit. The main drawback is that the insiders may have difficulty being objective, especially if colleagues or supervisors are criticized.

At Allied-Signal, team leaders notify a manager of a site one month in advance about the scope and specific dates of review. Corporate files are used to obtain and review information on the production processes. They may use flow charts, plant layouts, review policies procedures, and operational manuals.

ASSURANCE ACTIVITIES

At Allied-Signal, an on-site review starts with a meeting of the team and facility manager of an area to be audited, plus appropriate personnel, though each company's EA process can vary. At Allied-Signal's initial meeting, the audit team's objectives are reviewed and a brief tour is taken. Sometimes several preassurance activities are actually performed at the site. Regardless of where this occurs—at the site or before—several activities should be initiated. First, you will want to identify any management pollution control systems. These might include monitoring and record-keeping procedures and a review of plans for emergency situations. A careful review of internal inspection programs is also helpful.

Once you have control systems in place you will want to *assess* them. This involves determining how they are in meeting their objectives. Sometimes it is a matter of using judgment to evaluate the effectiveness of controls. To help aid judgment, gather as much evidence as possible. You will want to find out if the controls that are set out actually do what they are supposed to. For example, reviewing samples of effluent monitoring data seems wise. A review of training records will show you if the appropriate people have been trained. Purchasing records can be used to verify if approved waste disposal contractors have been used. All information should be recorded and whenever something is found that is not up to par it should be recorded as a "finding." Remember, the difference between an audit and an assurance activity is that everyone should feel this is a *service* not an indictment.

Once controls have been tested and verified, and team members have reached some conclusions, the team should meet to evaluate and draw conclusions based on all findings. At Allied-Signal, the team meets and completes its own questionnaire that helps to develop an initial understanding of the facilities' operations, processes, personnel responsibilities, and environmental management controls.

The team meets to integrate and evaluate individual findings and assess any inefficiencies or deficiencies anyone may have come across. The goal is to confirm that there is sufficient evidence to support findings. At Allied-Signal each person on the team gathers information and performs relevant tests. The team uses sampling techniques as well as use good judgment in selecting the type and size of samples.

POSTASSURANCE ACTIVITIES

With EA rather than audit, the service should be voluntary rather than mandatory. Findings should be reviewed individually with the person who is in charge of the site. A formal exit meeting should be held with site managers to report on the findings of assurance strengths and weaknesses. A final assurance report is then prepared by the team leader. The purpose of Allied-Signal's written report is to provide information to top managers on the most significant findings. The overall thrust of the report is an opinion about whether or not a facility is in compliance with its environmental needs. An EA report would be the same but the purpose is not on compliance but on maximizing environmental profitability.

At Allied-Signal, the written report has four parts. It could be a good format for an EA final report. Section 1 contains information about who, what, where, and why the audit is done. One section provides examples of significant incidents where regulatory standards were not met. This section would be significant as a record of profit potential rather than incidents of failure. Another section discusses the company's environmental policies and procedures and what is needed to encourage better environmental management (we will look at some of these initiatives in the following chapter).

The final section lists any incidents where inefficiencies or deficiencies in the control system make compliance with the law or company policies questionable. This might include improper record keeping, documentation, or unclean assignment of environmental responsibilities. Despite the breadth of the reports, they are typically four to five pages long. With an EA report, the same issues need to be examined, but the purpose should be on identifying life-cycle cost, not complying with the letter of the law.

CLOSING THOUGHTS

In the end, the length of the final EA report does not matter as much as the actions that result. Action plans should be drawn up to obtain management approval and to track improvements continually. Corrective action needs to be proposed. Follow-up should be encouraged so management knows corrective action has been taken.

Companies are slowly making the transition from audits where the objective is to manage for compliance to managing for assurance. It is here that the companies believe long-range success is best served by trying to identify tomorrow's environmental problems and risks. Changing the perspective from one of punishment to reward is essential. This must be voluntary, not mandatory. It should focus on documenting profit potential, not cost and legal compliance. It should be seen as a corporate service, and not a bureaucratic reporting system.

The EA team that is assembled should concentrate consulting services on examining if a site has clearly defined environmental policies and procedures and if they are being communicated to everyone effectively. The team should look at the day-to-day decision-making system that is in place and see if they can isolate areas where environmental considerations can be better integrated into the decision-making process. Later we will look at specific ways to improve and enhance this decision making so it leads to greater profit potential. Long-range financial and strategic decision making should also be examined to see if life-cycle costing and other accounting practices are being considered when developing future products, services, and business options.

In the final analysis, an EA process is the forerunner to reshaping an organization's structure. As we have noted, later in this book we will look at this new organizational structure which we call *Systematic Environmental Management* or SEM. In this section we will examine its components, then in Chapter 9 we will begin to tie all the pieces together to provide a comprehensive road map to organizational change. It is a change that brings the organization from the 1980s of compliance, cost, and regulations to one that focuses on improving the efficiency of environmental performance and profit.

6

USING WASTE REDUCTION AS A COMPETITIVE ADVANTAGE

$\mathbf{F}$rank McAbee, Senior Vice-President of Environmental and Business Practices for United Technologies, says waste reduction is to a large extent simply process engineering; it means operating processes at peak efficiency to reduce waste, cut costs, and improve quality and productivity. He then goes on to say that, in a sense, one can promote waste reduction through concepts like, "continuous improvement, total quality management, doing it right the first time and asset management."[1] He believes waste reduction reinforces the notion that protecting the environment and gaining a competitive advantage are *not* mutually exclusive. United Technologies has started taking advantage of this competitive edge by developing engineering standards that promote the use of environmentally responsible materials and processes.

DOW CHEMICAL'S WRAP

Dow Chemical would agree that the environment and, in particular, waste, is or will be a key to success in the 1990s. Perhaps Dow, more than anyone else, has been able to create one of the most famous systematic approaches to integrating and managing waste. Its formalized waste reduction activities began in 1986 through a program called Waste Reduction Always Pays or WRAP. It is more than a name, it is an integrated effort that has paid big dividends for Dow.

Dow's WRAP consists of *five basic goals* focused on the importance of improving both the management of the operational process of manufacturing goods and of the absolute necessity of extensive employee involvement. These goals include the need to:

- *Reduce waste to the environment* through continuous improvement in its manufacturing process so it can in turn reduce emissions and the volume of wastes.

- *Recognize excellence at eliminating waste.* By recognizing those efforts, Dow believes it sends a positive message that waste reduction is a top priority. When employee efforts are recognized, it motivates and encourages them to seek new methods of waste reduction.

- *Enhance the waste reduction mentality,* because waste reduction is employee driven. The approach is to try to promote, whenever possible, this attitude throughout the company.

- *Measure and track progress.* It is impossible to manage that which you cannot measure. Dow believes measuring waste reduction efforts is needed in order to track progress in each division.

- *Reduce long-term costs.* The company recognizes that all WRAP projects have a positive impact on its environment, but it wants to identify those projects especially that impact the bottom line through fuel, raw material and environmental control costs.[2]

DEVELOPING A LANGUAGE OF MEASUREMENT

Ultimately management must set up an effective operational process if goals are to become reality. It is setting up these operational initiatives that separates Dow from most. To begin with, each manufacturing division is responsible for developing and implementing its own WRAP program. This flexibility has produced a wide array of methods for implementing WRAP. Some of these include idea-generating contests and utilization of quality performance techniques. There are plant waste reduction reviews by teams of personnel, recognition programs, and communication initiatives.

While each division has the flexibility to tailor a WRAP program to suit its own individual needs, there needs to be common language that can be shared throughout the company. This need for a common link has been critical to improvement in quality and is critical to environmental management. Dow recognizes the necessity of this common language and has created a measurement they call the *ratio of waste versus production* which we will look at in a later chapter. It is used in assessing emissions throughout the entire corporation. Once these waste indexes are determined, performance can be tracked and evaluated for each area, regardless of the area's function. Once an area's performance is known, flow charts can be developed listing the steps involved in the WRAP process. Listing these steps helps the group identify and make improvements that will have the greatest impact on reducing wastes.

As part of this process, each plant was asked to develop an inventory of its waste stream. A waste stream consists of by-products produced when making any primary product. They usually have a negative effect on the air, water, or land. Once an area has identified its waste stream, each is researched to find out how it is produced. Next, each of these wastes is prioritized for further investigation and action is based on volume and toxicity. Individual targets or goals are established and resources are allocated to solve the most critical WRAP projects. Dow notes that tracking progress of improvements not only is fundamental to being able to improve, but provides a vehicle to communicate performance to both employees and the community.[2]

An example of this type of measurement system can be seen at a Dow subsidiary in Port Washington, Wisconsin, where a task force at the plant has identified and implemented a waste reduction program. The goal of the team was to reduce the polyvinyl chlorides (PVCs) and polypropylene plastic by-products. In order to do this, a material yield program was developed to keep track of weekly inventories and yield measurements. The key to the program's success was the daily collection and measurement of wastes at various points in the process. By using this data, it was able to establish both short- and long-term goals for waste reduction, recycling, and incineration. Milestone or baseline measures were established so it could measure progress.

Employee involvement is essential in any good waste reduction program and this was the case at Port Washington where the company trained employees in data collection, analysis, and goal setting. Feedback is important too, so it held weekly meetings between operators, quality assurance personnel and management during which they could share information and get the input from operational personnel.

Did emphasis on measuring performance and using employee involvement to improve performance help? As a result of this process, production became less wasteful once problem areas were identified. The production line waste has been reduced by 77 percent. Approximately 85 percent is recycled, 15 percent is incinerated, and no solid waste is sent to the landfill. The savings for this project are expected to exceed $300,000.

SUCCESS STORIES

Dow Chemical admits freely that effective waste reduction and being able to be cost competitive requires capital improvements. It may also require new equipment and upgraded facilities, but there can be a healthy return-on-investment. That is why each year the company invests about $150 million at its plants around the world.

There is no pat formula for a healthy return on this investment. What we know is that it takes an integrated effort. In Dow Chemical's case it was able to reap healthy dividends by implementing various operational initiatives including making process improvements, as well as making equipment changes and modifications. It also used involvement of suppliers and employees and used quality improvement tools like Statistical Process Control (SPC) to make a difference. Later we will look at how these problem-solving tools can be used to improve performance in greater detail. A good sample of how these techniques can be used can be seen in Dow's Freeport, Texas plant.

Process Improvements

At Dow Chemical's Freeport, Texas plant a waste reduction team recognized the opportunity to reduce the amount of product loss in a by-product stream. The objective was to improve the quality and utilization of a by-product called hydrochloric acid. They were able to get improved performance by *changing their production process*. As a result, the plant was able to eliminate the use of excess ethylene, which was contaminating its hydrogen chloride, thereby producing a higher quality hydrochloric acid. The team was also able to make modifications that improved the separation of a by-product. This improvement helped produce a higher quality hydrochloric acid and improved the recovery of other by-products. Savings are estimated at $2.6 million per year.

At Dow's plant in Pittsburg, California a waste reduction team identified opportunities to recycle and improve control of a chemical used in the production of agricultural products. By conducting experiments, it was able to find the *optimum operating conditions*. The team did it by developing a computer model that gave it the ability to monitor a number of variables such as pressure, temperature, rate-of-feed, and weight. Through these efforts they were able to reduce 2.5 million pounds of waste with a cost savings of $750,000.

At the Plaquemine, Louisiana plant the goal was to reduce asbestos being disposed of at an on-site landfill. Asbestos at the plant is used in a manufacturing process where "chlorine cell diaphragms" separate chlorine gas from caustic soda. Chlorine is used in the manufacture of plastics, solvents, and water purification systems. Caustic soda is used in the manufacture of paper, aluminum, and soap. A team at this plant was able to make the manufacturing process more consistent. To do this it used higher quality asbestos which in turn doubled its diaphragm's working lifetime. Higher quality asbestos thus meant it could be washed and reused. As a result of increasing the working lifetime of the diaphragms and by reducing the amount of asbestos used, the team was able to reduce what was going to the landfill by 3.3 million pounds or $1.1 million in savings per year.

THE ROLE OF TECHNOLOGY

Many assume that pollution prevention means excessive capital investment. As we will see, this is not the case, but *upgrading equipment and technology* can play a role in reaping long-term cost advantages. This was the case at Dow's Pittsburg, California plant. A team at the plant was trying to recover more solvent from their production process and reduce emissions. By upgrading plant equipment it was able to recover and reuse 210,000 pounds of solvent produced during production. The project also reduced air emissions by 15,000 pounds per year and reduced solvent costs by $8,000.

At the Minneapolis, Minnesota plant the savings due to a number of equipment changes and modifications were even more dramatic. A team was able to identify opportunities to recover and recycle methylene chloride by first brainstorming to determine potential solvents. It then implemented numerous process changes and capital projects. New equipment was installed which improved the separation of solvents. As a result, organic waste was reduced by 6 million pounds with an annual savings of $1.2 million. Dow notes it continues to make modifications and improvements and soon the company will be able to have 100 percent recovery of the solvent. Such improvements have led to the recovery of more than 360,000 pounds of solvent yearly with a savings of $112,000.

THE ROLE OF PEOPLE

In many cases, improved waste management has occurred due to improving equipment and process technology. While creating greater operational efficiency is one way to reduce wastes, that alone is not the answer. Technology helps, but it is simply a tool; it is the hand that holds the tool that matters most.

As you may have already noticed, the word *team* seems to appear a lot whenever improvement in reducing pollution is mentioned. One central theme running through these examples of most waste reduction programs is the use of teams and greater employee involvement to solve waste reduction problems. You may or may not need new equipment or better process efficiency to reduce waste, but you cannot have effective waste management if you do not have employee involvement. Invariably, it is one's operating personnel that form the core of these teams and provide critical insight and solutions. For instance, at Dow's Midland, Michigan plant a waste reduction team identified a waste problem. It was the operational personnel who came up with a suggestion for using a mechanical screening system to filter out fine product particles. As a result of efforts, its system now recovers 85 percent of product particles. Dow notes the project pays for itself every three weeks. There was a 56 percent reduction in emissions and an annual savings of $43,000 in raw materials cost—with *no capital investment*. Later in the book we will look at how to set up an effective employee involvement process that maximizes human resource efforts.

CORPORATE ENVIRONMENTALISM

Dow Chemical shows us that there are hard-nosed economic reasons to get everyone involved in waste management, but what about projects where costs and benefits cannot be as easily delineated. Selecting projects that show the most immediate enhancement of the bottom line may not be the best approach. What about those projects for which the savings are not as clear cut? Is there any reason, from a business point of view, that we should bother with them? Perhaps the answer revolves around corporate environmentalism.

Richard J. Mahoney, Chairman and Chief Executive Officer of Monsanto, at one time made a speech referring to a column written by Jessica Matthews of the World Resources Institute. The article had appeared in the *Washington Post*. In it she identified *four levels* of corporate commitment. Level 1 was where a corporation planned to exploit the "green fad" while it lasts. Such companies know of the public interest in the environment and stick biodegradable or recyclable labels on their products. Level 2 companies discovered that reducing pollution could buy one bragging rights at little or no cost. A Level 3 company believes environmentalism was here to stay. They knew they had to change their business in order to stay *in* business. A handful of companies are what she called Level 4. These companies see the environment as a strategic business opportunity and are striving to turn it into a competitive advantage.[3]

Mahoney believes that companies assume incorrectly that competition and environmentalism are mutually exclusive. Monsanto is learning how competition can serve the cause of environmental protection. He clearly sees Monsanto as positioning itself as a Level 4 company and believes the debate in the past has centered around protection versus cost. The public wants protection, and business has focused on cost and benefits, but he thinks the rules are changing.

Competition will make the environment a "wedge" that separates winners from losers. Using waste reduction as a cost-effective management tool is only the first shot. Waste, like so many other environmental considerations, is simply an overhead expense. We are just beginning to understand its long-term impacts. Better accounting and measurement systems will invariably help identify costs and benefits, but ultimately it is management's understanding of the intangibles of enviro-management that will dictate whether it will become a 1 or 4 level company. It is Level 4 that has the clear competitive advantages.

CLOSING THOUGHTS

These advantages, even if intangible, will be won when the public perceives a company as environmentally responsible. We buy products and services because of higher quality and the environment is no different. Typical of this new awareness of the competitive advantage of the environment is the approach used by ARCO.

The company recently received high marks for using a state-of-the-art procedure to reduce the environmental impact. While drilling an exploratory oil well in Ecuador, the company chose to do something other than bulldoze roads throughout the jungle. The company instead used helicopters to haul equipment and lumber into the area. Local Indians helped foresters select the trees for lumber used on the well pad that ARCO says was 25 percent the size of that usually cleared for such a project. After drilling was complete, banked topsoil was respread and vegetated with native plants grown at a nursery on-site. They also avoided any clear cutting of the forest and whenever possible cleared the land by hand and made use of trees that had been destroyed in storms.

The approach used by ARCO in this situation would be hard to justify on a balance sheet, but it is one that was chosen by an oil company, of all things! Why did they do it? Because they recognized that perhaps the best reasons for waste reduction and the best way to turn "green into green" may be a close accounting of intangibles. Even though they are intangible, they do have value which we will look at in closer detail in succeeding chapters.

However, first we will examine some of the *tangible* ways of reducing waste and inefficiencies. These techniques will provide a good start for anyone wanting to minimize costs. They will also provide a foundation for anyone willing to make the transition from one of cost avoidance to using environmental management as a profit measure.

ENDNOTES

1. McAbee, Frank, "The Bottom Line on Waste Reduction," *Waste Lessons*, Vol. I, No. 1, Summer 1992, p. 1–4.

2. WRAP package from Dow Chemical Company.

3. Mahoney, Richard, "The Environment Is Our Business," *Remarks at the International Institute of Synthetic Rubber Products*, Washington, D.C., May 16, 1991, p. 1.

7

GUIDELINES FOR PREVENTING POLLUTION

$\mathbf{A}$s we have already seen, often when managers think of environmental management, they think cost and when they think cost they are usually thinking about how they can react to their waste problem. Waste and how to reduce it in a cost-effective method is a big concern at management round tables. What most of these people may not realize fully is that often cleaner production doesn't cost, it actually can *save* money. Maximizing profits means maximizing yield. By obtaining more product from less raw materials, you produce less waste.

From a competitive standpoint if you lower your overhead below that of your competitor you have gained a significant strategic advantage. Currently the U.S. Office of Technological Assessment (OTA) thinks that we could cut industrial waste in the U.S. by 75 percent if we would only use advanced technologies, but this takes long-term commitment. A U.N. agency also reports that industrial countries could recycle more than 50 percent of their paper, glass, plastics, and metals if they had the proper infrastructure.[1]

One of the most famous examples of a company taking advantage of this preventative approach to waste management is the 3M Corporation. One goal of 3M is to lower releases to air, water, and land by 90 percent and to reduce the generation of solid waste by 50 percent by the year 2000. Economic reasons are why 3M, DuPont, AT&T, and others, are planning to move to a closed-loop production that emits no discharges.[2]

As organizations recognize the competitive advantages of waste elimination and reduction it becomes clear that they will need some guidelines for implementation. Luckily, some of these guidelines have already been developed by the President's Commission on Environmental Quality (PCEQ). The commission has studied waste and identified two areas, *source reduction* and *procurement of recycled-content products* as critical to the success of waste-management efforts.

PCEQ has developed a workplace waste reduction guide that can be seen in Appendix B. As part of the process, PCEQ tested the guidelines in a number of demonstration projects. Their revised *How-To Guide* in Appendix B in this book helps move organizations from initial waste reduction to the point where they can develop a full-scale reduction plan. The guide identifies four sources of waste reduction that include your suppliers, employees, technology, and customers. Furthermore, a series of questions has been designed to help managers evaluate and identify potential waste reduction opportunities. It was the opinion of the PCEQ task force that many environmental problems could be solved and that even monies could be made if organizations would simply change their purchasing practices. One surprising discovery the task force made was in the area of recycling. When recycling programs were in place, employees felt little more could be done. They assumed recycling was the extent of waste reduction responsibilities and ignored other potential actions. Contrary to this opinion, the task force found that several things could be done to make waste management a profitable operation. The three lessons learned from the experience were:

- *Within an organization there must be a champion of waste reduction who is in a position of authority (or has access to authority) to follow up and ensure that the project moves forward.* In particular, the task force noticed that while employee enthusiasm might be high initially, programs were *not* successful unless employees were empowered.

- In order to be successful, organizations must recognize that waste reduction involves more than just managing solid waste differently. *It requires a new attitude about how to conduct business.* A comprehensive waste reduction program involves purchasing, employee training, and supportive areas most would not associate with waste generation and disposal.

- *Collaborative relationships with neighboring businesses can improve cost effectiveness.* This might mean buying recycled content products, finding outlets for reuse of waste materials, or searching for low- or no-cost recycling options. The point is that there are economies of scale for working together.[3]

Now we will look at how some of the managerial actions identified produced economic rewards.

HOW TO DO IT

As already noted, 3M is one company that is making extensive use of the guides to waste reduction. It employs over 87,000 people and produces more than 60,000 different products including tapes, abrasives, film, and insulating material. Its efforts are on prevention rather than on dealing with waste after-the-fact. Their prevention efforts now referred to as *3P* (Pollution Prevention Pays) are renowned the world over. The program has been expanded to *3P Plus.* The "plus" has been a fairly recent addition to its "3P" efforts. It signifies greater commitment to reduce emissions through whatever means available, thereby reducing the source of pollution.

One of the most effective aspects of the 3P-Plus program involves the participation of the company's technical staff. Applications for eliminating or reducing waste projects are submitted to and reviewed by a coordinating committee made up of representatives from all technical groups. The purpose of the committee is to review the waste problem and to try to identify potential solutions while technicians provide needed expertise.

3M creates the employee collaboration so essential to success by establishing *waste minimization teams* in every operating division. The teams' purpose is to identify sources of reduction and recycling opportunities as well as to develop plans to meet them.[4] These teams are interdisciplinary in nature so they can develop the expertise for comprehensive solutions. The corporation also tries to multiply its efforts by sharing the results of a division's interdisciplinary team at pollution prevention with other 3M divisions.

So have all efforts paid off? From 1975 through 1991, 3M's pollution prevention efforts cut its pollution per unit production *in half.* It prevented more than 600,000 tons of pollutants and saved the company more than *$574 million.*[5]

"The Plan"

Employee involvement is critical to 3M's or any other business' chance to make prevention a profitable venture. However, desire alone is not enough

—you need a plan and you need a way of focusing your staff's efforts and thoughts. At 3M, the approach to eliminating pollution has been to concentrate on four fronts. They are:

- product reformulation
- process modification
- equipment redesign
- recycling and reuse of waste material

Product reformulation involves developing nonpolluting or less-polluting products or process. The company did this primarily by using different raw materials and feedstocks. Process modifications at 3M required changing the manufacturing process to control the production of by-products. It also occasionally involved incorporating nonpolluting or less-polluting raw materials or feedstocks. Equipment redesign at 3M refers to its efforts to modify equipment to perform better under specific operating conditions. It could also mean making better use of available by-products. Finally, 3M's resource recovery usually requires recycling of by-products for sale or for use in other company products or processes. Each of the four strategies used by 3M provides a framework for waste management that has been used, in one form or another, by a variety of organizations.

REDESIGNING PRIMARY PRODUCTS AND SERVICES

All of the techniques used by 3M and others are not equal. There is a hierarchy of choice when it comes to pollution prevention and your first choice should be *redesign of your products and services*. It would seem logical that when it comes to pollution your first choice and most comprehensive one should be to eliminate it. The best approach is to design pollution *out*. If preventing it altogether is impossible, then it may be possible to reduce the problem greatly by redesigning products and services so they are less polluting, by using different manufacturing systems, supplier systems, or raw materials.

For example, Robert Bosch, a German manufacturer, has developed a "super" electronic control chip which transfers all of a driver's instructions to the vehicle through a single cable—a second cable is enough for the entire electrical system. This redesign means a considerable decrease in the weight of the vehicle and resulting pollution.

In 1989, ARCO began selling "reformulated" gasoline in Southern California. This new gasoline can be used by older cars that run on leaded gas. ARCO says the gasoline can reduce air pollution in Southern California alone by 20 percent. This is because Olefin and other chemicals that react to sunlight to form smog have been lowered by one-third. Likewise, Benzene has been reduced by 50 percent and sulfur has been reduced by 80 percent in this new gasoline. ARCO's market share for older cars has increased from 33 percent to 35 percent in the first seven months the new gasoline has been available.

Earth's Best is another company trying to minimize the mark it leaves on the earth while at the same time making a profit. It introduced strained baby foods (in glass jars), cereals and juices grown organically without synthetic pesticides or preservatives. Even though the company's products are priced two to three times higher than conventional brands, sales have jumped from $1.2 million in 1988 to $5 million in 1989, and are expected to continue to rise.

Merck & Co. Inc., is a worldwide research intensive, health products company that has put extensive efforts into reducing the environmental impact of its products. A typical case of redesigning products to minimize waste production involved its manufacturing process for a drug called Primaxin. If it manufactured the broad-spectrum antibiotic drug as designed originally, it would have involved an 18-step process that generated a ton of waste for every pound of product as well as created a wide array of toxins. Before manufacturing began, Merck's chemists and engineers found a way to eliminate a half-million gallons of toxic waste each year. Solvent distillation and internal recovery of an acetone/water mixture cut the annual use of acetone by 80 percent. A new manufacturing plant to be placed at their Danville, Pennsylvania site will eliminate the toxic methylene chloride from major steps of this process.[6]

Another company that does a great deal of redesign work is 3M. At its laboratories it originally coated one of its medicine tablets with solvent. It was a necessary part of the process, but unfortunately emissions of the solvent at the plant had the potential to exceed its air pollution limits. The company eventually decided to use a water-based coating. The redesign cost $60,000 but eliminated the need to buy $180,000 in pollution equipment. Some solvents used in the old coating process were also no longer needed, saving 3M an extra $15,000 a year.

In another 3M facility in Aberdeen, South Dakota, staff was cutting round respirator masks from fabric sheets. Fully one-third of the fabric was wasted by this process. Resin sprayed on the fabric to help the mask keep its shape prevented the scraps from being recycled. Through a little rethinking, the company came up with a fiber blend that holds its form without resin. This change allowed the full recycling of 300 tons of fabric scraps per year and eliminated 400,000 gallons of dilute resin waste.

SUBSTITUTING, MODIFYING, AND RECYCLING

All these improvements occurred because of changes in operating conditions. Typical of this process is the one used by Northrop. Northrop Corporation's Aircraft Division in Hawthorne, California is the home of the company's manufacturing operation. Since 1989, it has reduced hazardous waste by over 60 percent through product and process redesign including *substitution of products, process modifications,* and *recycling.* As of 1993, its efforts have saved the company $2.5 million.

One typical case involved the mechanics on its F/A–18 fighter assembly line. The company found that touch-up paints and various sealants often hardened before the bottles and tubes were empty. The hardened materials were both wasteful and hazardous and as such required expensive special handling and disposal.

Its environmental solution, as is often the case, involved improving operational efficiency. In this case this meant improving inventory control. Because of changes in operating procedures, Northrop now buys these paints and sealants in smaller containers so mechanics are able to use all the substance before it hardens. As a result they discard less waste and have to buy less paint and sealant. The savings per year for this one action runs around $280,000.[7]

Not all redesigns reap such an immediate payback, but redesign should always be the first choice. Unfortunately, not enough attention is paid to redesign. This is especially true of services. One example of a service that needs redesigning is third-class mail. According to the U.S. Postal Service, 25 to 30 percent of all third-class mail is addressed improperly. It is often undeliverable and must be discarded. Of the 62.4 billion pieces of third-class mail sent in 1991, about 15.6 to 18.7 billion pieces of mail could not be delivered. Even if the Postal Service recycled all those billions of pieces of undeliverable mail, it would still represent a tremendous diversion of resources including paper, ink, energy, and time that could have been used elsewhere.[8]

Duplicate or unwanted copies of magazines and catalogs are equally wasteful, so the first solution should be to eliminate them. Publishers and catalogers could reduce the number of undeliverable magazines and catalogs by cleaning up the address problem. For example, Quad/Graphics notes that their Address Standardization reduces the number of undeliverable books by correcting addresses including street directionals (such as north and south), suffixes (avenue, street, boulevard), street names, cities and states of each address.

Being able to clean up the address problems will become even more important when bar codes are applied to mail automatically. Automatically mailing pieces of mail with bar codes will be heavily dependent on having clean mailing lists. There are currently programs that you can buy that identify duplicate names and addresses within mailing lists. Perhaps the best approach is the one used by the Direct Marketing Association. It offers consumers a mail preference service where people can request that their names not be sold to mailing lists. The file currently contains more than 2 million names.[8] Such an approach provides a good example of the redesign option that would be a preferred choice since elimination is often the best long-term solution.

HOW TO REDESIGN PRODUCTS AND SERVICES

The secret to being able to redesign products and services often depends on being able to *challenge your assumptions.* In order to redesign, never assume. A good example comes from plastics. Many assume plastic goods are the primary contributor to landfills and therefore should not be used. About 45 percent of landfill space is taken up by paper and paperboard while only 12 percent is plastic. Granted, 12 percent is nothing to be proud of, but it doesn't take up the space that paper does.

It is true that neither plastic nor paper easily biodegrade in landfills. Many therefore assume that because it won't biodegrade it is always toxic. A Dr. Rathie, Harvard-trained archaeologist, and his assistants examined landfills. He pointed out that a lack of biodegradability may actually be good. Being inert, plastic will not leak toxic chemicals into the groundwater as paper is susceptible to doing.[9]

Consider this point. Even if you recycle paper, there will be a time where it can no longer be recycled. Eventually, all paper fibers used in newspaper, cardboard, magazines and packaging breakdown and must end up in a landfill. Theoretically, plastic would be the best thing to print on. It is infinitely recyclable. John Morris, a manager in Quad/Graphics Finishing Purchasing department, points out that plastic can be recycled over and over again and will *never* lose its toughness.[10] It could be a milk jug one day and a fountain pen cover the next day. It might be possible someday to see the *Washington Post* printed on plastic over and over again.

REDUCING NONPOLLUTING PRODUCTS AND SERVICES

Quad/Graphics turned its Pallet Repair and Recycling area into a profit center by accepting wood waste from other companies for less than it would cost them to take it to a landfill. The old wood is then turned into mulch, and resold. It generates roughly fourteen 17-ton truckloads of mulch each month.[10]

In another case, Monsanto's Augusta, Georgia facility started using flammable process waste as fuel for its plant boilers operated by its food products subsidiary. This "waste" now generates 30 to 40 percent of the site's steam needs, and disposal costs have dropped.

Thinking about the practicality of eliminating pollution by using plastics to print on is pure speculation. There are, however, many organizations that are having a real and positive impact on its bottom line as well as the environment by reducing pollution through redesign.

Nordstrom, the retailing giant, has an aggressive waste reduction program that eliminates waste. One way it did this was through its credit card system. Annually they process 55 million Nordstrom credit card receipts that are produced on carbon paper, thus eliminating unnecessary trash. In a bit of innovation, its new credit card application form saves one million envelopes each year because it has been redesigned to fold into a return envelope. The result is a combination application/envelope that forms to make a new reduced-size form. Nordstrom's Data Processing Information group has also reduced its use of paper reports by over 45,000,000. Nordstrom has been able to do this by helping employees use on-line systems, thereby doubling the amount of information on each page and eliminating unnecessary reports.[12]

Packaging

One particularly rich source of waste reduction for services and manufacturers involves redesign of packaging. Americans land-fill 80 percent of their waste and recycle 10 percent. Of the waste sent to landfills, about 34 percent consists of discarded packaging.[13] Packaging engineers everywhere are studying the effect packaging has on the environment throughout its life span.

Packaging is no small thing; there can be big money in packaging redesign. Chrysler has eliminated 55 percent of the expendable packaging waste generated from its assembly plants through the use of returnable containers. It has been so successful that its new product programs plan to eliminate 95 percent of packaging waste.[14]

Former CEO of Chrysler, Lee Iacocca, has already noted that its new Jefferson North facility has reduced waste by 95 percent.[15] This includes such things as cardboard, wooden crates and pallets, plastic, and paper.

One of the more creative redesigns of packaging comes from DuPont. Because of DuPont's product, milk now served in school cafeterias often comes in flexible polyethylene, creating see-through plastic pouches rather than the milk cartons so familiar to all of us. With the plastic pouches, kids simply poke their straw into the pouch and drink. These mini-sip pouches are sanitary and collapse completely when empty. The new package provides a 70-percent reduction in waste disposal volume, lower environmental impact in manufacturing, and has energy savings because it takes less refrigerated storage spaces.[16]

Anyone looking to maximize resources and minimize waste such as packaging should probably start by challenging purchasing to be environmentally wise. A good guideline you can use could be adapted from the example of Quad/Graphics. Their *Purchasing Guide* is seen in *Figure 7–1*.

SECONDARY PROCESS MODIFICATION

Changing how your product or service is produced holds the greatest potential for eliminating pollution because it changes how day-to-day decisions are made. Only of slightly less significance is the need to *reexamine your secondary process modifications*. This usually involves controlling by-products of your primary services, and production processes. Again, the idea is to eliminate the problem by finding nonpollution functions, services or raw materials. If that is not possible, then it may be feasible to come up with less polluting (or costly) alternatives. Often it only requires a little innovative thought as in the case of the grass at Rodale Press.

GRUFF'S PURCHASING GUIDE

Suggestions for incorporating environmental
responsibility into purchasing decisions

Ask Yourself, Ask Your Vendor:

"Is it good for business? Is it good for the environment?"

Green Purchasing

When making a purchase: 1) find out whether a recycled version of the product would work, and 2) reduce waste. Periodically, ask vendors about alternative materials and ways to reduce packaging. New products are constantly being added to the list of recycled goods.

Close the Loop

Consider how much of what we buy goes directly to a landfill. Cut out waste (such as excess packaging). It will help control handling, storage, and disposal costs.

Be Aware

When making a purchase, consider the economic and environmental costs associated with the product, including packaging, transportation, and disposal. There are many hazardous chemicals that may be in the products you buy. Certain hazardous chemicals are being phased out because they destroy the environment. To accelerate the phaseout, taxes are being applied to products containing the hazardous chemicals. Early work with our vendors to find safer alternatives will ensure we do not bear the additional cost.

Get Gruff With Your Vendors

Use the examples on the other side of this guide as an aid. Ask tough questions. Make the vendors work with you to "Be Gruff . . . Recycle Stuff!™"

For more information, please E-mail GRUFF.

Ask Your Vendors:

- Is it possible to make the product from recycled materials? What is the difference between the two manufacturing processes? What by-products does each produce? What is the difference in cost and quality? What is the percent of recycled content? Of post-consumer content?

- Is it recyclable? What can it be recycled into? What market is available for the recyclable product?

- Do we currently recycle it? How could we start?

- Does the vendor know of, or currently have, a recycling program for the product?

- Does the Material Safety Data Sheet (MSDS) contain hazardous chemicals that must be reported under the Superfund Amendments and Reauthorization Act (SARA), commonly known as the Community Right-to-Know Act? Become familiar with the MSDS for each product. Look for these hazardous chemical key words: Corrosive, Ignitable (Flammable), Reactive, Toxic, Acute, Chronic, Inhalation Hazard, Explosive, Lethal, Mutagen, Poison or Carcinogen. Request an alternative product.

- Does the product contain VOCs (volatile organic compounds), CFCs (chlorofluorcarbons), or chlorinated substances? VOCs contribute to ground-level ozone problems and add to air emission levels. CFCs deplete the stratospheric ozone layer. Chlorinated substances are toxic and some are also ozone depleters.

- Can chemical containers be reused, recycled or returned to the vendor for further use?

- Does the vendor have a container pickup program? If so, what is done with the containers?

- What category of plastic is the container or product? There is currently a market available for No. 1 PET (2-liter, bottle-like) and No. 2 HDPE (milk jug-type).

- Can chemicals be bought in bulk or in concentrated form to reduce packaging?

- What waste by-products result from the use of this product? How can the waste be prevented? How can we properly dispose of it?

- What is the energy-efficiency of the product? Is there a more energy-efficient product available?

- Challenge the vendor to suggest new products or ways of using products that will decrease our environmental impact.

- Remember, ask yourself: "Is it good for business? Is it good for the environment?"

Figure 7–1

The grass grows slower in Emmaus, Pennsylvania at Rodale Press's newest building. According to their Vice-President, Tom Stonebest, the company planted slow-growing grass on purpose because it needs to be mowed less. Because of the redesign, they use less gasoline, don't use their lawn mowers as much and reduce pollutants.[17]

Merck's Tom LaBuz, Environmental Manager at the Cherokee plant, recalls how one by-product, bottom ash and fly ash, generated from their site's coal-burning power plants, were put to productive use. At one time ash, from their coal-burning power plant went off-site for use in concrete block manufacturers. LaBuz said that Merck was informed that the manufacturer would no longer need the ash. As a result, Merck was faced with finding other viable alternatives.

Ken Caputo, one of the site's senior environmental engineers, was one of those evaluating available options. Ken had already spent eight years as a manager for the Bureau of Waste Management. As such, he was very familiar with the mine reclamation program. Federal and state laws require strip mine operators to restore mined lands to the lands, original contours after they have finished extracting coal. Because of Caputo's experience, they were able to use the ash to help coal companies reclaim lands by using it to restore strip-mined lands to their original contours.

Manufacturers are not the only ones that are making innovative use of their by-products. Nordstrom, like any retailer, is in the business of selling consumer goods. One service or by-product of this service is gift-wrapping. Gift wrapping is not a primary feature of its business but it can be a profitable one. Being environmentally conscious, Nordstrom tries to make sure its gift boxes contain post-consumer content. From 1991 to 1993, the company used recycled paperboard for its gift boxes. This meant it eliminated the need for 8.1 million pounds of virgin fiber.

While eliminating the need for virgin fiber may be noteworthy, it is probably more impressive to learn of Nordstrom's gift box design. In many department stores you get a white box, then you choose gift-wrapping for your present. Nordstrom gift boxes are beautifully designed so there is no need to gift-wrap them.[13] Eliminating wrapping paper eliminated the risk of gift wrap becoming trash for their environmentally conscious customers.

Challenging the ways things are done often produces new solutions. This happened in a division of Quad. The company was under pressure from employees who were questioning the use of styrofoam in its cafes. Many wondered why the company didn't wash dishes instead of tossing them. Using china and silverware proved to be practical in some plants. Others have implemented styrobeam recycling programs.[9]

Upjohn was also able to improve waste management by *challenging old assumptions* about the way business had been done in the past. By working with the purchasing and office service's departments, it was able to find a recycled paper almost identical to what it had been using. The new paper eliminated the need for new virgin material and the company discovered the recycled paper was actually less expensive.[18]

TECHNOLOGICAL SOLUTIONS

As we saw in Dow Chemical's case, often environmental operational strategies simply involve investing in new equipment and technologies rather than using obsolete ones. For example, studies have shown that the newest lighting fixtures, air conditioners, furnaces, and refrigeration units are 50 percent to several times more efficient than older models. The International Energy Agency in Paris estimates that industrial countries could cut energy demand by 20 percent by the year 2000.[6] Upjohn saved $123,000 on its electric bill by simply replacing light fixtures and bulbs with more efficient alternatives such as mirrored reflectors that increase reflectivity by 94 percent and reduce the number of bulbs required to light a room.[19] Technological solutions are also the reason why new herbicide plants are producing 90 percent less pollution than ones already in service.[20]

Equipment and technological solutions can also prevent pollution. By modifying your equipment to perform better or by optimizing its performance you can reduce by-products and waste. Some technological solutions are high tech, others are simply good common sense. On the high end would be Merck's use of an experimental expert computer system called Environmental Assessment System (EASY). It gives Merck a systematic way of evaluating manufacturing process concepts in advance for the amount and type of waste and emissions.[6]

There are control technologies that physically trap substances before they are released into the environment. Waste can then be recycled, destroyed, or landfilled. Minimization technologies improve the design or equipment used in the manufacturing process so that waste can be eliminated or reduced. As part of its constant Performance System, Goodyear created the first "smart tires" for the trucking industry. A tiny integrated circuit or "chip" imbedded in medium commercial truck tires enables them to "report" by radio frequency such information as tire pressure, temperature, and revolutions. The technology helps truckers to maximize fleet fuel economy and extend tire life, keeping them from premature entry into the waste stream. The objective is to have high yield, a small volume of benign waste using the fewest control technologies.[6]

Prevention technologies seek to avoid waste. A good example can be seen in Quad/Graphics use of electronic page and image processing instead of the older photomechanical, film-based technology. The growth of electronic page and image processing, like many paperless systems, is enviro-friendly. Publishers who use electronic page design and production now skip intermediate steps such as use of art boards and galley stages that consumed paper and other resources. When the design is complete, it is sent on diskette over phone lines to Quad/Imaging and processed into final films directly.[10]

Aircraft manufacturer Northrop got the same positive results from its film processing when it converted its photography department from conventional chemical photography to electronic photography. It reduced its waste, decreased hazardous waste water, and eliminated film purchases. It also saved their B–Z Division about $500,000 annually.[7]

There seems to be no end to the emerging environmental technology. Already researchers have developed a new method for processing pulpwood that may reduce the energy and production cost at paper mills by 80 percent. It may double yields and cause virtually no air or water pollution. Scientists have also developed a new approach to pesticide waste disposal that uses ultraviolet irradiation and ozone to break up the pesticide molecule so that it can be metabolized easily by microorganisms.[21]

These examples might give you the impression that technological solutions to pollution must be high-tech with a high-investment cost. Technological solutions can be low-tech and low cost. Sometimes it just takes a little creativity.

Quad/Graphics had faced a common business problem. They had stacks and stacks of broken wooden pallets but didn't want them to end up in a landfill. These stacks of pallets would pile up in a corner of the plant parking lot during certain production cycles. Vendors would ship hundreds of them filled with cards and inserts, which were then put into the magazines and the catalogs printed.

Many of these pallets became damaged or were too weak to be used for stacking their magazines, catalogs, and other commercial products. Every year it needed to get rid of 1,400 tons of pallets. Luckily for Quad/Graphics there was an *antipollution champion*. His name was Ben Erdman. He worked for their Facilities department and wanted to fix those pallets that were possible to fix. He convinced others it could be economical to establish Pallet Repair Stations. Now pallets are repaired when possible and returned to production. In 1992, Quad/Graphics repaired 53,000 pallets and put them back into use. It would have cost $318,000 to buy this number of pallets. But this is not the real story.

Quad/Graphics also purchased a $50,000, 177-horsepower diesel chipper, similar to what groundskeepers and groomers use. When pallets are beyond repair, they could be sent to landfills. Instead they are fed through the chipper. This reduces their volume by two-thirds, then the chips are fed into a tubgrinder that removes nails and turns the chips into landscaping mulch. Keeping the material out of landfills saves $50,000 a year in tipping fees. Quad/Graphics offers its mulching service to other businesses too, which reap a similar benefit.

Quad/Graphics is also looking into making even better use of this by-product. Ben Erdman at Quad/Graphics is exploring ways to remove more of the nails and refine the wood waste further to produce compressed wood products.[9]

RESOURCE RECOVERY

The last option in this hierarchy of pollution prevention choices is *resource recovery*. It is the least desirable choice because you are in a reactive rather than proactive mode. Naturally, prevention rather than control is always the preferred method. Recycling should never be the goal of waste management, because it's not the last choice! It would be better to recycle less because you waste less. The goal is waste reduction, not recycling, which means the focus should be on efficient use of *all resources* including energy, tax dollars, and landfill space. Sometimes people and government lose site of the goal of pollution management. As a result, recycling and collection efforts often end up costing more than the recyclables are worth. Despite its drawbacks, recycling by-products for sale still can remain a viable and economic alternative.

Needless to say, while resource recovery and in particular recycling may not be the first choice, it is an essential one. In 1960, Americans produced 88 million tons of trash. By 1988 that amount had risen to 180 million tons or roughly 4.5 pounds per person per year.[22] To give you a better sense of how much garbage that is, consider this perspective. If you were to put all that garbage each year into garbage trucks and put them end to end, it would stretch more than halfway to the moon![12] If this trend continues, America will generate 216 million tons of trash annually by the year 2000. Looks like we will need more garbage trucks.

Despite our ever increasing mountain of trash, landfills are decreasing almost as fast. In 1978, there were 20,000. By 1991, there were less than 6,000 and most will be closed by 1995. Assuming current disposal rates continue, there will only be 1,594 landfills by 2003. The closing of these landfills is not an environmental issue, it is an economic challenge for business. Recycling is obviously going to be part of the solution.

One ton of recycled paper saves about 17 trees, 7,000 gallons of water, and 4,000 kilowatt hours of electricity, not to mention keeping three cubic yards of landfill space while keeping 60 pounds of pollutants from the air. Additionally, Ron Pool, waste control manager at Upjohn, notes that the recycling program reduces energy consumption as well as avoids incurring landfill cost.[23]

Even modest environmental initiatives like recycling paper products can pay big dividends. The Upjohn Company reported that in 1990 it recycled 910 tons of waste paper, carton board, loose-corrugated and corrugated bales. Not only did this paper-recycling effort help the community by saving an estimated 2,992 cubic yards of landfill space, preventing 54,413 pounds of air pollution and saving 15,420 trees, it also helped the company's bottom line. Because of the recycling effort it was also able to save 3,809,033 kilowatt/hours of electricity and 6,348,388 gallons of water.[19]

Any recycling efforts are valuable. For example, recycling packaging can have a dramatic economic impact. Valvoline packaging plants have recycled more than one million pounds of plastics, corrugated stretch wrap, banding, and paper, thereby reducing the amount of landfill material by nearly 3.4 million pounds. Likewise, the Disneyland Resort recycling efforts produced impressive numbers. They collected over 2 million pounds of cardboard, 24,000 pounds of aluminum cans, over 133,000 pounds of glass and 302,000 pounds of paper. Their *paper* efforts alone saved 2,571 trees and 4,000 kilowatt hours of electricity.

Anyone thinking of implementing a recycling program could learn from Rodale Press Vice-President and chief financial officer, Tom Stoneback. When asked about the company's successful recycling program, he said it had three rules. First, make it easy and convenient for employees to recycle. To drive home this point he used an example of their routine recycling paper. The company's main waste was mixed paper, and the wastebasket material in offices was called mixed, recyclable paper. High-grade computer or other valuable paper is collected in control areas close to where used. At the end of the day newspapers are placed beneath wastebaskets to ensure they remain separate.

The second rule is, if you don't have to bring it into the company you don't have to get rid of it. In other words, if you don't buy it you don't have to dispose of it. The last rule reflects the importance of employee involvement. He said you should try to give employees an opportunity to make the right decision. By this he meant that the company felt recycling was the right thing to do and it encouraged their employees to "do the right thing."[17]

Separating By-Products

The process of recycling, as seen in the Rodale Press case, is in theory very simple. It starts with good sorting. Separation adds value to waste. If you have a garbage bag full of crumpled papers, aluminum cans, and glass bottles, that is exactly what you have—garbage. On the other hand if you have one bag for paper, another for aluminum cans and still a third for glass bottles, then you have *resources,* not garbage. They are now by-products that can be sold. There are some companies that have taken their recycling efforts far beyond this and have raised the art of separation into a science.

In most chemical processes, about 80 to 90 percent of the steam is intended by-product while the rest is unintended by-product. Many chemical companies have treated these by-products as waste. After the oil shock of the 1970s, DuPont recognized the need to conserve resources so they adopted a policy of "no process steam is waste." The key was to *match product value to customer need.* It then began separating and capturing Dibasic Acid (DBA) from its process steam. DBA is now added to limestone scrubbers at coal-fired power stations to reduce acid rain emissions because it makes the scrubbers more efficient.

The company continues the research and development on the by-product DBA. It began converting DBA into another chemical called DiBasic Ester (DBE), a solvent first sold to customers in the coating industry. Today, DBE is the preferred solvent replacing many acetones and methylene chloride solvents that have a greater environmental impact.

The company's specialty chemicals made from by-products have been implemented to create a thriving business. If the company had not pursued this, business disposal cost would have exceeded $100 million a year. DuPont's Paul Tebo sums up this philosophy—they (by-products) are no longer viewed as environmental problems but as "business opportunities."[24] Waste is seen as a potential new business opportunity.

At Disneyland, a portion of the polystyrene foam cups are now being recycled into such products as flower pots, garden rakes, and building installation. Employees return used polystyrene foam cups to drop-off receptacles where cups are compressed by a densifier into 40-pound disks. These disks are then taken to reprocessing plants where material is turned into plastic resin beads. In turn these beads are used to make items like flower pots, benches, parking bumps, rakes, and so forth.

Never assume separation and reprocessing is small change. Reprocessing by-products can be both big business and a profitable venture. DuPont represents one company where by-product sales are big business. One by-product called "Dytek A" provides a good example. It is a by-product of the company's nylon manufacturing process. Today, it is used to improve the flexibility and toughness of polymers.

Dytek A is on the market only because DuPont decided it makes more sense to sell by-products than to pay to dispose of them. Selling by-products is a mind set of DuPont's Paul Tebo, Vice-President of Safety, Health, and Environment. He emphasizes that environmental solutions do not have to be cost prohibitive. Rather, it can add to the bottom line thereby helping a company better meet customers' needs while remaining profitable.[25] DuPont recognized the opportunity when it sold its first pound of by-product over 18 years ago. Currently there are efforts underway by Volkswagen and BMW to make cars 100 percent recyclable. It's simply a matter of economics and customer awareness.

CLOSING THOUGHTS

DuPont, and those like Volkswagen and BMW, show us that recycling can be a profitable business. However, all this discussion may be a moot point. As landfill space continues to decrease, recycling will become a required business activity. Eventually the public will demand better waste management. It is likely that most products and many services will have to be redesigned so that they are easily reused or reprocessed for the next generation of products. Already in Germany there are auto disassembly plants. Cars may soon be sold on the basis of how recyclable they are. Tipping fees for landfills overseas are 10 times or more what they are in the United States. If the U.S. intends to sell overseas it probably will not be too long before customers buy all products based on how recyclable they are. Disassembly tools and technology will become a growth industry. Product design will also change. Instead of the hodgepodge of different types of materials for products, it may be far more economical to reduce not just the number of component parts of a product but also the variety of materials being used to make those products.

ENDNOTES

1. Smith, Emity T., "Growth vs. Environment" *Business Week.* May 11, 1992, p. 66–75.

2. Smith, Emity T., David Woodruff and Fleur Templeton, "The Next Trick for Business: Taking a Clue from Nature" *Business Week.* May 11, 1992, pp. 74–75.

3. *Partnerships to Progress: The Report of the President's Commission on Environmental Quality.* President's Commission on Environmental Quality. Washington, D.C. January 1993, p. 24–25.

4. Zosel, Thomas W. "Case Study: How 3M Makes Pollution Prevention Pay Big Dividends" *Pollution Prevention.* Winter 1990–91, p. 71–72.

5. *3M Pollution Prevention Pays.* A booklet published by 3M, no date, p. 2–3.

6. *Merck and the Environment.* A booklet published by Merck & Co., no date, p. 9–11.

7. *Northrop's Environmental Efforts Make Good Business Sense.* Northrop Bulletin, no date.

8. Mother Earth says, "Clean Your Mailing List" *Quad/Views Special Update: The Environment.* Fall 1992, p. 18.

9. *Quad/Graphics 1990: Taking Better Care of Our World.* Annual Report Quad/Graphics. 1990, p. 9–20.

10. "The Business of Protecting the Environment," *ENVIRO/FACTS,* Quad/Graphics in-house publication, 1993, p. 2.

11. "Environmental Annual Review, July 1991," Monsanto in-house publication, 1991, p. 7.

12. *Earth Focus: Environmental Efforts Company Wide.* Nordstrom Newsletter, March 1993, p. 2.

13. *Merck and the Environment: A Progress Report.* A booklet of Merck & Co., 1992, p. 17.

14. *Environmental Programs Pamphlet.* Handbook of Chrysler Corporation, 1992, p. 10.

15. "Chrysler Announces 1992 Electric Vehicle Production, Cites Company's Alternative-Fuel Vehicle Leadership," Press Release, Wednesday, April 15, 1992, p. 2.

16. *We Don't Inherit the Environment from Our Ancestors; We Borrow It from Our Children.* DuPont's Environmental Respect Awards pamphlet, 1991, p. 15.

17. Rich, Cary Peyton, "Think Green!" *The Magazine for Management Annual.* 1992, Vol. 21, No. Guide, p. 241. p. 253.

18. *Inter-Comment.* Upjohn Newsletter, Vol. 20, No. 12, April 5, 1991, p. 1.

19. *Upjohn and the Environment: A Global Company Acting Locally.* In-house publication, 1991, p. 11–13.

20. Bhat, Vasanthakumar N., "The Green Corporation: How to Plan for It" *SAM Advanced Management Journal.* Summer 1992, Vol. 57, No. 3, p. 8.

21. *Science and Technology Report and Outlook—1985–1988.* Office of Science and Technology Policy and the National Science Foundation, 1988, p. 3.

22. *Environmental Quality.* 22nd Annual Report: The Council on Environmental Quality. U.S. Government Printing Office. Washington, D.C., March 1992, p. 109.

23. "Recycling Efforts Make Environmental Impact" *Inter-Comment.* Vol. 20, No. 22. September 20, 1991, p. 1.

24. "Making and Marketing Recycled Resins" *DuPont Magazine.* September/October, Vol. 85, No.5, 1991, p. 19.

8

THE ENERGY FACTOR

$\mathbf{T}$ rivia question: What do the following three facts have in common? Pacific Gas and Electric has decided that energy conservation is more profitable than investment in nuclear power.[1] Scientists at G.E.'s Research and Development Center and those at Ford Motor Company are jointly trying to beat a deadline called the California Standards. They are rushing to create cars that do not use petroleum since the California Standard calls for 2 percent of the cars in the state to be emission free by 1998, 10 percent by 2003.[2] Meanwhile it's Europe, not the U.S., that leads the world in recovering the energy content of plastics. Called thermal recycling, the modern waste-to-energy incinerators recover as much as 70 percent of the original energy in plastics.[3]

Obviously, what each of these three incidents has in common is energy. More specifically, each group has seen energy conservation and conversion as a critical component of their businesses. In the Pacific Gas and Electric case, it's a matter of dollars and cents. Its return on investment is simply greater with conservation than with investments in new sources of energy like nuclear power. G.M. and Ford, on the other hand, are trying to be in less of a reactive mode. As demands to reduce pollution increase, alternatives like electric cars become a viable alternative. G.M. and Ford are also involved in joint ventures to create electric powertrains for electric vehicles.

The reference "Europe leading the world in recovering energy content" comes from Dow Chemical. In the U.S., Dow and seven other plastic manufacturers have formed the National Polystyrene Recycling Company (NPRC). By 1995 they expect to be recycling 25 percent or 250 million pounds of polystryene used in food services and packaging application in the U.S.[3]

Good energy management, found in all these cases, enhanced the bottom line. Either through conservation or conversion, wise energy management made dollars and cents. Ford and General Motors are not the only automakers concerned about energy management. Chrysler has been more successful than most at turning energy into cash. During the 1980s, energy usage per Chrysler vehicle built was reduced by 40 percent. It was accomplished by downsizing vehicles and using more energy-efficient equipment, processes, and energy conservation programs. Each Chrysler plant also has a conservation committee, whose goal is to reduce energy usage and cost. Some of the projects these committees oversee include highly efficient lighting systems and heating and ventilating modifications.[2] G.M., Ford, and Chrysler, among others, are looking for the competitive edge. They recognize that energy saving can have a big pay off.

ENERGY AS THE COMPETITIVE EDGE

Energy use can be a significant factor in competition. Consider the steel industry in Japan. This industry is a big energy consumer and accounts for over 10 percent of the country's total energy consumption. If you could reduce this operational overhead, it would make both the country and any company operating within its borders more competitive. When you hear that a focus on energy efficiency in the Japanese steel industry has led to a savings of nearly 20 percent, it is a big deal![4]

Like Japan, some industries within the U.S. also recognize the importance of energy. The chemical industry for one recognizes the potential for energy profits. The U.S. chemical industry, from 1974 to 1990, experienced a 43 percent gain in energy efficiency.[4]

PRIORITIZING ENERGY SAVING

We know that our greatest opportunity to reduce cost and improve competitiveness comes through both *changing energy use patterns* and *better energy technology*. By retrofitting coal plants there has been at least a 15 percent increase in efficiency. New technology in some countries has also increased the average vehicle energy efficiency by at least 50 percent.[4]

One of the most likely areas for reducing cost reductions is better *lighting management*. At Upjohn, its utilities and energy conservation unit replaced 9,200 fluorescent light fixtures in its main manufacturing facility in Portage, Michigan. This action alone conserved enough electrical power for Upjohn's Portage facility to serve 300 homes for a year and saved the company $123,000.[5]

Smart companies recognize that they have to concentrate their energy-reduction efforts in order to maximize effectiveness. Energy-efficient lighting is one of the first areas where prudent management should concentrate their efforts. It is an area that is in constant change with new ground being broken yearly. Consider what is happening at General Electric. The company makes a line of electronic compact fluorescents that provide good lighting at a fraction of the energy. One fluorescent bulb is 20 watts, but delivers light comparable to a 75-watt incandescent bulb and has a life of up to 10,000 hours. Such savings ought to "light up" the eyes of even the most hard-nosed managers.

GREEN LIGHTS

Reducing cost and making money by reducing lighting overhead is easier when you participate in the United States Environmental Protection Agency's (EPA) Green Lights program. The purpose of the program is to encourage major corporations to adopt energy efficiency as a *profitable* means of preventing pollution. The EPA believes that energy-efficient lighting and better lighting design allows the user to illuminate its operation, thereby using less energy.

Many businesses do not fully appreciate the potential savings just from better lighting management. Lighting and the air conditioning needed to remove heat generated by lighting accounts for about 20 percent to 25 percent of the nation's electrical demands. The EPA notes that high efficiency lighting technologies have been developed which can dramatically reduce energy consumption while getting better illumination. The Electric Power Research Institute estimates that if highly efficient lighting were used to its full potential nationwide, the electricity required for lighting would be cut by 50 percent.

Aggregate demand for electricity would be cut by 10 percent and at least $18.6 billion would be cut from ratepayers' bills. From the pollution standpoint there would be a four percent reduction in Co_2 and there would be reductions in boiler ash, scrubber waste, mine tailings, acid mine drainage and radioactive waste.[6] All of this comes from simply improving how to light our facilities.

A corporation joins Green Lights by signing a Memorandum of Understanding (MOU) with the EPA. The MOU commits the corporation to survey the lighting in all its facilities and to retrofit wherever retrofitting is profitable. In return, the EPA will help a Green Lights corporation in several ways. It arranges public recognition for Green Lights corporations. Exposure includes making sure customers, stockholders, employees, and the public are aware of the corporation's environmental achievements. EPA also says it will provide "substantial" technical support to benefit its Green Lights Partners so companies can lower the barrier to energy-efficient lighting.

In the works is a computerized support system that allows Green Lights Partners to rapidly survey the lighting systems in their facilities. It also helps you assess your retrofit options and select the best energy-efficient lighting upgrades. The EPA also conducts a lighting information program that provides information so purchasers are better able to select energy-efficient products. They also provide case studies that show successful retrofits and provide details on the products used.

The EPA has also developed a project to identify financing resources for energy-efficient lighting. Green Lights Partners are given rosters of financing sources such as utility programs, energy service companies, government grants and low interest loans, banks, and leasing companies. As part of the financial side, the EPA also circulates information about the profitability and quality of energy-efficient lighting. They have also been collecting case studies of economically successful investments. These cases detail equipment and technology used and what will be available to Green Lights corporations. It is good energy information so if you want to check into it you can call 202-479-6936. You can also find out more about its program by referring to material in Appendix B.

HOW TO LIGHT UP THE BOTTOM LINE

A little lighting conservation and conversion can make a big difference and you do not need EPA's Green Lights Program to do it. A good case in point is the work of The Upjohn Company. Its energy efforts have paid off handsomely for the company. In one particular example, employees in an area known as "building 41" substituted light fixtures, ballasts, reflectors and bulbs with innovative cost-saving replacements. They expect to save The Upjohn Company about $123,000 annually on its electric bill.[7]

Upjohn's savings in one of its areas is impressive, but it is really quite easy to achieve such savings when the latest technology is used. The newest lighting fixtures, air conditioners, furnaces, and refrigerators are from 50 percent to several times more efficient energy users than older models. In fact, the International Energy Agency in Paris estimates that industrial countries could cut energy demand by 20 percent by the year 2000 if they would use more energy-efficient equipment. Others estimate that in years to come, solar power could provide 30 percent of our energy needs.[8]

Anyone looking to make money from energy conversion could also learn a thing or two from the Nintendo Corporation. Some of the things it did for profit included:

- replacing magnetic-type ballasts in fluorescent fixtures with energy-efficient electronic ballasts

- replacing incandescent light fixtures with compact fluorescent light fixtures

- installing occupancy sensors to control light in selected areas of the building (occupancy sensors detect people in an area and control light accordingly)

- replacing four-lamp, lensed light fixtures with energy-efficient three-lamp paracude light fixtures

- replacing individual thermostats with central energy management controls

- removing electric duct heaters

- installing economizers to roof-top units, equipped with fixed outside air dampers (save energy by modulating the amount of outside air brought into the building)[9]

ENERGY MANAGEMENT

It would be a mistake to assume all conversion and conservation efforts should be directed toward lighting. Even in Nintendo's case, three of its changes (see the last 3 in the previous list) were not related to lighting programs.

Walt Disney provides a good example of how to maximize energy savings. There are several projects and plans that demonstrate well-thought-out energy management. One of these involves expanding the use of computerized energy management systems throughout its parks, resorts, and office buildings. Management always seems to be involved in research involving ways to save energy through better refrigeration systems, kitchen appliances, pumps, motors, heat pipes, and heat recovery systems.

Potential energy savings for the smart company or manager are everywhere including your very own personal computer (PC). Earlier we mentioned that Walt Disney uses computerized systems to save money, but there is another way to save money using computers—turn them off! The EPA estimates that PCs are responsible for five percent of the commercial consumption of electricity in the U.S.

The waste is due mostly to ignorance. Most of the nation's 35 million PCs often are simply left on, unattended when they are not being used. It is estimated that 30 to 40 percent are left running all night and on week-ends. However, this is beginning to change. For instance, new PCs are on the market that dramatically reduce this energy demand.

REAPING ENERGY SAVINGS

The good news is that the changing behavior of people and corporations can occur and when it does, big savings are possible. From a competitive standpoint, the good news is that while energy savings are everywhere, few people or corporations take advantage of them.

When you do choose to take advantage of better energy management, it can have a profound effect. At Dow Chemical, the amount of energy required to operate its manufacturing process has dropped by 55 percent for its major petrochemical and plastic products. New Dow plants coming on line will further reduce energy use 30 percent to 40 percent below the current average. One of the reasons for these projects involves cogeneration. Dow Chemical is a big advocate of cogeneration, which relies heavily on gas turbines, heat recovery units, and steam turbines. Combinations like these are about 20 percent more efficient than conventional plants which use boilers and steam turbines.[10]

Laboratories have gone one step beyond Dow's cogeneration, by eliminating the need for a boiler altogether. By equipping hundreds of laboratory hoods with electronic sensors and better individual management, it has been able to coordinate air supply and exhaust. This hood project has helped to eliminate the need for a new boiler and water chiller at the company's research complex in downtown Kalamazoo; the process saved $13 million.

This $13 million savings is also due in part to the energy-conserving design of their "Building 300," which is a recently completed research facility. What is interesting is that it was able to eliminate a planned boiler and chiller, not because it reduced their heating or cooling needs, but due to an entirely different reason. It redesigned the way air at the facility was circulated and controlled and because it could do this it was then able to eliminate the boiler. You see, ventilation hoods are used to protect people from potential exposure to various chemical vapors. Often the *entire* volume of air in the facility is replaced 30 to 60 times every hour.

This case points out the interdependent nature of poor or good energy management. Energy inefficiencies often create a lot of problems, so when you solve an energy problem you often end up not only improving the bottom line, but you also solve pieces of the pollution puzzle.

In Upjohn's situation it was looking for a better way, a more efficient way to safely control the air supply and exhaust rather than by simply flushing the facility with air. The company knew it had a great deal of energy inefficiency, but little else. Using computer models, it soon discovered that its air-handling system was working at nearly full capacity around the clock. Because of this discovery its new facility is equipped with electronic sensors so a building's supply and exhaust will be balanced automatically.

Upjohn's case also demonstrates one additional point. It was able to eliminate waste overhead by doing what has become a common theme in enviro-management: involve its people in the process. You see, its $13 million savings was not due entirely to technological improvements that involved automatically regulating the air supply. Judgment is almost always a factor and scientists are also asked to gauge the openings of their hoods based on their needs. Because of both technological improvements and greater employee involvement the company not only saved $13 million, but also saved at least $600,000 annually on energy bills.[12]

CLOSING THOUGHTS

The greatest opportunity for reducing energy (or any other environmental) cost and improving your competitiveness comes through making better use of technology and changing people's day-to-day work patterns. While Upjohn's case demonstrates what can happen when these two conditions occur, such savings cannot be expected unless environmental management is approached in a *systematic* manner.

Companies like Disney have a good track record at handling pollution problems because they approach problems systematically. Disney has a Corporate Energy Conservation Committee that augments existing energy conservation programs and that makes a difference. It is the committee's role to develop a wide variety of energy plans and procedures like its computerized energy management system.

The reason things never work out as they are planned is because they are not planned. It takes an integrated approach to pollution prevention to prevent the jigsaw piecemeal approach so common in industry. Next, we will try to avoid this piecemeal approach by laying out a systematic plan for turning pollution prevention into profit. It is an integrated approach that has a beginning, middle, and end. It is an approach that will fit all the pieces into a coherent and integrated action plan.

Some people have discussed the environment in terms of using a process similar to the TQM approach in the quality movement. TQM is an integrated approach that has both a philosophy and a systematic application of problem-solving tools and techniques and it is hard to argue against such an approach. Employed alone, a TQM type of approach will not be enough. It helps, and can help reduce overhead and make you more competitive, but does not comprehensively address or completely change the real raw materials of organizations—and that is how decisions are made. TQM shows us that we need greater employee involvement, and in some cases even provides some tools to help them make decisions, but it does not look at the decision-making process itself. Creating waste, or rather not creating waste, is challenging. Good quality can come about when we are smarter about how we use all our resources, and TQM is one piece of the puzzle that can help both here and in preventing pollution. Ultimately, we must develop a way to organize our approach to pollution management so that all the pieces are in place. Identifying these pieces and assessing what is in place and what is needed is critical to turning environmental green into monetary green. First, we will look at the pieces of the puzzle, then we will draw them together to create a "pollution wheel" that turns pollution from cost to a revenue generator.

ENDNOTES

1. Kleiner, Art, "What Does It Mean To Be Green." *Harvard Business Review*, July–August 1991. Vol. 69, No. 4, p. 38.

2. Chrysler Corporation Environmental Programs, (in-house publication. no date) p. 11.

3. Special Reprint from 1989 Annual Report, Dow Chemical in-house publication. February 12, 1990, p. 9.

4. Williams, Jan Olaf, Ulrich Golüke, *From Ideas: To Action Business and Sustainable Development*, International Chamber of Commerce (Ad Notam Cyldendal Publishing), 1992. p. 54–64.

5. "Pollution Prevention Eliminates Waste at Source." *Upjohn Intercom*, June 1992, p. 9.

6. *United States Environmental Protection Agency Green Lights: A Bright Investment in the Environment*, United States Environmental Protection Agency flyer.

7. "Lighting Project Reflects New Technology." *Inter-Comment*, January 25, 1991, Vol. 20, No. 3, p. 1.

8. Smith, Emity T., "Growth vs. Environment." *Business Week*, May 11, 1992, pp. 66–75.

9. *Executive Summary Nintendo of America Design Plus Energy Study,* in-house document, (no date) p. 2.

10. *Environment, Health and Safety*, Dow Chemical brochure, (no date) p. 2.

11. "Pollution Prevention Eliminates Waste at Source." *Upjohn Intercom*, June 1992, p. 9.

12. "Conservation Plan Could Save $13 Million." *Upjohn Inter-Comment*, September 7, 1990, Vol. 19, No. 10, p. 1–4.

9

A MONEY-MAKING MODEL: SEM

In the traditional organization, everyone's attention is focused on those above and below them. Each knows the pecking order and most everyone knows you need money to stay in business. Beyond that, though, things are a bit fuzzy. It knows its customers are supposed to be kings and queens. Some even talk about their internal customers and suppliers, but beyond that it's pretty vague. Do your job, watch out for yourself, and at least appear busy. It also does not hurt to do a little "brown nosing" every now and then.

What's missing is a deep understanding of how things really work. Some suspect that work is somewhat haphazard. Oh, things get done, products are produced, and services are delivered, but there are a lot of inefficiencies, a lot of backtracking and missteps. The flow of goods and services has a lot of ebbs and undercurrents. Eventually something does come out the other end, but a lot of physical, not to mention psychological, waste occurs in between.

Sounds familiar, doesn't it? Unfortunately, it sounds all too familiar to many people. That is one of the reasons to push for a flatter, more horizontal approach to management. The attempt is to smooth out the flow of information and resources so the organization runs in a more adept, less wasteful manner. Vertically oriented organizations concentrate on the organizational chart. A more horizontal approach shifts attention to the production process. The reason this shift is important is because a poorly defined production system not only is "improfitable," but it creates overhead and pollution like excess inventory, scrap, and rework.

HIGH INVOLVEMENT PRODUCES HIGH DIVIDENDS

Delegating decision making downward can improve productivity because it gives everyone a sense of ownership and accountability so essential to improvement. Long-term pollution prevention will always be a problem as long as it's perceived to be the environmental manager's job. You cannot turn even the best recycling and waste reduction efforts into profitable ventures unless everyone believes it is their job to do it! Moreover, recycling programs, as noted earlier by the President's Commission on Environmental Quality, can often be distinctive because many believe that once there is a recycling program they are doing all they need to do to reduce waste. Waste reduction thinking is not integrated into their decision making. When the majority of people around you feel like you do, namely that it's *your* job to find more efficient, less polluting ways of working, then things will really change. Everything else is just smoke and mirrors.

Granted, a case can be made that an exceptional CEO or group of highly talented vice-presidents can make very good decisions without participation, but there's a high cost. People simply do not care! There are also strong reasons why as many need to participate as possible—regardless of the quality of the decision. High involvement by all levels, functions, and individuals creates a greater understanding of decisions by everyone. If you have ever been involved in the deciding, you know you are a lot more likely to be committed to implementing those decisions. After all, you have a stake in making it happen, plus you have a greater understanding of corporate (or otherwise) objectives.

High involvement also fulfills strong psychological needs and creates a greater team identity. We all know that we are a lot more likely to cooperate when we have been involved in deciding what to do. In addition to all of this, there is one more reason for high involvement, and it's the one that some might question. Although it probably is not always the case, it is a fact that high involvement decision making can create *better* decisions. When you bring a team of people together with different viewpoints and knowledge, you can create more comprehensive solutions.

A SYSTEM FOR MAKING PROFITS

Desire for change is never enough. There must be some way, some vehicle for creating the high involvement. It's one thing to know there's a good idea, it's another thing to have a logical way to implement it. We have to create a system to do it. Such a system should aim to keep everyone informed about what is expected—they should know where to "fit in."

Vertical types of organizations with their "bosses," pecking orders, dichotomized functions, and multi-levels are not really conducive to communications or pollution control. Directives, requests, and orders for pollution control or any other actions flow downward, but it is extremely difficult for ideas and communications to flow upward. If you doubt this, think about how and why brainstorming works. Brainstorming is meant to generate ideas and solutions. It works in large part because participants share ideas without labels or barriers, but in vertical organizations those barriers are built in.

Such highly-structured organizations had probably been useful (they are easy to build) when things did not change a lot or when it was difficult to get critical information to a lot of people. In today's highly competitive marketplace, information, thanks to computers, can easily be shared with a wide range of people. Incremental improvements are essential, and to have these we need everyone's help. One case in point is Dow Chemical.

The power of getting everyone involved in continuous improvement is critical to turning pollution concerns into profitable pollution management. For instance, at Dow a team of workers and supervisors made a few simple changes in pipes and production equipment and improved housekeeping techniques including making sure certain valves were closed when they were supposed to be. In the process the company eliminated 60 percent of the material that was going to landfills and saved $310,000 in annual fees. But the story does not end there. More efficient latex production, another benefit of these changes, saved an additional $420,000 a year.[1]

CREATING POLLUTION OWNERSHIP

As we have already seen in early chapters and in the case of Dow Chemical, employee involvement is essential to pollution management. There are teams, suggestion programs and antipollution champions, but people do not feel a real sense of ownership unless they feel *personally* responsible for pollution control.

At United Technologies, Vice-President Leslie Carothers makes this point when he says, "the most important activity we can accomplish, both this year and the next year is getting everybody thinking about pollution prevention and waste reduction." He feels the *key* to his company's success thus far has been the involvement of its workforce.[2] A good example of what employee involvement can do is provided by Joseph Cannon, who started Geneva Steel in Utah in 1987. At the time the plant barely met EPA requirements, which stated that at least 90 percent of all coke-oven doors must seal perfectly against leaks. Cannon asked his employees to work toward improving their track record. In fact, it turned out that the best solutions to this pollution problem came not from executives or environmental scientists, but rather from the blue-collar employee. By redesigning and making it easier to clean door plugs, and through their union employees' dedication to carefully cleaning oven seals, the plant was able to have 97 percent of its oven doors with perfect seals.[3] Carothers and Cannon know that as long as it's the "corporation" that is polluting, then it's not their problem. True, profitable pollution management cannot occur until we can create a more empowered, more horizontal structure so that people are drawn into the decision-making and solution-generating process.

Our customers, as we have seen, have rising environmental priorities. When you use your short-term and long-term customers' needs as a focal point you begin to transform your organization or area. Job descriptions and performance appraisals should be based on meeting these expectations. Raises, promotions, and other rewards should be based on meeting our internal or external customers' needs. Dow is one of the few companies that has begun to integrate environmental priorities into day-to-day decision making. One incentive is the fact that salaries and bonuses are tied in, along with other things, to how well environmental goals were met.[1] It has also added an environmental category to everyone's job appraisal form. If this is the case, purchasing provides supplies that hopefully do not add to the waste of other departments. If purchasing does not do this, then it is not supplying its internal customers (like production) with what they need. On the other hand, production control (as their customer) may have initially asked purchasing to supply them with materials. Who's at fault when product control did not allow purchasing the opportunity to innovate?

Seeking recyclable options or using newer technology are only a few of their options. If we are free to choose, who knows what pollution breakthroughs might be made? It is easy to lose sight of what is really important if you do not know your internal customers' needs. Remember the nurse and the syringes. Purchasing was never brought into the process until the problem was brought up to the doctors. If the company had identified its internal customer and suppliers, it would have been resolved earlier or maybe not have been a problem.

Pollution problems will be reduced when you create responsive systems that identify your internal customer and suppliers. Choose your most important internal customers. Tell your internal suppliers what you need to reduce pollution and cost. Find out your customers' needs as well as what information you need to supply to your internal suppliers so they in turn can meet your environmental needs.

You are almost through, but not quite yet. Once you have identified your internal customers' and suppliers' environmental needs, the last step is to find ways of measuring them. In a later chapter, we will look at how to use something called a waste ratio as well as other assessment tools that have been used by companies like Dow to measure pollution performance. Regardless of whether you identify your internal customers and suppliers, it is essential to measure things like waste, excess scrap, inventory and unintended by-products.

Some innovative companies recognize that in order to improve you must come up with measurable characteristics, then assess how you measure up. For those with customers as a focus, there is already at least one way to do it. Since 1986, the EPA has required all plants of the some 10,000 U.S. manufacturers to report the annual releases from their facilities into the air, ground, and water of some 317 toxic chemicals and 20 toxic chemical categories referred to as the Toxic Release Inventory or TRI. The main reason for TRI is to provide the public with an annual environmental benchmark. Dow's TRI releases of per dollar of sales, a common measure used by environmental groups to avoid penalizing large companies, is among the lowest in the U.S. Chemical industry.[1] It's a competitive advantage and one that relates directly to one of its long-term customers' concerns.

If you do not use hazardous chemicals, it will still be important to find measures that both your internal and external customers consider important. The best advice is to ask them, then make those measures the universal language used throughout the organizations. Everyone ought to be measuring the same things—what is important to your customers. If push comes to shove, your external customers' requirements must override internal customer needs. Then find out why your internal and external customer pollution reduction needs do not match.

FOCUSING POLLUTION EFFORTS

Your internal and external suppliers, your customers, and the company must be on the same wavelength if waste reduction is to be maximized. Ask yourself some very basic questions such as, "What do I do?" "What do I need from my suppliers to reduce pollution?" If you have too many customers to count, then identify who your *major* customers are and assess their performance. If you are not getting the pollution reduction performance you need out of your people or your suppliers' people, then teach them how to solve environmental problems using tools similar to the problem-solving tools in Chapter 13 and by using Appendix B.

Choosing antipollution champions for each major (internal or external) consumer transaction can also be an option. Duties would include responsibilities for applying pollution concerns to the day-to-day work area. If you feel a more involved process is needed, you could create cross-functional green teams to handle broader pollution problems. Such teams might be involved in addressing issues to improve recyclability, reduce waste, by-product, and other inefficiencies.

Improving pollution performance does not require that you identify internal suppliers and customers, but it can help to get people focused. There are, however, other ways to pull people together. A very popular way some innovative companies are using to draw attention to pollution issues is by combining pollution concerns with concerns for quality.

One of the concepts getting a lot of attention is applying TQM to pollution prevention. What happens when you do this is a fundamental restructuring of the way decisions are made. TQM implies that you will replace the traditional chain-of-command vertical organization with greater levels of employee involvement. Employees are given the freedom to solve problems and implement corrective actions without having to get their supervisor's approval at every step. TQM advocates want more decision-making authority from employees.

Proctor & Gamble is one of the world's largest producers of consumer goods. It believes there is a direct connection between quality and environmental issues. To that end, it uses TQM principles to help the company better manage environmental issues. As part of this process, it uses the continuous improvement cycle (Plan, Do, Check and Act) that we will discuss in the problem-solving chapter. It tracks waste generated at each site, then sets corporate wide goals so comparisons can be made. Such comparisons put everyone on the same wavelength as well as provide a means for waste elimination.

P&G approached the process comprehensively through a Lifecycle Analysis (similar to that described in Chapter 3). Before P&G introduces a new product, Lifecycle Analysis is done to determine the amount of energy and waste products produced at every stage of the supply chain. This includes material sourcing, manufacture, distribution, and customer use and disposal.[4] Dramatic savings can occur by rethinking the product design process in this manner. For instance, "ultra" detergents were redesigned to be concentrated. There was an immediate 50 percent reduction in packaging, and P&G environmental coordinator Karen Ellen also noted other impressive benefits. She said these included 9,000 fewer truckloads per year, which means the company used 900,000 less gallons of fuel each year. By using a concentrated detergent it also saved 3,000 tires and about $16.5 million annually in direct product and transportation cost with their "ultra" product line.

AT&T provides another excellent example of a company that is using TQM principles to solve pollution problems. First, it established a paper reduction goal (to reduce by 15 percent by 1995). Then it created a TQM team to help figure out how to meet this. Next, it used TQM techniques (like those found in the problem-solving chapter) to identify the heaviest paper users. It called these "fat rabbits." These fat rabbits then formed their own teams to try to meet corporate goals.

Once the problem was identified and people focused attention, solutions soon came. Some simple ways the company found to reduce paper consumption by 22 percent included eliminating cover pages and using electronic, rather than printed, media.[1] The long-distance division also compressed spacing on some 12 million bills to major customers on its Pro Wats and Custom Net lines. As a result, it was able to save three million fewer sheets of paper and had lower postal rates. The net outcome was *$4 million* annually.

A MODEL FOR POLLUTION MANAGEMENT

A lot of companies have been trying to figure out a way of integrating pollution efforts into their decision process. That is why many, like P&G and AT&T, have looked at TQM as a way of pulling pollution efforts into the 1990s. Still, though, it is surprising to see success stories on pollution because efforts are often so disappointing that it often seems like random selection. Many companies do not even seem to have a cohesive idea of where they want to go with the pollution issue, much less, how to get there. What we need is a model or framework for consistent and logical pollution decisions.

A good model for pollution management must take several variables into account. It would need to help you decide where you are at and what's needed to move from one point to the next. It would account for the different *degrees of employee involvement* in the management of pollution. Some companies see no need to have people involved other than to make sure they do not openly violate any environmental regulations that can get them in legal trouble. Some companies recognize that pollution efforts are costly and hope to minimize costs by seeking employee participation. Still other, more progressive organizations have recognized, probably through older quality efforts, that high involvement is essential to successful change. A good model would be able to discriminate these levels of participation and help frame your understanding of which types of participation is appropriate at this "stage" of your development.

Another variable a good model should be able to discriminate is the *type of problem solving* used. One point we already know is there can be a wide range of participation from total consensus to more autocratic lower involvement. Before setting up a pollution-prevention process consider how much freedom should be given for making decisions. In some cases, employees are asked to investigate and make suggestions. It is more rare for employees to be asked to actually "decide" what to do. Thus, there are different types of problem solving. Some individuals believe there is value in finding out what people know, but still reserve the right to decide what to do to managers. Some believe you actually end up with a better decision if the group decides, rather than one manager. Self-directed work teams are an outcrop of this type of philosophy.

ENVIRONMENTAL WHEEL

The environmental wheel seen in *Figure 9–1* is an attempt to draw some of these variables together so that an organization can approach pollution problems in an integrated manner. The model in *Figure 9–1* consists of three stages of environmental growth. Within each stage are five separate considerations. These consist of the *degree of employee involvement*, which *operations management* techniques are employed, what *strategic initiative* is adopted to deal with environmental issues, how environmental *costs* are assessed, and what is the *marketing perspective*.

The hope for the model is to solve corporations' piecemeal approach toward environmental management. Some companies have employee suggestion systems in place that hope to encourage employees to provide ideas of how to conserve or recycle. On one hand, the CEO talks about environmental issues being everyone's responsibility, but what he/she is really worried about is avoiding environmental liabilities or cost. People may be encouraged to recycle, but are not given the rewards or incentives to back up those claims. Setting a goal of "zero waste," then not changing the way you do business, prostitutes the whole idea. It is an unworthy cause that it is doomed to failure. If you change your strategy (zero waste) you must change the way marketing, accounting, operations and employees interact or it's just a lot of babble.

The Environmental Wheel attempts to show how various aspects of an organization are interconnected, but it does not advocate one best stage or type of pollution-management effort. It is possible to have an effective com-

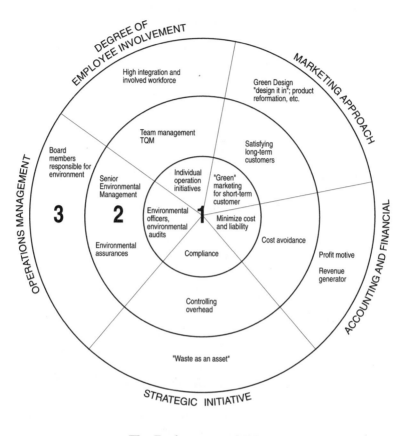

The Environmental Wheel
Figure 9–1

pliance or Stage 1 approach to management as long as mixed signals are not sent. A Stage 2 or more horizontal management and employee involvement approach can give you a competitive advantage much like TQM does in the quality area, but only when key pieces are not missing. If your organization is highly integrated, flat, fast, and empowered, you have a golden opportunity to use Stage 3 to make money from better pollution management, but it cannot happen unless there is total integration of environmental issues into the decision-making process. In the next few pages we will look at the components of each of these stages and how some of them have been used to improve environmental practices. Later you can see a questionnaire and color in your own "wheel" to see what stage you are at and what pieces are missing and in place.

STAGE 1 ORGANIZATIONS

The components of Stage 1 pollution efforts are seen in *Figure 9–2*. Employees are often asked to separate and recycle at their work areas. In many cases they are also encouraged to change energy-use patterns. A very good example of this approach is Upjohn's Resource Recovery Program that has already been mentioned. DuPont's and Disneyland's approach to separating by-products is another case where employees have been engaged actively at the Stage 1 level. At Stage 1, you can also encourage individual initiatives by recruiting antipollution champions (remember Quad/Graphics wooden pallet story?). The point is that at Stage 1, companies seek to employ at the individual level. The theme at Stage 1 is that it is "everyone's responsibility" but no significant structural changes are made in how decisions are handled. Stage 1 employee involvement is a good approach for a company wanting some environmental awareness but lacking the desire and/or resources to institute significant cultural changes.

From a strategy standpoint, Stage 1 companies perform environmental audits to make sure the corporation complies with all necessary regulations. The emphasis is on minimizing the cost of environmental pollution and avoiding any significant liability that might occur due to pollution. Since the focus is on the legal aspects, paperwork is an important part of Stage 1 efforts so they often hire, or more likely appoint from within, Environmental and Safety (E & S) officers. These E & S departments concentrate on evaluation, compliance, and employee education efforts. Job duties include assessing waste, tracking its movement, and trying to teach others of its importance. The use of PCEQ's Waste Reduction Guide seen in Appendix B is a good tool to use for this purpose. In addition to training aids, a lot of time is often spent using "management-by-wandering-around" (MBWA) to encourage employee help in actions and ideas. Well-run Stage 1 companies make extensive use of environment audits initiated by corporate headquarters. The purpose is to ensure compliance with environmental regulations.

In Stage 1, if there is an awareness of consumers' environmental needs, it's their short-term external customers who draw the attention of marketing and sales. The emphasis is to try and identify then exploit the "Green" Marketing approach discussed in Chapter 4. DuPont's "match product demand to consumer need" is a good example of this type of thinking. Those companies that believe they have a more environmentally beneficial product than a competitor will try to get recognition for them through organizations like Scientific Certification Systems or other similar programs. Those that do not feel the product is environmentally superior at least try to make sure their product does not violate any laws, and try to follow the marketing guidelines outlined in Appendix A. The Home Depot's approach to green marketing is perhaps one of the best examples of green marketing in action.

**Stage 1 Organization
Figure 9–2**

Empowered Stage 1

You should not get the impression that Stage 1 environmental efforts are bad. A poorly organized Stage 1 is bad, but so is a poorly organized Stage 2 or 3 effort. A well-thought-out approach to environmental compliance can be a powerful friend when your competition does not have a plan. A well-thought-out Stage 1 management has an understanding and awareness that environmental management with its current mode of operation is a cost. Like any overhead, it should be controlled and minimized.

At Stage 1, financial implications of environmental matters are starting to be recognized. In an attempt to comply with regulations and protect the environment, costs of pollution are being identified, measured, and attempts are being made to reflect those costs in corporate decision making and reporting. There is a growing recognition, in Stage 1, that there are environmental obligations being incurred from current practices. These Stage 1 people know that the prospect of environmental liability operates in such an emotionally-charged atmosphere that the cost from litigation might well be greater than the cost of the cleanup.

To have an empowered Stage 1 company, these financial costs, including potential legal costs, will have to be estimated and allocated to periods and products. Capital improvement plans will need to be drawn up to finance them. The drawback to all of this is that such obligations are naturally hard to assess since lengthy forecast periods may be involved. Other questions will also need to be answered in Stage 1 such as "How should we report the potential cost of decontaminating sites?" "Should environmental lawsuits be considered a contingent liability or should they be disclosed in notes to financial statements?" In the last chapter we will examine some of the more innovative and effective ways of doing this so you will have a more realistic idea of the true cost of pollution. Assessing the true cost is essential to an empowered Stage 1.

Some actions at this stage of environmental management include developing and publishing an environmental policy. Short-term goals for improving pollution control are necessary. There must also be specific long-term goals for controlling pollution, thereby minimizing legal risk. Discussion should be held on preparing an agenda of actions. Senior management needs to send a strong signal that pollution control is very important to the survival of the company. This means that it also needs to allocate adequate resources to the job, and there needs to be an ongoing program to monitor, audit, and report the status of waste reduction efforts.[1]

One of the differences between a well run and a poorly run Stage 1 company is how well all these pieces are tied together to form a unified approach. Using a common measurement system like *waste ratio*, which will be discussed later, can be a tool for drawing people together. If every person, every department, and every function has these it becomes a common focus and language for everyone. As such it provides a means of communication across functional and departmental lines.

To be an empowered Stage 1 company you will want to maximize your human resources so you do not waste your material resources. This means getting as many as possible involved in the green movement. Asking them to reduce, reuse, and recycle is one thing, getting their commitment to do this is another. Basing raises, promotions, and other rewards in part on how well subordinates perform their environmental and other responsibilities can enhance their commitment. When your people know they are being judged on environmental performance as well as other organizational concerns like cost, productivity, quality, and customer service, then you can have an empowered Stage 1 organization. Otherwise, you can only hope your competitors do not have a more empowered company or that your customers perceive that you do a better job of minimizing environmental impact than actually is occuring.

STAGE 2 ORGANIZATIONS

In the Stage 2 organization there is the first real change in organizational structure. Up until now, the old vertical-boss-subordinate structure where management "tells and sells" has been the method of operation. In Stage 2, organizations are similar to those that have begun to de-layer, streamline, "fatten" and empower so they can get more inclusive decision making. A natural outcome of these organizational changes is often more fluid decision making.

A Stage 2 model is seen in *Figure 9–3*. It is here that a revolutionary step has been made, going from the vertical decision making of Stage 1 companies to the more horizontal decision making of Stage 2. In Stage 1, employees were asked for their opinion about how to reduce pollution. Their input was sought, and in some cases they were given additional environmental responsibilities. The more innovative companies also rewarded employees for their participation, but no structural changes in actual decision making had occurred.

It is at Stage 2 where the true rearrangement of decision making occurs. These decisions, that at one time were the exclusive domain of management, now are assumed by employees. This involvement usually takes some form of team management. Increasingly companies are giving teams of employees the responsibility and authority of front-line supervision. "Line of sight" teams (responsible for everything within their sight) or semiautonomous work groups decide how work at their site is to be organized. In some situations they even decide who is hired or fired. More common are teams that do their own preventative maintenance and quality assurance, determine how work is scheduled, and decides who assumes what responsibilities. The success of this team approach in the quality area is well documented.

Ownership

Robert C. Whiteman, Manager, Environmental Health and Safety and Support Engineering for the Printed-Circuit Board Headquarters at Richmond, Virginia for AT&T, notes that reduction of toxic emissions at Richmond were the result of *teamwork* across the board; process engineering, facilities engineering, environmental health and safety engineering, and

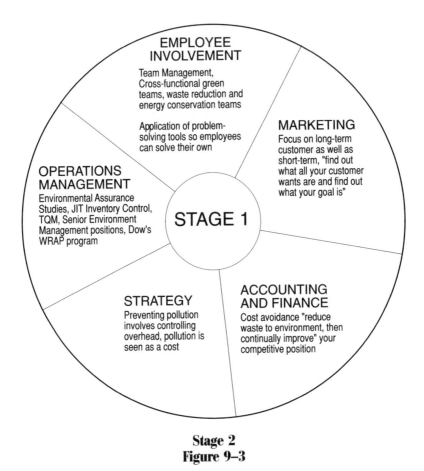

Stage 2
Figure 9–3

operation personnel.[5] It is true that teamwork has to exist for pollution to be reduced, but there must be a real sense of ownership within the team for it to be a Stage 2 approach. The real power of a Stage 2 approach can only occur when there is a sense of ownership among team members. At Stage 1, people are informed about what is expected of them, but work is still dichotomized. Directives flow downward in Stage 1, but it is communication that goes back and forth and up as well as down that is needed for better pollution management. In Stage 2, ideas can be shared without labels or artificial barriers. There are powerful psychological forces at work when we empower people with a strong sense of ownership.

Earlier we mentioned Quad/Graphic's savings from reducing ink waste. It is easier for you to get this degree of involvment when your people assume ownership of pollution concerns. Such ownership at Quad dates back through the early years of the company. In 1973, when the company started adding presses, it refused to put anyone in charge of the pressroom. The point was to make everyone a full partner, each pressperson running his or her own press.

Teams that are given the power to decide produce a greater understanding of those decisions. Members will be a lot more likely to be committed, as well. People may half-heartedly recycle if they are told to do so, but they will not try to find better ways of reducing pollution if they do not make the connection between work, pollution, profit, and a sense of ownership.

If your people do not perceive that they have a stake in the organization or in the outcome of decisions, they will only give half-hearted efforts. They are much more likely to look for opportunities when they feel they have a personal stake in the outcome. It is only when they do this that they are likely to continually try to reduce pollution as well as other overhead items. A Stage 2 organization moves people from the sense of cooperation that exists in Stage 1 to one of collaboration.

Restructuring

Bringing different people together with different viewpoints increases the knowledge essential to improving productivity and to reducing inefficiencies and waste. From a training standpoint, a great deal of cross-training must occur in Stage 2. Everyone must have a better understanding of their role and how they fit in. They must have the strongest identity with the process of production. They must know how and where they are most valuable.

In Stage 1, the purpose is to control pollution, to monitor it through audit techniques like management-by-wandering-around (MBWA) to hopefully pick up ideas on how to reduce pollution. The purpose of a Stage 2 company is quite different. There is a conscious effort at *assurance* rather than audits. An audit's focus is on compliance and monitoring waste. An assurance process concentrates more on pollution training and assistance. In Stage 2 it is the employees' job to reduce pollution at the site and management is there to help and provide assistance, not to oversee, as it is with audits.

Restructuring changes many things. Employee involvement methods like JIT inventory are often used so operational personnel can be given greater responsibility for controlling overhead. As material is pulled through by internal customers rather than being pushed through as it is in Stage 1, inventory begins to drop. Inventory levels and excess should drop because those people upstream control what is needed. That is good because they are in the best position to know what they need. Internal customers do not want to "buy" more than they will need. JIT is obviously not the only way to reduce inventory, but inventory must be kept at a minimum through some means.

As the amount of excess inventory drops because of better communications, so does waste. We have already discussed the Northrop Corporation's aircraft story where cans of paint were being wasted. Inventory (and waste) was only reduced when it matched production rates to supply rates. Matching these production and usage rates is one of the things internal suppliers and customers do. It is a better, less wasteful process but does require a great deal of trust, training, and internal communication. Those upstream must be empowered with the responsibility and *authority* to "stop the line" so problems can be solved immediately and waste and mistakes can be prevented.

Principles of TQM recommended by the President's Commission on Environmental Quality (PCEQ) and those used by several innovative companies in this book provide a good example of Stage 2 management. They are Stage 2 because the shift is to a restructuring of management decision making where greater responsibility and accountability are assigned. It is management's job to assess and support (quality or other operation initiatives), not to direct and control as it does in Stage 1. The PCEQ initiatives mentioned earlier and the WRAP program are good examples of the TQM approach being applied to pollution control.

Managerial Initiatives

From a strategic viewpoint, management moves from a commitment to comply with legal requirements that is common with Stage 1 companies, to a new realization. The realization is that pollution is an overhead similar to bad quality or poor inventory control. Typical thinking for this frame of mind comes from Kent Kresa, Northrop's chairman and CEO who in discussing the environment said that business should take the initiative to gain a competitive advantage that comes from having greater control of destiny. The thinking goes, if it is a cost to us and our competitor, it can become a competitive advantage. For it to become a competitive advantage, you must control pollution cost better than your competitor. In Stage 2, there is a recognition that it takes more than compliance or avoidance to use it to a competitive advantage. It takes more efficient use of resources, including human resources.

In Stage 1, someone is probably given a title of Environmental (and Safety) Officer and the CEO may make occasional reference to the importance of environmental issues. In Stage 2, corporate actions are more substantial. Allen F. Jacobson, 3M's recently retired chairman and CEO, advises to make environmental concerns part of the routine business planning.[6] Some of these actions include some restructuring of the organization and staffing so lower operational people have a greater sense of ownership and participation. The company should actively invest in worthwhile environmental science and technology so that they can lower their long-term environmental cost—thus gaining a competitive advantage. To this end, more effort will need to be spent on educating people on why they need to participate and how to do it. Every day greater efforts need to include building bridges to various groups. Environmental committees may be selected to oversee strategic issues. Xerox's senior management Environmental Leadership Committee might serve as an example of this approach. We will look at other examples of this high-level commitment in the next chapter.

The financial end of the business is also beginning to change. The approach has gone from one of cost minimization that was the hallmark of Stage 1 to one of *cost avoidance* or *competitiveness costing*. In Stage 1, accounting looks to reduce short-term cost by keeping capital investment down and avoiding long-term legal losses. Accounting in Stage 1 believes pollution concerns are of minimum importance or value to an organization's success so little material, technological, or human resources are committed to it.

In Stage 2, the perspective is completely different. Through life-cycle costing and similar processes, management is better able to understand the true cost of environmental overhead. With a competitive-costing approach there is recognition that total pollution and waste cost are a major overhead, similar to excessive poor quality. Dow's WRAP and 3M's 3P approaches are examples of well-run competitive-costing programs. A number of corporations like Monsanto, 3M and DuPont are betting those that stay two steps ahead of environmental regulators will stay one step ahead of the competition. That is Stage 2 thinking.[7] Untypically successful was 3M's 3P approach. It undertook 3,000 projects, achieved a 5 percent waste stream reduction per unit of production, reduced pollution by 1 billion pounds over 15 years, and realized a total savings of $500 million. At this stage, management wants to avoid overhead so it may be necessary to invest in capital technology or human resources in order to get a lower overhead and return on investment later.

In Stage 2, marketing has also changed its thinking. In Stage 1 there is recognition of their short-term customers' green needs. Stage 2 marketing efforts have broadened definitions to include long-term customers such as the community at large. Even governmental regulations can be thought of as long-term customers. Marketing at this stage is beginning to recognize that their customers include the public, and can even include the publics of other countries where one expects to do business. If you plan at any time in the future to do business in Germany, then you must be aware of its "green" packaging and environmental requirements.

Dow Chemical was one of the first to recognize the need to bring all their customers into organizational decision making. It has community Advisory Panels at many of their manufacturing locations. These panels meet regularly with Dow representatives on things like emerging preparation and other environmental programs. The German company, BASF, as far back as 1970, set up a twenty-four-hour hotline to deal with complaints from neighbors.[8]

Dow has been one of the most impressive at bringing long-term customers into its decision process. Four times a year, eight environmental advocates from around the world gather at its headquarters in Midland, Michigan to spend 1 1/2 days with senior managers and board members.[1] Their plant managers do the same thing with local environmental groups.

As we have already seen, in many cases, European customers' environmental expectations are higher than American expectations. Stage 2 marketers recognize that it seems better to market to your customers' highest expectations rather than your lowest customer expectations. It makes little sense to have one product for German customers and another for American customers. Marketing people know that the only safe approach is to be a world-class competitor. Being the best in your city, country, or even hemisphere is a risky decision in a world where new competitors are coming on-line every day.

STAGE 3 ORGANIZATIONS

The last stage on this continuum is one of total integration of pollution components into the fabric of corporate decision making. A model is seen in *Figure 9–4*. Stage 3 requires complete integration of environmental considerations in all corporate decisions, from major ones like whether to build a new plant, to minor ones, like recycling paper. In Stage 3, environmental issues are a part of everyone's day-to-day decision making. The theme of Stage 3 is that given enough effort, coordination, process, and product understanding it is possible to create profits from antipollution efforts, from closed-loop production, and operational efficiency.

From the production side of management, there is already one example of Stage 3, namely mother nature. In nature nothing is wasted, everything is reused, nothing is landfilled. In human terms we can think of nature as a closed-loop system. The goal here is different than in Stage 1 or 2. It is no longer to minimize or contain cost, but rather the point is to maximize resources—all resources, including waste. Even the term waste is incorrect. There is no waste, only by-products.

**Natural Integration Stage-3 Model
Figure 9–4**

There was a great story in *Forbes* magazine that illustrates this new thinking. It seems a man named Robert Smee believes he is an "industrial dating service" or a "corporate garage sale." He directs Pacific Materials Exchange in Spokane, Washington, one of the nation's largest waste exchanges. As such, it is a matchmaker for manufacturers, municipalities, and waste brokers that want to get rid of their own waste, or use someone else's for raw materials. In 1990, he exchanged 600 different materials at an annualized rate of 4.5 million tons. About 15 percent of it (buyer/sellers) changed hands and he only charges users a $48 subscription fee. He estimates that the national waste exchanger saved $27 million in reduced disposal cost where someone used waste as raw material. He notes that as the cost of virgin materials and waste management go up, large-scale exchanges are going to become more and more feasible. These were the efforts of an individual.

There is no telling what revenues are possible when more people begin to find ways to reduce by-products and greater efforts are made at finding markets for those by-products.

The first approach is to turn 100 percent of your true raw material which are *decisions* into finished goods and services without any pollution. Every decision should be examined, every assumption should be challenged. For instance, why assume you must *make* things to turn cost into profits; you might have to *disassemble* rather than assemble. If by-products remain, there must be a continuous effort to maximize this resource.

Management already knows the battle cry "zero waste" even if it does not understand the method for doing it. For zero waste to be more than an empty phrase, you first have to redefine waste. In Stage 3 it is not a liability, it's an asset. J. Kirk Sullivan, Vice-President for governmental and environmental affairs at Boise Cascade (a huge Idaho papermaker), points out that many environmental problems can be solved by not generating waste in the first place. He emphasizes that if you define it in broad, generic terms you can't get anywhere.[10]

In other words, it's not enough to say your objective is zero waste. You have to define operationally what is expected. This means no extra processing, minimum cycle times, no rejects, no extra inventory, no waste motion, and no lagtime. Operationally defining zero waste in all aspects of operation is the Stage 3 call to arms.

It is critical to establish specific environmental policies. Saying you are dedicated to ensuring the conservation and prudent use of "resources" means nothing. Do not be vague. Be specific about intermediate as well as long-term objectives. Divide the philosophy into objectives, like reducing emission of chlorofluorocarbons by "x" amount, then identifying strategies for reaching them. An example of quantifying expectations comes in the quality area from Motorola's *Six Sigma* approach. It gets high standards, and expect no more than 3.4 defects in one million opportunities for errors. From white collar to blue collar, the standard is the same. Pollution Management efforts need something similar if they want to create profits from antipollution efforts.

Lack of a good quantifiable measurement system impedes attempts to produce profitable environmental management. Another restriction involves life cycling. Life-cycle costing, as seen in Chapter 3, does attempt to quantify environmental cost, but at present this is still an emerging science. Currently, there are no true or highly accurate ways of assessing life-cycle cost. The eco-balance sheet is accounting's way of beginning to assess true cost. The company that is first able to develop a more comprehensive eco-balance sheet, true life cycle costing approach, or use the capital-budgeting process mentioned in Chapter 14, will have a major new competitive tool to use against its competitor!

Concurrent Marketing

Concurrent marketing refers to the practice of production and process engineers working closely together to produce designs that are highly produceable. If pollution efforts are to evolve into profitable, rather than cost-avoidance efforts, then marketing must develop a close relationship with production and product design. The phrase "green design" must mean more than adding in environmental components.

Level 3 marketing recognizes that there are enormous profits in marketing products that make a real and genuine difference for the planet. The effort involves substantial research and development. Especially in the world of consumer marketing, every month spent awaiting EPA authorization to operate a new factory means lost profits.[7]

Marketing knows, or should know, customer needs. It should work closely and swiftly to design in customer needs. It can be the ultimate competitive advantage. It was just noted that a comprehensive eco-balance sheet would be a competitive advantage. The same can be said for better design in customer needs. The better you can identify specific consumer environmental needs, the better off you are. If you can tie these needs into design parameters, you can gain the competitive advantage, and there is already a way to do it.

Adapting the Quality Function Deployment (QFD) efforts to include your customers' environmental concerns is such a tool. In order to achieve Stage 3, marketing must work closely with design when decisions are made about product reformulation, substitution, and modification. Nonpolluting designs are of little value if the customer does not value them.

QFD is a systematic approach that ingrains the customers' needs into the design of products or services. Companies like AT&T, Digital Equipment Corporation, Eastman Kodak, and Proctor and Gamble have used QFD to set competitive performance goals and create products and services that meet customers' needs. QFD cross-functional teams start with a ranked list of customer needs. There is also a customer rating of your company's and your competitions' current performance. By analyzing the result, you can set performance goals and design your customers' requirements.

QFD uses cross-functional teams so you are more likely to avoid the mistakes that normally occur when you're trying to figure out what the customer wants. QFD does increase the upfront development time—especially if you have not already collected detailed customer and competitor information. It does reduce later engineering changes by 30 to 50 percent.[12]

If you would like more information on QFD you should contact the American Suppliers Institute (ASI) at 15041 Commerce Drive South, Dearborn, MI 48120 (313-271-4200). ASI is a nonprofit spin-off of the Ford Motor Company and a leading proponent of QFD. Another non-profit QFD group is GOAL at 13 Branch Street, Methuen, MA 01844 (508-685-3900).

Design For Environment (DFE) will be a part of Stage 3. With DFE, all relevant and ascertainable environmental considerations and constraints are integrated into product and process engineering. This involves pollution prevention, waste minimization, and toxic use reduction. It also involves product life-cycle analysis and the so-called Design For Disassembly (DFD). Mercedes DFD efforts to design a car for *disassembly* in Germany has already been noted. Among recent reports are those of the Motor Vehicle Association in the United States that estimates that 90 percent of all materials in a modern 2,400-pound car may be recyclable. At the North American International Auto Show in Detroit, Dodge introduced the Neon, a concept car with virtually every component recyclable. Coded body parts identify plastic for sorting.[11]

When it comes to design there are continuing efforts to close the loop, so to speak. Researchers are having increasing success at doing what was once thought to be impossible. In one case, researchers at Argonne National Laboratory have developed a process to create large quantities of biodegradable polylactic acid (PLA), a plastic used for biomedical products. The plastic is made from the starchy food waste of potato processing. When exposed to water, sunlight, or bacteria, PLA breaks down into harmless chemicals. Likewise, researchers at Battele in Columbus, Ohio have produced a high-strength and elastic plastic from castor bean oil. They hope it will be a renewable raw material with applications in electronic components, cable insulation, and injection molding components.[11]

CLOSING THOUGHTS

In Stage 1, employees were asked to participate. In Stage 2, greater responsibilities and accountabilities for pollution were given to employees, usually through team management. Most of these green teams, as we will see, revolve around work area issues or those issues affecting several functions within a plant or site. At Stage 3, involvement becomes integration. Most of the Stage 1 employee involvement is limited to individual initiatives like antipollution champions and employee suggestion schemes. People are encouraged to recycle and conserve energy.

At Stage 2 involvement is broadened to include accountability and responsibility for pollution, usually at one's work area. Autonomous work groups that replace supervisors are already in many places. They set environmental goals, measure waste performance in their work areas, and work across functions. So what's left?

Integration is the next step beyond involvement. At this stage, operational personnel are not being limited to work area issues. Their participation in decisions can involve design considerations or even financial or strategic issues. Their input could help decide what products to produce, what capital expenditures to make, and so on. The point is to continually expand their participation so that artificial boundaries are washed away so everyone works in a more cohesive and integrated manner.

If you would like to find out where you are at in the pollution management continuum, or to find out what pieces are missing, a "Green Survey" and a visual way of scoring your responses is provided at the end of the chapter. If you fill out the questionnaire and "pollution wheel" you may find some surprises. At least it should give you a rough idea of areas in which you can improve. Next, we will look at how to improve some of those areas.

GREEN MANAGEMENT SURVEY©
(Do not reproduce)

Company _____

Name _____ Position _____

Type of Business _____ Size _____

Answer the following questions by circling the most appropriate response. For each question ask yourself to what degree the statement is true. You can then score the "wheel" at the end to see what type of pollution program exists. If you feel a question is not applicable (N/A) to your situation, circle the * on the sheet. Before circling the *, first try to see if it applies in a general way to your situation. When you fill out the "wheel" at the end, shade N/A questions in a different color than ones where the question was applicable.

	Always	Frequently	Occasionally	Rarely	Never	N/A
STRATEGY						
Stage 1						
1. Within our organization we have *written* an environmental policy and short-term goals for improving our environmental performance.	4	3	2	1	0	*
2. A clear and strong signal has been sent from our senior managers that better environmental management is not a choice, but a mandate.	4	3	2	1	0	*

	Always	Frequently	Occasionally	Rarely	Never	N/A
3. If applicable, we would voluntarily participate in EPA's voluntary programs such as 33–50 (which aim to reduce releases of 17 targeted chemicals 33% by 1992 and 50% by 1995 from a 1988 baseline).	4	3	2	1	0	*
4. We have a senior environmental officer in our corporate headquarters.	4	3	2	1	0	*
5. A key part of our environmental planning is compliance with all legal and governmental regulations.	4	3	2	1	0	*

Stage 2

6. Committees or other high-level management initiatives are used to oversee environmental strategic issues, an outcome of which are *specific* long-range goals for pollution control including eliminating pollution-related cost.	4	3	2	1	0	*
7. Management adequately invests in worthwhile environmental science and technology so we can lower our long-term environmental cost.	4	3	2	1	0	*
8. Management understands that pollution is a cost to both our competitors and us. As such, the one that best controls this overhead is the most competitive.	4	3	2	1	0	*

Stage 3

9. Our organization has a corporate wide philosophy for the total elimination of waste (e.g., zero waste or similar approach) and we have been effective at getting that message across to our people.	4	3	2	1	0	*
10. Environmental concerns have been integrated into the decision making of our Board of Directors (senior environmental officials on the Board of Directors is one example of how you might integrate green concerns).	4	3	2	1	0	*

	Always	Frequently	Occasionally	Rarely	Never	N/A
11. Our Board of Directors and/or senior managers meet regularly with environmental advocates and other "outsiders" to discuss environmental issues.	4	3	2	1	0	*
12. Our plants and local sites meet regularly with local community and environmental groups and other "outsiders" to discuss environmental issues.	4	3	2	1	0	*
13. My organization believes it must not compromise the ability of future generations to sustain itself through good natural resource management.	4	3	2	1	0	*
14. Senior management sees better pollution management as a revenue generator and corporate asset.	4	3	2	1	0	*

OPERATIONAL MANAGEMENT

Stage 1

	Always	Frequently	Occasionally	Rarely	Never	N/A
15. We have ongoing environmental audits in order to determine if we comply with all governmental and legal requirements.	4	3	2	1	0	*
16. We have management people who have environmental responsibilities at the local or plant site area.	4	3	2	1	0	*
17. We have an extensive reuse and recycle program.	4	3	2	1	0	*
18. Staff understands our priorities at work are to reduce, reuse, recycle, and landfill as a last resort.	4	3	2	1	0	*
19. Do you feel like your environmental assurance process is designed to *assist* and provide a resource for the plant or site level to better reduce environmental overhead cost (emphasis should be on assistance, not auditing; it should be on reducing cost rather than simply meeting legal obligations).	4	3	2	1	0	*

	Always	Frequently	Occasionally	Rarely	Never	N/A

Stage 2

20. We are constantly looking for advances in technology to reduce pollution.

| | 4 | 3 | 2 | 1 | 0 | * |

21. We use inventory control methods similar to JIT or other pull methods where employees, as internal customers, are ultimately responsible for controlling inventory.

| | 4 | 3 | 2 | 1 | 0 | * |

22. Within my organization it is management's job to support and assist pollution efforts of employees rather than simply to direct and control pollution efforts.

| | 4 | 3 | 2 | 1 | 0 | * |

23. Our operational employees have the authority to "stop the line" if they perceive there is an environmental risk occurring.

| | 4 | 3 | 2 | 1 | 0 | * |

24. We use TQM to solve our pollution problems (e.g., TQM teams, Pareto's analysis, cause and effect diagrams, etc.).

| | 4 | 3 | 2 | 1 | 0 | * |

Stage 3

25. Does purchasing have an ongoing and comprehensive evaluation system designed to eliminate waste?

| | 4 | 3 | 2 | 1 | 0 | * |

26. Our organization focuses more on source reduction (e.g., eliminating pollution at the source) rather than recycling efforts.

| | 4 | 3 | 2 | 1 | 0 | * |

27. Our products, services, and production processes are designed, reviewed, verified, and controlled to meet the environmental needs and expectations of our internal and external customers.

| | 4 | 3 | 2 | 1 | 0 | * |

28. Workplace teams of a cross-section of employees are used to help the company decide strategic and financial initiatives that affect environmental concerns.

| | 4 | 3 | 2 | 1 | 0 | * |

	Always	Frequently	Occasionally	Rarely	Never	N/A

EMPLOYEE INVOLVEMENT

Stage 1

29. We use "green teams" to solve local work-site environmental problems.

    4   3   2   1   0   *

30. Our raises and promotions are based in part on how well we perform our environmental responsibilities to control waste and recycle. An environmental category is part of every employee's job.

    4   3   2   1   0   *

31. We conduct employee idea-generating contests that encourage employees to give us ideas on how to recycle, reuse, or consume energy, and recognize them for their contributions.

    4   3   2   1   0   *

32. We use a systematic environmental training and recognition plan that trains employees to *identify* and *classify* environmental problems (e.g., Pareto analysis, cause and effect, histograms, etc.).

    4   3   2   1   0   *

Stage 2

33. We have cross-functional green teams in operations, whose goals are to get a group together to reduce a specific environmental problem that crosses functional and divisional lines.

    4   3   2   1   0   *

34. When it comes to eliminating pollution, our employees have a real sense that pollution is their problem as much as it is the company's problem.

    4   3   2   1   0   *

35. Ideas on pollution management are shared freely among lower, middle and upper levels within the organization. It is a collaborative effort.

    4   3   2   1   0   *

	Always	Frequently	Occasionally	Rarely	Never	N/A
36. We have a systematic environmental employee training and empower-ment plan that teaches employees how to make good environmental decisions. (This plan should not only teach them how to identify problem areas, but most importantly how to make the decision about what to do.)	4	3	2	1	0	*

Stage 3

	Always	Frequently	Occasionally	Rarely	Never	N/A
37. Our workforce has a high degree of decision-making involvement and integration in *plant-level* green deci-sions (e.g., help make the actual deci-sions, as opposed to simply identify-ing problems or providing solutions).	4	3	2	1	0	*
38. When it comes to decision-making authority in *corporate decisions* about what green strategies, products, and services we offer, our employees are involved in identifying problems, developing solutions, selecting the best choices, implementing them, and evaluating results.	4	3	2	1	0	*

ACCOUNTING AND FINANCIAL

Stage 1

	Always	Frequently	Occasionally	Rarely	Never	N/A
39. We measure whether we meet or exceed our internal or external customers' envi-ronmental priorities and needs.	4	3	2	1	0	*
40. All of the departments and functional areas assess and measure waste out-put using some quantifiable measure like waste ratios, etc.	4	3	2	1	0	*
41. We try to contain the cost of pollution by making sure we do not violate var-ious environmental codes and laws.	4	3	2	1	0	*

Stage 2

	Always	Frequently	Occasionally	Rarely	Never	N/A
42. Our goal is to reduce the *long-term* (5 years or more) cost of energy, waste, and other environmental cost.	4	3	2	1	0	*

	Always	Frequently	Occasionally	Rarely	Never	N/A
43. When we calculate the cost and savings for proposed capital projects, the time frame we use is five or more years rather than the usual three to five years that is often used by companies.	4	3	2	1	0	*
44. Senior management recognizes that environmental costs are a cost to our competitor as well as to us. It knows if we lower our cost relative to theirs, that we gain a competitive advantage.	4	3	2	1	0	*

Stage 3

	Always	Frequently	Occasionally	Rarely	Never	N/A
45. Environmental managers or those chiefly responsible for environmental management have adequate authority over capital investment decisions.	4	3	2	1	0	*
46. We do extensive life-cycle costing, or use eco-balance sheets on our products and services.	4	3	2	1	0	*
47. When it comes to generating profits, environmental concerns here are held in the same regard as productivity and quality.	4	3	2	1	0	*
48. Our overall environmental goal includes exploring how to generate revenue through better environmental management.	4	3	2	1	0	*

MARKETING AND CUSTOMER SERVICE

Stage 1

	Always	Frequently	Occasionally	Rarely	Never	N/A
49. We are constantly looking for ways to develop partnerships with our suppliers to reduce waste.	4	3	2	1	0	*
50. Our marketing department seems to always be trying to explore our external customers' green needs and concerns by, whenever possible, making sure we highlight our products' and services' environmental benefits.	4	3	2	1	0	*

	Always	Frequently	Occasionally	Rarely	Never	N/A
51. We use a variety of effective and sometimes innovative methods for obtaining feedback about our external customers' environmental needs.	4	3	2	1	0	*

Stage 2

	Always	Frequently	Occasionally	Rarely	Never	N/A
52. We look for ways to sell our by-products to other companies so we can eliminate waste.	4	3	2	1	0	*
53. People in my organization recognize that our external customers also include the community at large, environmental advocates, and governmental agencies' environmental needs.	4	3	2	1	0	*
54. We use a variety of effective, and sometimes innovative, methods for obtaining feedback about how we are satisfying the environmental needs of the community and environmental advocates.	4	3	2	1	0	*

Stage 3

	Always	Frequently	Occasionally	Rarely	Never	N/A
55. Our marketing department works closely with our product and service designers so that environmentally friendly products can be made that add value and satisfy our external customers' needs.	4	3	2	1	0	*
56. Our design engineers try to "think green" and create products that are designed for disassembly or otherwise aim to close the loop on production.	4	3	2	1	0	*
57. In our capital budgeting process our focus is more on enlarging market share through "green" product and services (as opposed to simply avoiding liability).	4	3	2	1	0	*

---

* Copies of the questionnaire can be obtained by writing to D. Keith Denton, Department of Management, Southwest Missouri State University, Springfield, MO 65804.

"PIECES OF THE PUZZLE"

Shade the wheel according to how you filled out the Green Management Survey. For instance, if you circled a "3" on question #2, you would shade it as seen below. If you answered "not applicable" to any question, shade this. Any white spaces can indicate pieces of the pollution puzzle that need to be addressed before you can have an integrated and effective Stage 1, 2, or 3 program. Stage 1 is the inner circle, Stage 2 is the middle circle, and Stage 3 is the outer circle.

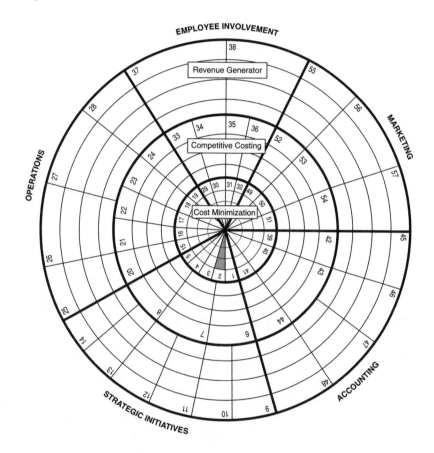

The Pollution Wheel
Figure 9–5

ENDNOTES

1. Rice, Faye, "Who Scores the Best on the Environment," *Fortune*, Vol. 28, No. 2, July 26, 1993, pp. 115–116.

2. "Measure of Environmental Success Often Intangible," *United Technologies News*, January–February, 1992, p. 1.

3. Boroughs, Don L., Betsy Carpenter, "Cleaning Up the Environment," *U.S. News and World Report*, March 25, 1991, p. 19.

4. Muller, E.J., "The Quest for a Quality Environment," *Distribution*, January 1, 1992, p. 32–34.

5. *A Healthy Balance: AT&T Environment And Safety Report*, 1992, in-house publication, p. 4.

6. Taravella, Steve, "Employee's Ideas and Efforts Can Make Hospitals' Environmental Program Thrive," *Modern Healthcare*, February 24, 1992, p. 28.

7. Boroughs, Don L., Betsy Carpenter, "Cleaning Up the Environment," *U.S. News and World Report*, March 25, 1991, pp. 17–18.

8. Henne, Hans Jörg, "Ecological Responsibility and Corporate Activity: The View of a Chemical Company," (*Paper at the International Symposium 'One Future World'*) Tokyo, Japan, November 17-18, 1992, p. 13.

9. Zweig, Jason, "Garbage In, Garbage Out," *Forbes*, November 11, 1991, p. 390.

10. Gardner, Elizabeth, "Teams Can Solve Environmental Quandaries," *Modern Healthcare*, February 24, 1992, p. 29.

11. Baker, Andrea L., "Green Revolution Comes to Engineering," *Design News*, September 9, 1991, pp. 102–103.

12. Mellina, Catherine, "Getting Started With Quality Function Deployment: An Annotated Resource Guide," *Corporate Quality Environmental Quality II Measurements and Communication Conference*, Arlington, VA, March 16–18, 1992, p. 98.

10

MOVING TO EMPOWERED POLLUTION MANAGEMENT

Earlier we mentioned the fact that any good model should address the issue of what type of decision making is occurring. To have a highly integrated model of employee participation, you have to know not only what decisions are made, but also *how* they are made. When you talk of sharing decision making, you must first examine how much *power* will be shared. Decision making includes several steps including (1) identifying pollution problems, (2) developing pollution solutions, (3) selecting the best solutions, (4) implementing them, and (5) evaluating the results. The scope of lower-level involvement varies dramatically from organization to organization and also within areas of an organization.

The least involvement in decision making would be employees being asked to simply identify pollution problems in their work area. This Stage 1 type of involvement often carries the lowest sense of ownership. The result is a low sense of integration. Most will feel little sense of unity of purpose.

At the other end of the scale is high level of involvement in all aspects of a business and a resulting strong sense of ownership. This creates a high integration of purpose within an organization. In order to reach this high integration, personnel must do two things. First, participants must be involved in all five steps of the decision process (identify problem, develop solutions, select the best one, implement and evaluate it.) They must also be involved in more than deciding on simple work area issues like maintaining a clean work area or good preventative maintenance. Other broader pollution issues they could explore might include dealing with employee scheduling of work and coordinating pollution efforts with those of other areas. At the highest corporate level, employees can help select capital investments to reduce pollution or participate in strategic sessions to identify new products, services or environmental niches. In fact, this is one of the criteria for Stage 3 pollution managment efforts.

When managers talk of "giving the line first shot at it," it should mean not only identifying pollution problems, but should also mean encouraging them to generate solutions, planning how to implement them, and then evaluating results. Anything less is pseudo-involvement. That is one reason why suggestion schemes do not work. If they had a chance to implement those decisions, then they would have a sense of closure. For people to truly "buy in" to the pollution prevention process, they must have this type of full-time participation.

This kind of participation, as seen in *Figure 10–1*, can range from partial decision-making responsibility to full decision-making responsibilities including obligations to fully implement decisions. The authority to make decisions can also vary from simple workplace decisions, like the need to recycle, to broader issues involving planning and even corporate green policy making. It is possible to have full participation in decision making at one's work area or at your work site, but only have minimum responsibilities at higher areas such as your plant or corporate headquarters. In Stage 3 there is a full participation at all levels including corporate green decisions. As an organization moves toward Stage 3 the objective is to raise and extend this level of participation from full participation in green workplace issues to full participation in corporate green concerns.

AN INTEGRATED ORGANIZATION

The scope and degree of participation in workplace, site, plant, or corporate pollution management decisions determine whether Stage 3 is truly being implemented. But, participation in the process of decision making is not enough to ensure an empowered organization. How well the various com-

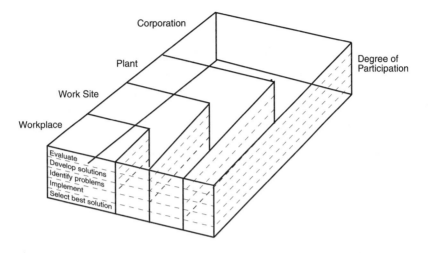

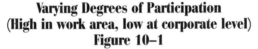

**Varying Degrees of Participation
(High in work area, low at corporate level)
Figure 10–1**

ponents (employees, operations, strategy, accounting, and marketing) communicate also affects your ability to turn waste management into a profitable venture. For there to be profits, you must concentrate on creating barrier free, open communication. Functional and departmental walls must disappear for there to be better free-flowing communication and pollution management.

There are many ways to reduce this barrier to communication and pollution management. Computer technology is one such tool that can be used to help reduce the mistakes and misunderstanding that creates much of the pollution. Computers can hold enormous amounts of information. If you are going to have good decisions made about environmental issues, you are going to need good information transferred between internal customers and suppliers.

Good communication and computers can help any organization improve pollution performance, but this is not unique to any stage of pollution development. In order to move to Stage 3 you will need something more unique. You will need some way to increase the circulation of information and knowledge throughout the organization. You will need to *upgrade knowledge* within the entire organization. In order to turn pollution management into profits all those within the organization must understand the entire production and delivery process as well as its financial and strategic components. The reason is simple: in order to move from Stage 1 and its concern for cost minimization to Stage 3's focus on profits, you must not only get everyone's help, but you must also provide staff with both the knowledge and skill to make good resource maximizing decisions.

When CEOs talk of the need to try to control pollution and that it is "everyone's responsibility" to do so, it is just an empty phrase, a lot of hot air. It means nothing to someone who feels left out of the loop. CEOs can have a "vision" till they are blue in the face, but people will not get it if they don't understand how all the pieces fit together. By understanding the whole production and delivery process and their place in it, they can make good decisions. Capturing their minds alone is not enough, you must also capture their hearts. If you can give them a stake in the outcome, some personal and financial reason to manage pollution, you can then profit from the experience.

Capturing your employees' hearts and minds is critical to profit making. To do that means restructuring decision making so that those who produce products, services, and pollution have a chance to, at least, affect how and what is done. In the 1990s, letting subordinates know what pollution responsibilities are expected is a start. Holding them accountable for them is even better, but empowering the organization can only occur when everyone, as much as possible, is involved in not only deciding how it's done, but also what should be done in the first place. This is the type of thinking needed to move to a Stage 3 organization.

It is doubtful that full equity and consensus decision making will be a reality in our lifetime, but the important thing to remember is that it does not have to be an either/or situation. If your organization or area has a greater sense of equity and sharing of knowledge and responsibility about pollution, it is more integrated. A more integrated organization produces some nice by-products like greater productivity, quality, profits, and marketshare because it has less inefficiencies, cost, and pollution.

MOVING FROM STAGE 1 TO STAGE 3

Using the Pollution Management Wheel in the last chapter, we have discussed the stages of pollution management. We have looked at its potential for turning a cost into a more profitable venture. The next step is to lay down the groundwork for moving from Stage 1 to 3. It will depend on several factors and the first one you can probably already guess. After all, nothing really significant happens without a high degree of top management commitment and it's the same case for pollution management.

Pollution prevention involves changing the corporate culture and that involves everybody accepting pollution prevention as part of their daily job.

Such a change takes time and it takes more than talk. It involves a real commitment from the top to change the direction of the organization. Top commitment alone is not enough, but it is critical to any change.

One essential for moving from Stage 1 to 3 is for top management to change the way it views environmental issues. In Stage 1, management assumes a pollution control liability, or a cost. In order to move toward Stage 3 you must think of it as an *asset*, not a nuisance. As we have already seen in early cases, good environmental management, even when it is in piecemeal form, makes money rather than costs money. But, before money can be made in a consistent manner, management must change its thinking. The point may have been most succinctly expressed by Sir Denys Henderson, Chairman of Imperial Chemical Industries, who said environmental performance is not an extra.[1]

Pollution management need not be difficult. In Stage 1, senior managers can have a dramatic effect on environmental management by frequently speaking about the importance of better environmental management at employee meetings and at other external settings. CRS Limited, headquartered in Australia, understands the importance of this type of communication. It makes extensive use of videotapes and reinforces its environmental messages from senior management through printed handouts. It notes that senior management also makes a lot of use of another Stage 1 process, namely management-by-wandering-around (MBWA). Additionally, CRS Limited uses a Stage 3 technique where a committee of its main Board of Directors oversees environmental efforts. The committee, as part of its responsibilities, makes visits and talks with local managers. It also employs a formal reporting system that gives the people in the organization the opportunity to make environmental issues known.

This brings up an important point, namely that actions speak louder than words. Hype is everywhere, people have heard it all before. Simply saying it is important to be environmentally conscious will not make it so. People must be convinced it's a high priority. Resources, personnel, and time must be devoted to it. Time is the most critical of these resources because everything else depends on time. It takes time to organize people and resources. A videotape, printed handout or mention in an annual report is not enough. A coordinated attack needs to be made. Policies, training, and oversight committees need to fit together like pieces to a puzzle, and that takes time.

ASSIGNING ENVIRONMENTAL RESPONSIBILITIES

One of the pieces needed for any type of environmental effort is some type of oversite committee that can be used to coordinate environmental efforts. Such a committee is often called an *Environmental Steering Committee*. It usually consists of key senior managers who participate actively in developing environmental organizational plans.

Deere and Company has formed what it calls its "Green Company Steering Committee." It consists of a group of the company's environmental personnel. They attempt to guide the company's goals and programs. Thus far they have:

- developed an environmental symbol for use within the company to promote environmental awareness (Stage 1)
- begun implementation of a facility audit program (Stage 1)
- implemented a quarterly environmental measurements report covering process water, nonhazardous waste, hazardous waste, and volatile organic emissions (Stage 1)
- set several corporate environmental goals (Stage 1, 2 or 3 depending on whether liability, cost, or revenues are being emphasized)
- achieved selection of the environment as one of six communication priorities for the corporation this year (Stage 1)
- initiated a design for environment program (Stage 3)

In a Stage 3 move, Dow put its senior environmental officer on its board of directors. At Xerox, a senior management Environmental Leadership Steering Committee was formed to guide environmental programs. This steering committee has representation from the heads of Manufacturing, Engineering, Supplies, Research, Quality, Real Estate/General Services, Marketing, its Worldwide Operating Companies and the Environmental Health and Safety department. Monsanto's Environmental Policy Committee makes policy recommendations to top management and its Board of Directors. The committee includes representatives from law, finance, accounting, manufacturing, marketing, communications, and environmental. The company believes its policy committee serves two purposes. First, it helps upper management gain a perspective on environmental concerns. Second, it believes the committee's integrated approach helps to educate all functional areas on the significance of environmental concerns in its area. If this is so, then it is at least an early indicator of a potential Stage 3 company.

Monsanto, among others, found it to be effective to create senior management positions with responsibility for environmental issues. It discovered that these positions should be equal in stature to finance, human resources, and other key senior executives. If a committee is impossible to assemble, it is wise to at least identify senior environmental positions that can coordinate such activities.

The German chemical company BASF doesn't just have an environment committee or senior environmental officer; it has a whole division. Since 1973, its Functional Division has been responsible for environmental protection, safety, and their Works Fire department. The Works Fire department is a group of technical people who pump out tanks, cover overshafts, mop up liquid spills, and do other emergency procedures. The Environmental Protection, Safety and Works Fire division employs more than 2,100 people. Most noticeably the division is assigned to the second level in the company hierarchy, just below the BASF Group Board of Executive Directors. This means the head of the division automatically has the right to make direct submissions to corporate management.[2] While the sheer number of BASF's environmentally-related personnel may be impressive, it is Volkswagen that may have made the most significant move. It was the first European car producer to appoint a board member *solely* responsible for environmental issues.[3] This puts environmental considerations at the highest possible level within an organization.

YOUR CORPORATE OBJECTIVES

Regardless of whether it is a board member or a senior environmental officer, it is essential for senior-level leadership to stress the *relationship* between environmental initiatives, productivity, and profits. The objective should be to keep the environmental agenda a part of normal senior management and board meeting conversation. It also involves communicating the environment message to the masses. Creating an environmental culture in an organization depends on leadership from top to bottom.

Almost every organization begins its commitment to environmental initiatives by developing policy statements and directives that come from the top. Companies have adopted a variety of initiatives designed to change the corporate culture and move toward environmental excellence. Often the initial impetus for change begins with a strong statement by the CEO, followed by a set of guidelines or principles established as corporate policy and widely communicated throughout the organization. Jack Welch, CEO of General Electric, provides a good example of what the typical top management directive is when he says, "Every person at GE has to be an environmentalist."[4] Such a statement can mean only one thing and that is that the environment is a top priority in the CEO's eyes. Welch's directive leaves no doubt about where he stands but it alone is not nearly enough. Problems occur when there is little senior-level responsibility for the environment. If there are no explicitly stated corporate objectives, or motivated people and well-trained experts, it's just talk. In order to implement this policy, GE has developed long-term objectives that include improved employee education and training that it hopes will create an environmental mindset for all job activities. GE management feels employees must "buy in" to solutions. When this happens, a by-product of this process will be reduction or elimination of waste streams, improved working environment and reduced operating cost.[4] Reducing operating inefficiencies is a reoccurring theme of many environmental statements.

THE STAGE 3 GOAL

Chevron's Perth Amboy Refinery expanded its pollution prevention goals by also focusing on reducing environmental cost throughout the facility. It felt a broad environmental policy statement would help increase its employees' feelings of responsibility for environmental issues. Chevron notes when it issued these statements, its people felt greater responsibility for environmental management throughout the workplace. The company's sense of responsibility is similar to the way safety is thought the responsibility of employees.[4]

One of 3M's facilities, the Medical Product Division in Brooking, South Dakota, has already taken the parent company's desires for continuous improvement in environmental performance one step further and may have developed the ultimate environment Stage 3 goal. It simply says its objective is *zero waste*. This is a concept much like Motorola's Six Sigma approach to quality. The concept behind zero waste is that while in the short term it may be impractical for the entire facility to achieve zero waste, it may be possible to achieve zero waste in many of its individual operations.[4]

Another company that has adopted the zero-waste, zero-effect goal is Monsanto. Achieving zero waste means first finding out where you stand and that means collecting comprehensive data on waste emissions. It maintains its own waste database that provides management with objective and quantifiable means of seeing if it truly is in a state of continuous improvement rather than simply in a state of continuous change. It is for this reason that every August, Monsanto publishes a report titled *Environmental Annual Review*, which contains information on its waste elimination programs.

As we noted, the ultimate goal for those seeking continual improvement is zero waste or *zero effect* from their operations on the environment. Monsanto, rightly so, does not see any difference between this environmental goal and its quality goal of zero defect in product manufacturing. The rationale behind zero effect is that zero waste is the only goal that mandates continuous improvement.

The top priority of this zero waste process, as it is with quality zero defect, is on prevention of problems rather than to reaction on environmental problems. A Stage 3 company has the objective of trying not to create waste in the first place rather than reacting after the waste has been created. In the last chapter we will look at some ways of doing just this; creating opportunity, not waste.

DEVELOPING SPECIFIC OBJECTIVES

Zero waste is a goal for anyone wanting to emphasize continual improvement, but as we've noted earlier it will take more than decrees to move a Stage 1 company to Stage 3. An organization's people must be informed about a goal, be trained on how to get it, and be informed of progress. All of this must be tied together through strategic planning. Every organization must have some form of strategic management. Strategic management does not have to be fancy but some basic questions have to be answered so that everyone understands the answers and where they are headed. One of the first answers you want to know is "what do we want to be and where are we now?" Secondly, if you are not where you want to be, decide what actions must be implemented so you can get there.

A company's Stage 3 environmental agenda should also include focusing on "which products to market?, how they will be packaged, how much open disclosure of pollution and health information the company should provide, and finally, how the company can reduce waste at its source." Unless these issues are addressed, you cannot expect an integrated approach to environmental management.

Very few organizations have gone as far as 3M in incorporating their policies, objectives, and standards into the company's operations on a day-to-day basis. Senior managers at 3M are required to incorporate environmental policies, objectives, and standards into their operation, including R&D, long-range planning, capital and operating budgets. Summary reports are presented each month to the Corporate Operations Committee by the Vice-President and other high-ranking officers.

Senior management's environmental policies are then reflected in the environmental plan of each operating division. To this end, each of 3M's operating divisions has an environmental management plan, developed by the division management committee that guides each division operation. These plans focus on both short- and long-range concerns.

The company has also developed several programs designed to implement senior-level policies, objectives and standards. One of the most famous of these programs has already been mentioned. Started in 1975, it is called the *3Ps* and stands for Pollution Prevention Pays. The program has reduced air emissions by 134,000 tons, water pollutants by 16,900 tons, sludge and solid waste by 426,000 tons and saved $537 million. Another of its programs, called Resource Recovery, projects by the year 2000 that waste generation will be reduced by 50 percent and that all pollution discharges to air, land and water will be reduced by 90 percent from 1987 levels. Beyond 2000 it wants to approach zero pollution.

A great deal of 3M's success that we looked at earlier can be traced to its comprehensive approach. For 3M, environmental management is not simply an operational objective. Senior management responsibility for compliance to corporate policies and objectives goes beyond daily operations and includes research and development, long-range planning, capital and operating budgets decision making. To this end, 3M has always had a healthy commitment to research and development (R&D). About 6.6 percent of its sales budget ($865 million) is devoted to research. Of that amount, about 12 percent ($100 million) is directed to such environmentally oriented projects as removing hazardous chemicals from its products and production processes.[5]

Senior policies are also ingrained into the company's long-range planning. To make sure its year 2000 goals are more than idle conversation, senior management includes the necessary funding and allocated resources too. For example, $170 million was allocated for installing air pollution equipment by 1993. Corporate and 3M product divisions' operating budgets also reflect senior management policies and objectives. In the Pollution Wheel Model, 3M's approach would be a very good example of implementing Stage 2. It is not Stage 3 because it still focuses on reducing cost rather than revenue generation for the long-term. The company also still remains very much vertically integrated with most of the power at corporate and little *broad* decision-making responsibility at the bottom. Employees can give ideas, but little real concerns and decision-making exist for strategic or financial issues.

CASE STUDY OF INTEGRATION

The Swiss-based corporation SANDOZ is an international organization with global activities in pharmaceutical, chemicals, agrochemicals, seeds, nutrition, and environmental engineering. It has strict standards of environmental protection and makes a significant investment in this area. Fifteen percent of its capital is invested in the environmental and safety protection area.

It funded the first chair in Management and the Environment that was established at a European business school. In many ways, it provides a good example of environmental management. Some of its principles and strategies of environmental management can be seen in *Figure 10–2*. It provides an example of a starting point for an integrated Stage 1 corporate commitment to environmental management because its focus is on reducing risk, cost, and liability. The objectives, basic rules and tasks that managers must do to meet their corporate environmental objectives are seen in Figure 10–2. These objectives and basic rules form a system that leaves little doubt about what is expected and how to do it. It is clear and well thought out and can be an effective tool for integrating environmental considerations into day-to-day actions.

STRATEGIES ON SAFETY, ENVIRONMENTAL PROTECTION AND INDUSTRIAL HYGIENE (S+E)

The environmental mission of SANDOZ is to integrate S&E into corporate decision making that includes the following points:

Objectives

1. All our companies take initiatives to safeguard health and safety of employees, customers and the public as well as the environment. They ensure that their products can be manufactured, handled, stored, transported, used, and disposed of safely and without unacceptable risks for the environment.

   The divisional companies manage the inherent risk of their businesses so as to achieve an acceptable, small-remaining risk in all their activities and at all sites. Thereby they follow and, when appropriate and feasible, contribute to the state of the art in their industry.

Basic Rules

Basic rules for this integration includes the following 9 points.

1. *Undivided Line Responsibility.* The responsibility for S+E lies with line management. S+E staff functions support line management.

2. *Total Management Involvement.* Managers of all functions and levels integrate S+E in their activities and encourage responsible attitudes. S+E is part of the regular goals and management evaluation.

3. *Integrated Approach to S+E.* Safety, environmental protection and industrial hygiene are closely linked and interdependent and should be approached in an integrated way.

4. *Complete S+E Coverage.* S+E covers all aspects of the business system, from R+D, purchasing, production, waste management and infrastructure, to transportation, warehousing, marketing and distribution, including emergency management and, in an appropriate manner, contractual third-party activities. It comprises not only safety, environmental protection and industrial hygiene, but also related topics such as biosafety, radiation protection, toxicity, and security.

5. *Comprehensive Risk Knowledge.* Effective S+E management requires comprehensive and systematic risk knowledge. Risk portfolios are recommended as tools for developing and documenting risk knowledge.

6. *Priority Setting.* Priorities for corrective measures are set as a result of risk assessment.

7. *New Activities and Changes.* New projects and related activities, new or modified processes, products and installations do not start unless the S+E impact has been assessed adequately and the acceptable, small remaining risk has been attained. The divisional companies define the respective responsibilities and evaluation procedures.

8. *Measures Beyond Official Requirements.* S+E measures which go further than official or corporate requirements are encouraged to the extent that they are in proportion to the risk and are feasible economically. Management encourages and promotes R+D and other efforts to find optimum solutions for processes and products.

9. *Cost Transparency.* In order to achieve cost transparency, S+E costs should be assessed separately.

Figure 10–2

SANDOZ gives us a very good example of an integrated Stage 1 commitment to environmental management. It is Stage 1 because the focus is on cost and risk minimization. If it had been on competitive costing, or profit and resource maximization, then it could have been a good example of Stage 2 or 3. The nice thing about its approach is the way all of the pieces are connected. The focus is risk assessment and the objective has been translated into specific operational initiatives.

SANDOZ has also given a great deal of thought to its Environmental Protection initiatives. A summary of its policy, the rules to follow and specific tasks to be completed is seen in *Figure 10–3*.

ENVIRONMENTAL PROTECTION

No Unacceptable Effects on the Environment. Companies conduct their businesses in consideration of ecological needs, minimizing the effects on the environment and the public.

Basic Rules

The following 17 points are the basic rules for implementing the "No Unacceptable Effects on the Environment" policy:

1. *Optimum Use of Resources.* Companies preferably purchase and use raw materials, energy, technology, and equipment in a way that helps to preserve natural resources and does not harm the environment.

2. *Customer Advice.* Appropriate advice for safe handling, use, and disposal of products is provided to customers if the products might lead to an environmental hazard.

3. *Emission Control.* Material and immaterial emissions from activities into the environment are to be minimized by constant efforts to avoid or reduce them.

4. *Priorities in Waste Management.* Wastes are minimized by measures in the following order of priorities:

   —Avoid
   —Reduce
   —Recycle and reuse ·

   Wastes that cannot be avoided are to be treated and disposed of according to the state of the art.

Tasks

   a) Management Tasks

5. *Information and Training.* By providing information and appropriate training, managers ensure a high level of awareness on the part of all employees towards environmental matters.

6. *Environmental Protection Goals.* Management of the companies is encouraged to establish environmental protection goals and to communicate these to the employees involved in order to foster awareness of and dedication to environmental issues.

7. *Assessment of Wastes and Emissions.* The assessment and characterization of all wastes and material emissions are prerequisites to efficient waste management. Waste stream evaluation and material balances (e.g., ecograms) are basic tools for waste assessment.

8. *Data Collection and Availability.* Companies determine, collect, validate, update and document the data and information relevant to the assessment of the possible impact of substances and processes on the environment. They make these data available to other SANDOZ companies, and in an appropriate form to third parties, customers, employees, authorities and the public, consistent with the practice of comparable leading companies.

9. *Research Projects and Associations.* Companies show their dedication to environmental issues by participating in and supporting research projects and associations and by cooperating with authorities.

   b) Technical Tasks

10. *Avoid and Reduce.* Products and processes have to be designed so as to keep emissions to the environment and the formation of wastes at a minimum. Products and processes are reviewed constantly for opportunities to reduce wastes, emissions, and energy consumption.

11. *Recycle and Reuse.* Site management ensures systematic evaluation of the possibilities for recycling and reusing wastes and energy.

12. *Waste Disposal.* Wastes may only be disposed of in secure, authorized landfills. Sea dumping and export of wastes to developing countries are not acceptable.

13. *Waste Disposal Plan.* Each site characterizes, separates, collects, treats and disposes of its wastes according to a written waste disposal plan, that includes an inventory of the waste streams into the air, water, and landfills. Regular manufacturing of a product may not start before an acceptable waste disposal plan has been established.

14. *Waste Documentation.* Storage, transportation, and disposal of wastes have to be documented adequately. These documents should be retained for an unlimited period.

15. *Safe Disposal.* Substances that could produce noxious, malodorous or explosive decomposition products or other hazards may not be drained or disposed of without adequate pretreatment.

16. *Contractors.* Only contractors who comply with our standards and the local regulations are acceptable for waste transportation and disposal. Dependence on a single external disposal channel should be avoided.

17. *Local Environment Monitoring.* Depending on the activities and circumstances of a site, the local environment, such as water, soil, and air in the vicinity, should be monitored in order to identify changes in the relevant environmental parameters.

Figure 10–3
(Courtesy of SANDOZ)

Again, the impressive thing about SANDOZ's approach to better environmental management is its systematic and integrative nature. It all fits, and is well thought out.

CLOSING THOUGHTS

Senior-management support and direction are critical to the success of any cultural change. If an organization is to reap the cost advantage of better enviro-management, then senior management must be the main force. Coherent policy objectives and an effective and systematic reporting system are essential. Measurement systems like 3M's serve to benchmark where you are at, what happens when you take action and helps define what is needed to meet senior-management goals. SANDOZ provides an excellent case of a well-thought-out top management initiative to pollution management, but it is not the only approach. Every organization is different. It's not always wise to try to be a Stage 3 organization. You will have to decide what resources are available, and what it takes to compete. If your competition is not at Stage 1, then you have a competitive advantage. Whether it's Stage 1, 2, or 3 that you feel you need to stay ahead of your competition, one constant is absolutely critical. It must be integrated and systematic. It's unknown whether SANDOZ is as operationally efficient as its strategic planning process, but it is clear that you can't be operationally efficient environmentally unless the planning similar to that used by SANDOZ has been done.

In the next chapters we will examine how to implement these strategic goals. This will include information on greater employee empowerment, teaching those who must make decisions how to make better environmental choices.

ENDNOTES

1. Anderson, Sir Denys, "Investing in the Environment" *Speech delivered at* The Financial Times *Conference*. Petrochemicals in Europe—The New Scenario, London, November 28, 1990.

2. Henne, Hans Jörg, "Ecological Responsibility and Corporate Activity, the View of a Chemical Company" *Paper presented at the International Symposium "One Future World."* Tokyo, November 17–18, 1992, p. 4.

3. Williams, Jan Olaf, Ulrich Golüke, *From Ideas: To Action Business and Sustainable Development*, International Chamber of Commerce (Ad Notam Gyldendal Publishing), 1992, p. 94.

4. *Total Quality Management: A Framework for Pollution Prevention*, Quality Environmental Management Subcommittee, President's Commission on Environmental Quality. Washington, D. C., January 1993, pp. 66–70.

5. *3M Quality Environmental Management Program booklet*. St. Paul, Minnesota. p. 8.

6. Kleiner, Art, "What Does It Mean to Be Green?" *Harvard Business Review*. July–August 1991, Vol. 69, No. 4, p. 39.

MAKING SURE
ENVIRONMENTAL POLICIES
MEASURE UP!

If the ultimate environmental management goal is zero waste or zero effect, then naturally you would want to know, "How can we prevent pollution and eliminate waste, so we can strive for zero waste?" According to William Bitters, the Packaging Technology Manager at Proctor and Gamble in Lima, Ohio, the solution lies in gathering the proper information so you can really eliminate problems.[1] It involves understanding the impact of your organization's production processes, waste and emissions and deciding what needs to be done and what improvement projects should be undertaken.

There is no way to know what processes to change or what materials to substitute if you do not have data. Without good data you may unintentionally create more problems when you try to eliminate pollution. For instance, if you do not have enough information on chemical substitutes that decrease air emissions you might accidentally increase wastewater. Dick Scott, Environmental Manager at Procter and Gamble's Lima, Ohio location says, "you must dig into a problem to determine its root cause."[1] He went on to say you do not always find what you expect. By collecting data on waste streams and emissions you and your team are able to determine your best pollution prevention projects.

Good data collection begins with a good definition. When 3M created its Year 2000 program, it made sure to create *specific definitions and objectives.* For example, all waste streams including solid, hazardous air, water products, and by-products must be measured by weight and reported on a quarterly basis. This allows management, including senior officers, a chance to measure programs by each product division. By having such objective data, management can adjust its R & D and other expenditures to maximize pollution-prevention efforts in order to reach their long-range goals.

The best opportunities for pollution prevention can be determined by examining three areas. The first of these is *sources of waste.* Every raw material brought into a facility becomes part of a product or waste. All materials should be identified, including cleaning agents, water, chemicals, packaging materials, process scrap, greases, scrapped equipment, oil, and other debris.

The second area to examine is the *quantity of waste material.* Although data on waste quantities is not normally available, *baseline data* can often be determined from a list of materials purchased and manufactured. Ford Motor Company has found that the weight of waste is a more accurate measure than volume because it is not affected by packaging or storage.[1] Likewise, because waste varies with production level, it is best to measure waste generated per production unit.

The third piece of information that can be used is the *cost of waste practices.* After waste streams have been identified and measured, then their true cost should be calculated. The following are some of the costs of wasteful practices.

- *Wasted raw material* including the cost of raw materials to replace the disposed-of material.

- *Waste handling* including all labor costs involved in removal, treatment and disposal of waste material.

- *Waste storage* including the cost to store waste materials at the site of generation in holding tanks or salvage areas within the plant or in a drum area.

- *Waste transportation* including the cost to haul materials from where they are generated in the plant to a salvage area, and the cost to ship it offsite.

- *Waste disposal* such as landfill cost, incineration cost, etc.

- *Intangibles* such as reduced environmental effects, reduced liability, and reduced exposure to regulations.

Given the diverse and sometimes hidden environmental costs it is easy to see how some environmental overhead can be overlooked. That is why it is often wise to go over cost for a second time. At Proctor and Gamble's Lima, Ohio plant, cross-functional teams do a second more in-depth assessment to determine whether additional data or resources are required.[1] In one case they expected to find opportunities to reduce waste in its manufacturing processing area. However, it was its packaging process that was the greater generator of waste.

CHOOSING A PILOT STUDY

A critical but often overlooked area of assessment is practicality. Sometimes an assessment will show that there is a need for new technology. What some companies noted was that they were sometimes frustrated to later learn that some needed technology was not readily available. Ford has practically overcome this risk by encouraging its plants and divisions to undertake *pilot tests* so that major process changes could be tried out before large capital expenditures were made.[1] Ford also made a point of providing technical support to any of its groups willing to start pollution prevention projects.

Pilot studies give you a chance to explore technological options. They also give you a chance to debug everything before wholesale changes are made. The emphasis should be on experimentation. International Paper emphasizes experimentation whenever it implements projects by encouraging employees doing projects to *assume* that some tests will not succeed. It believes that these projects should be viewed as educational experiences rather than as failures.

Any project you are considering should be chosen based on some criteria. Some factors to consider when establishing project priorities could include:

- Waste volumes
- Raw material cost
- Regulations
- Disposal methods
- Feasibility
- Toxicity
- Health and safety

- Handling time
- Potential liability
- Disposal cost
- Cost/unit produced
- Treatment cost
- Environmental concern
- Product quality

Not all these criteria are appropriate, nor is one the best way for ranking projects. Deciding which project has the greatest potential varies from one organization to another. Each area, department or organization has to decide individually what concerns and environmental issues are of utmost importance. While some of the data is measurable, other information is anecdotal in nature. For instance, it may be subjective, but no less valid if you choose a project because it has greater opportunity for transfer of knowledge in one area over another.

One way to help you establish priorities is by using a *pollution prevention hierarchy* that you construct. In rank order this usually includes first *source reduction*, then if this option is not possible consider *recycling and treatment* as a last option. The reason for ranking projects based on their ability to reduce the source of pollution over recycling or treatment of pollution is that elimination of a problem should always be the preferred choice. In Chapter 14 we will see the dramatic affect source reduction can have on the bottom line. Some of these elimination or source reduction techniques include modifications of technology and process or procedures to eliminate the hazard. Ways of doing this include substituting one type of material for a less toxic raw material. Even simple improvements in housekeeping maintenance, training and individual control can also be a way to eliminate pollution.

WASTE MEASUREMENT INDEX

Having chosen a project, it will be critical to properly measure performance. Measuring performance is essential if you plan to show or want to find out if you are meeting or exceeding expectations. Measurement also shows others what you expect a pollution-prevention project to do.

There are many ways to track your progress. One might be referred to as a *waste measurement index*. The index might involve measuring your pound of waste generated per unit of production or output. Such a ratio would not be influenced directly by production increases or decreases. Therefore, it would be easier to measure your TEM goal of continuous improvement. 3M's Medical Products Division in Brookings, South Dakota along with the rest of the 3M organization uses a ratio that it has found very useful in judging the effectiveness of its pollution efforts.[1] It can be written mathematically as:

$$\frac{\text{WASTE}}{\text{Waste} + \text{By-Product} + \text{Product}} = \frac{\text{WASTE}}{\text{Total Output}} \times 100 = \underline{\qquad}$$

One good thing about this and other ratios is that each is amenable to establishing continuous improvement goals that are not related to your production rate. Consequently, your action taken to reduce the rate of waste generation will be reflected in the ratio.

One drawback to waste indexing is that it does not relate to the absolute amount of waste released into the environment. If the rate of waste production per unit produced goes down but your production level increases, then the absolute amount of waste may remain constant or even increase. Therefore, another valuable measure of pollution is the amount of waste (or releases) into the environment. This measure of performance is of concern because it is one of utmost concern by surrounding communities. Although environmental organizations prefer ratios, the general public tends to focus on waste released into the air, water, and land. For this reason alone it is wise to have at least these two types of measurements.

Cost-related metrics provide another good measure or source of information about environmental operating cost. Of course, these costs will vary from one waste stream to another. One company that has done some work in this area is Chevron. It arrived at its cost-related metrics by considering the cost of disposal, permits, inspection, fees, operation, and maintenance of environment equipment, lab analysis, lost product, operations downtime, avoided capital investment, environmental liability, and public image.[1] Proctor and Gamble's Paper Product Plant in Mehoopany, Pennsylvania also identified other potential costs, including raw materials lost, production losses through scrap product waste handling, and treatment cost.

HOW THE RATIO WORKS

3M is using the ratio in conjunction with its waste-minimization programs. These programs hope to reduce waste dramatically in the manufacturing process by reformulating modifying procedures, and by redesigning equipment. Through these efforts it plans to reduce waste by 35 percent by 1995.

3M is using a waste measurement index ratio because it felt it was imperative to come up with a simple method to track changes. As part of this process it identified what was good output and what was waste. Good output was defined as one of three things. Finished goods were defined as those shipped from the plant. This included all packaging, but excluded pallets and totes. Finished goods shipped to another plant for shipment were classified as semifinished.

These semifinished or partially finished materials would be shipped from one 3M facility to another for further processing. Semifinished material was assigned to the division that produced it. The only exception was when semifinished material was shipped internationally, in which case it was considered finished goods. Since it was not tracking materials across country borders, the company decided to include it in the finished goods category so the producing division could get credit for it.

The third and last good output was by-product. This would include any material that would have a productive secondary use. Testing to see if a material is a by-product consists of three steps. First, there must be no undesirable impact on the environment. Second, there should be no treatment or disposal cost, and finally, you must receive money or something of value (including charity) for the material. Some examples would include materials sold or materials that could be transferred for recycling. Using materials as an internal or external fuel is not a by-product.

3M has defined waste as residual from its manufacturing process before it is subjected to any treatment. Its manufacturing process included manufacturing operations and related support functions such as offices and labs. Residual waste from energy generation was excluded. Waste that it did measure included chemical waste, trash, organic air and water waste, particulate air waste, and discharged water waste.

3M classified waste as any material that had an undesirable impact on the environment. Likewise, if cost was incurred for treatment or disposal, then it was waste. It was measured through one of several ways. One way was to measure the weight directly. 3M felt it was essential to weigh its chemicals and trash. It also used a metered measurement of waste and something it referred to as Material Balance. The Material Balance approach is used for calculating solvent waste. It recommended its divisions take beginning inventory of all solvents, add any receipts of solvents, then subtract ending inventory as input. Next, subtract sold solvents and solvents that go out in products as well as those that go to waste disposal sites. The difference from this addition and subtraction is your solvent waste.

Finding ways of measuring performance is essential to improvement but so is the need to *time* the achievement of goals. It is important to decide *when* to expect improvement as well as know *what* and *how* to measure environmental performance. A sample Waste Minimization Report can be seen in *Figure 11–1*.

CLOSING THOUGHTS

The problem with pollution is that for far too long it was not measured. An essential part of any pollution effort, including Stage 1 organizations, is to begin to measure waste output. It has no value without a number. That is why using a form similar to that in Figure 11–1 is essential. A document like it should be used throughout any company that is serious about reducing environmental risk and cost. When waste is measured, you can assign accountabilities, you can give incentives for reducing it, and you can reduce cost. But you must first measure it.

Measuring waste can be the common language so essential to drawing people together. Everyone produces some by-products; it's a matter of identifying these operational inefficiencies and focusing management's and employees' attention on them.

You can measure waste without involving employees, but you cannot hope to involve employees in continual waste reduction if you do not measure performance. Measurement is the *universal language,* and that is what makes it essential in Stages 1, 2, or 3.

WASTE MINIMIZATION REPORT

Reporting Period   ————
Plant Code   ————
Division Code   ————   ————   ————   ————   ————

Good Output (thousands of pounds, one decimal)
Semifinished   ———.— ———.— ———.— ———.— ———.—
Finished Goods   ———.— ———.— ———.— ———.— ———.—
By-product   ———.— ———.— ———.— ———.— ———.—

Waste (thousands of pounds, one decimal)
Chemical   ———.— ———.— ———.— ———.— ———.—
Trash   ———.— ———.— ———.— ———.— ———.—
Organic   ———.— ———.— ———.— ———.— ———.—
Air (particulate)   ———.— ———.— ———.— ———.— ———.—
Water (solids only) ———.— ———.— ———.— ———.— ———.—

Figure 11–1
(Courtesy of 3M.)

ENDNOTE

1. *Total Quality Management: A Framework for Pollution Prevention,* Quality Environmental Management Subcommittee, President's Commission on Environmental Quality, Washington, D.C., January 1993. pp. 23–80.

12

THE POWER OF
EMPLOYEE INVOLVEMENT

Barbara Cunningham, a Lab Technician at Procter and Gamble in Mehoopany, Pennsylvania provides one shining example of the power of employee involvement. She came up with the idea to recycle containers used at its facility for cleaning products. She and others collected data on the type and quantities of chemicals used in pressurized and nonpressurized containers. She took it upon herself to reduce waste by questioning suppliers about which containers were available in bulk gravity systems. She then contacted employees who worked with the various chemicals to see if they would be receptive to using refillable containers instead of the pressurized disposal containers they were currently using. She also contacted supply room staff to make sure they would be willing to work with bulk gravity containers.

Once she had done all the footwork, she then contacted management about the project. Because of all the work she had done she was able to get their support and the funding to buy the necessary equipment. Since all of the parties involved had bought into the project, it was relatively easy to secure formal approval. The outcome of this antipollution champion's effort was that Procter and Gamble used less landfill space. They also saved *$25,000* a year from this single project.[1] There were no formal policies here, just simple employee involvement.

All of the policies, goals, and objectives mentioned in the last chapter have been attempts to tie pollution efforts together into a cohesive plan. It certainly beats simply calling a meeting and asking for suggestions. Hopefully, an outcome of this planning will be a greater desire to participate in reducing pollution.

Often knowing what to do is easier than knowing how to do it. Policies, goals, objectives, and procedures are very scientific, very black and white. Maybe that is why managers like to pass decrees. It is easier than dealing with people. Stage 3 procedures can be set up fairly rapidly; it is the Stage 3 "interpersonals" that pose more of a problem for managers.

Rules and regulations are one thing, but if people feel powerless, they will do something, they will disengage, resist, form a union. If they do not feel a sense of ownership they will not participate or feel committed to pollution control efforts. That is bad news for anyone wanting to control something as subtle and widespread as pollution. It tends to be an inverse relationship. The more stratified we feel, the less likely we are to care about what someone higher up is saying to us. It is not just a matter of reducing levels within an organization. After all, it's been said that the Chinese army has one General (god) and the rest peasants, yet no one would think that it is an empowered horizontal organization. Lack of status in most organizations does not occur because there are too many levels. It occurs because many, maybe most of the people, lack information and knowledge. Typically, a few have a lot of information and influence and most of the others in the organization have little. Reducing the knowledge gap increases the effectiveness of employee involvement. One of the most famous examples of the power of knowledge can be found in Ford Motor Company. Long noted for adversary roles with their unions, Ford started sharing information and in some cases actual decision making. The results were greatly improved quality and commitment within the organization.

Sharing information does help create the knowledge needed to make good decisions, and it also does one other important thing, it creates *trust*. People are a lot more likely to get involved if they feel you trust them. Sharing information shows you trust them. If you provide accurate information, sound judgments, and follow through on promises, it creates trust. Years ago a study of over 40,000 managers reported that as few as 20 percent of those surveyed had a basic trust in the competency of their employees. Quad/Graphics, like other companies, need people to be on time, and on hand, but they use no time clocks for their blue collar workers. Workers are trusted to show up and fill out their own time clocks. Quite a change from most thinking. Consider your own situation. Do employees run their own suggestion program or does management run it? Do employees decide how to recycle or conserve energy or are they told how to do it? If you do not create this basic trust, you will remain at square one. No amount of policies, procedures, rules or regulations will help pull one from Stage 1 to Stage 3. In Stage 1 and 2 managers do the pulling; in Stage 3, employees do the pushing. It is up to managers to figure out how to make it easy for people to push.

MANAGING POLLUTION EFFORTS

The purpose of Stage 3 management is to first define the threat, and once the threat is defined it is then up to management to provide the resources for people to solve their pollution problems. In order for people to push pollution efforts they must have a sense that it is their organization and it is in their interest. When people wonder about their roles and importance or the organization's importance to them, how can we expect them to care about quality, customers or corporate pollution problems?

It is up to managers to define the threat and make them understand how they can contribute. This is a key point. What Ford and others have discovered is that formulating mission statements or having a "vision" is not enough. You have to be very specific in deciding what needs to be resolved and what to do about it.

Defining the Threat

Before you define the threat for employees, it is necessary to do the same thing for upper managers. A series of seminars could be organized so upper management could better understand the problems facing managers and operational personnel trying to be productive and control pollution. It might be beneficial to do an analysis to determine what forces are encouraging and discouraging greater participation and more autonomous pollution management. Have lower-level people participate and ask them "How are things around here?" Anonymously, review their responses, write them on a board so all can see. Look for things like, "They say one thing, but do another." Through a frank discussion try to identify your culture and how decisions are made. Give your managers leadership analysis like the Myer-Briggs Temperament Indicator (MBTI). By analyzing leadership you can identify categories of leaders, like *promotor, traditionalist, visionary* and *democratic.*

Once you have assessed what exists and what to do, it is then, and only then, that management can galvanize the threat. The threat might be customers, competition, profits, marketshare, or something else. There is always a threat. In Stage 3, it is management's job to draw a line in the sand and get people to concentrate on it. Things like waste ratios are one such focal point. But keep in mind that *the numbers are not the main thing*. From an environmental standpoint, that line in the sand is your internal and external customers' environmental concern, so make those numbers mean something to your customers. The next step would be to get the troops to incorporate this threat into their day-to-day decision making.

FOCUSING ON CONTINUAL IMPROVEMENT

Earlier we noted the Monsanto approach involved integrating environmental practices into its ongoing business activities. It also emphasized the need to focus on continuous improvement. Monsanto's third and last principle is to try to involve everyone in reducing environmental inefficiencies. Monsanto, like many others wanting to make environmental management more profitable, tries to incorporate environmental decision making into the daily responsibility of all personnel. For instance, at its Georgia pharmaceuticals plant, it was a team of employees who developed the industry's only known alternative to cleaning process equipment with chemical solvents. The water-based cleaning procedure cut toxic air emissions 90 percent and liquid hazardous waste 70 percent, while saving $500,000 in 1992.

TQM says everyone can make a difference. It is the same story for Stages 2 and 3. For environmentalism to be a competitive tool, everyone must develop a sense of environmental ownership of the process. Even a Stage 1 organization draws on operational personnel to identify not only products and services, but also wanted and unwanted by-products. It means everyone knowing their external and internal customers' environmental needs. It means sitting down with those internal and external suppliers to identify your incoming environmental quality needs (e.g., packaging, and so on). This means that we must work closely with both people inside and outside the organization. For instance, Dow Chemical was able to work with its vendors on sampling technology. As a result of its vendors' *product* expertise and its own *process* expertise it was able to create a prototype system that met its requirements.[1]

AT&T's Network System's Columbus Works organization in Columbus, Ohio had a 90% reduction in solid manufacturing waste disposal. It also eliminated many other chemicals. It was able to do this because of greater involvement and input by outside representatives early on in its pollution-prevention process.

What we know is that moving to higher stages of pollution management requires a focus on continual improvement. You must create close communication between the various functions within an organization as well as between you and your suppliers and customers if Stages 2 and 3 are to become a reality. Stage 3 cannot occur unless everyone has a sense of ownership and knows how to solve problems. One good example of this type of ownership comes from Quad/Graphics.

EXAMPLES OF EMPLOYEE INVOLVEMENT

The results of good employee involvement can be dramatic. Quad/Graphics prints a variety of products including brochures, papers, reports and so forth. It has been able to eliminate printing ink waste by making everyone aware of the problem and finding ways to implement solutions. It discovered that its pollution problem was not the result of any one person pouring out gallons of ink. Rather waste, as it often does, accumulated quickly as each person threw out a little too much.

Management made sure its people knew the areas where too much was being wasted. It was then up to employees to become more attentive. Departing crews also started informing arriving crews of ink use so an exact accounting could be made of ink that was being transferred. At the end of every production run, left-over fresh ink is shared with others so it can be used immediately. Quad's presspeople took it upon themselves to pinpoint problem areas and redesign their system so problems could be prevented. One example of this involved their ink drums. In the past, ink drums were stationed at each press. They decided to have better control by setting up a central Recyclable Ink Station. As ink is disposed, each pressperson notes the amount of ink and reason for disposal on record-keeping logs. Because of individual accountability and responsibility for pollution control, common problems can be tracked and improvements can be made in the process. It is this individual accountability and acceptance of responsibility for waste reduction that is at the heart of continuous improvement. The cost of the waste reduction program? *Nothing.*[2] The payback for employee involvement for Quad/Graphics was $510,000 in one year.

3M's Medical Products Division in Brookings, South Dakota is also able to prevent pollution because it had top management approval and because of employee involvement. The reason prevention works so well at the plant is that everyone accepts pollution prevention as part of their daily jobs. This attitude is common in 3M facilities. In general, 3M's environmental efforts have been fruitful. Its 3Ps over the past 17 years have saved the company more than $500 million and eliminated more than 600,000 tons of pollutants. It will tell you that its savings are in large part due to employee involvement.

More specifically, 3M believes it has been successful because it has (1) an understanding of the connection between good practices and environmental responsibility, (2) involvement of workers at all levels, (3) corporate, supervisory and production worker flexibility, and (4) a willingness to make significant capital investments. Through these efforts it reduced waste by 10 percent. By 1995 the projection is a 35-percent reduction in waste. By the year 2000 it plans for a 90-percent reduction in waste.

WELL-RUN EMPLOYEE SUGGESTION PROGRAMS

One obvious way to involve people is through a well-designed and *well-run* suggestion program. Well run is highlighted because most suggestion programs are not well run and are generally a "waste" of time. One that has not been a waste of time involves Upjohn's Dry Products Packaging area. The company's operation was experiencing a great deal of waste. On this particular process, it uses cartons to package some of its products. Cartons were passing too quickly on its production line. The line was also being stopped because suppliers ran short. Due to these two causes, excessive numbers of cartons were being wasted. One of the packaging area employees, Ann Marie Edwards, made a suggestion through the company's Quality Improvement Process (QIP) Suggestion Program. A seven-member quality work group was formed because of Edwards' suggestion. Within a month the group had determined the cause of the waste. It discovered it was due to the timing of two pieces of equipment which were not properly synchronized. When the timing was adjusted, the line ran smoother and waste was reduced. Because of the reduced carton waste, the company saved $10,000 and the job in the packaging area was safer and easier.[3] This Stage 1 activity produced positive results. Employees looked at the problem, found its cause, and hopefully were the ones who made the decision about what to do. It is this sense of ownership that is needed to move not only from one stage to another, but from a piecemeal approach to an integrated, empowered approach. Another example of an integrated approach is provided by Upjohn.

Upjohn's 900 employees in the Pharmaceutical Manufacturing Operation generated 3,000 QIP suggestions in 1991. The reason, according to Dave Farnham of their Quality Administration, is "Since people have discovered that their suggestions will be responded to and recognized, the numbers have just taken off."[3]

Nippondenso's manufacturing suggestion program has experienced a tripling of suggestions from 1990 to 1991 and that number is expected to triple again in 1992.[4] It did this by making sure that *rewards were not the focal point.* Linda Topolsky, senior human-resource specialist, noted that there were too many disadvantages to using dollars as a reward. The amount would generally be so small that it would not be reinforcing.

Nippondenso's rewards are now given in points which can be turned in for gifts. Its average gift is eight points, or about eight dollars' worth. It has a 73% rate because it focuses on small improvements. No suggestion is too small. Employees get points for implementing ideas. Points, in large part, are determined by effort. Intangible ideas employees suggest can result in five, eight or 15 points based on one's effort put forward and the originality of the idea as well as its impact. The maximum offered is 10,000 points.[4] The main lesson that Nippondenso learned was that employees' motivation increased the more frequent and immediate the contact. Because of this insight, it made sure that it responded to suggestions within four or five workdays.

Textron Aerostructure, like Nippondenso, also found it effective to reward incremental improvements. When its employees felt like they had to hit home runs to get rewarded, there was little participation. The focus is on singles, not home runs. It believes the message it sends employees is that ideas are valuable no matter how small, and that everyone should participate.

At Textron, 50 people handle suggestions and can approve them. Employees get a face-to-face response to their suggestion within 21 days. It is, however, the employee, acting as the champion, who is responsible for making sure the idea is implemented. Its goal is to create ownership of the idea. As in the previous example, Textron's approach is to emphasize employee recognition rather than cash. Employees do receive a $50 gift certificate when an idea is implemented. A $500 end-of-the-year award is given for the most innovative idea in such areas as work simplification, communication, environment, and so forth. The company concentrates on recognition rather than cash because before the employees felt the idea was worth more than their compensation, and therefore the company seemed to be taking advantage of them. However, an employee task force found that employees were more interested in prompt feedback and getting ideas implemented than being rewarded financially.[4]

THE ROLE OF TEAM MANAGEMENT

Increasingly, teams are becoming the cornerstone of any employee involvement. Both Stage 2 and 3 organizations use teams to get greater involvement. Several types of teams are worth noting. One of the most common is a *green team.* These teams are responsible for dealing directly with specific environmental issues or processes.

AT&T uses these types of green teams through its TQM efforts. At their Warrenville/Westwood, Illinois location, eight employees formed the Westwood Ecology Quality Circle in 1990. The mission of the team was to institute ecological programs and increase environmental awareness. Its most successful program has been Westwood's paper recycling project. Beginning in April 1991, the project recycled over 29 tons of paper by year end.

The AT&T green team is typical of green teams because it deals with a specific issue or process, in this case, recycled paper. Often the work of green teams produces the need for other types of teams. One of these is *the investigation team*, which is usually formed because of something that a green team discovers. Members of investigation teams are often not formal members of other environmental teams or groups. Rather, each has an interest in a specific environmental topic under discussion. Using the AT&T example, if in the process of looking at recycling efforts the team discovers that something in its customers' or suppliers' processes had an affect on the amount of waste it was generating, an investigation team might be formed of concerned individuals to see if it could solve the problem. When this does occur, one of the members of the investigation team is usually one of the people from the green team that originally discovered the problem. The reason of the green team member on this new investigation team is so that he or she can keep the green team informed of any actions taken or deliberated that affects them.

Cross-functional green teams are another common type of team. As the name implies, they are formed to deal with issues that cross departmental or functional lines. As such, members come from all those areas or functions that will be affected by the pollution problem including engineering, environmental management, accounting, purchasing, maintenance, and operations. The team's main purpose is to share information and knowledge critical for effective decision making. The common denominator is to assemble people together who have a strong interest in improving the environment and want to make a difference.

Procter and Gamble's Mehoopany, Pennsylvania plant provides a good example of the operational cross-functional green team. It created one team to focus on air and water issues and another team to look at solid and hazardous waste issues. Both teams used members with TQM experience who also had knowledge of environmental issues and plant operation. Procter and Gamble accomplished this by *selecting members based on their knowledge of environmental and operating systems and their ability to analyze data and to identify pollution prevention opportunities.* Anyone planning to create cross-functional teams should follow Procter and Gamble's advice. Find members with a wide range of experience. All participants should have insight into potential pollution-prevention techniques and activities. Together these members need to have the engineering, operational, and cost expertise to analyze specific processes and product changes. Making the extra effort and staffing teams with the best people can produce big dividends. Savings from cross-functional teams can be astronomical and this has been the case with the Procter and Gamble teams. Their solid waste minimization efforts produces a value to the company of $25,000,000 per year.

Environmental cross-functional green teams have made dramatic changes in how business functions. At Chevron's Perth Amboy Refinery in Perth Amboy, New Jersey, cross-functional teams in six areas identified more than 300 opportunities for improvement. From this list they narrowed it down to 10 waste streams for immediate action. Some of the changes included replacing an old boiler/powerhouse with a smaller unit that had lower air emissions and higher stream efficiency. They also redesigned a fuel gas scrubber.[1]

Manufacturers are not the only ones making good use of environmental teams. Boots, a leading United Kingdom retailer, uses teams to integrate its environmental policy into daily decision making. Their teams were initially set up in the merchandise area. Now its green team members are environmental specialists in their areas. Responsibilities range from establishing recycling facilities to helping develop "greener" products and packaging.[4]

Creating teams and having them participate in real decision making is a reward in itself, but should not be the only reward. ARCO has Stamp Out Waste Awards Program. The program offers ten $2,000 awards for the best employee ideas in the area of waste minimization. Projects implemented have produced a cost savings of $2 million per year and reduced waste by $50,000 per year.[5]

STAGE 3 TEAMS

If an organization is going to move from Stage 2 to Stage 3, it will be necessary to form more strategic-oriented green teams. *Steering teams* can be used for policy making. These should consist of the highest level personnel.

Browning Ferris Industries, a leading waste management company, has set up several of these steering teams. One team is the Environmental Policy Committee that has focused on policy issues. It is composed of corporate level personnel from legal, operations, engineering, environmental, and risk management departments. It is the committee's responsibility to look at controversial environmental policies. It also is involved in strategic planning and develops an annual environmental report.

Another one of Browning Ferris Industries' cross-functional and strategic-oriented green teams is its Issues Management System. It is used as an early warning system for developments and issues that might affect the company's ability to do business. A third and higher level environmental cross-function green team evaluates environmental business opportunities and markets.

Any steering committee should know where it is headed, how to get there, and what to accomplish. Members should also have received enough planning so they are able to plan and implement the changes needed.

Other Stage 3 teams include occasional use of *change teams,* which are ad hoc in nature. They are usually created because of upcoming work-related changes (for example, new technology, product changes, and facility modifications). *Design teams* may be created in the final stages of the product and process development. They are designed to improve communication and bridge the gap between those vital to the success of product design. One last Stage 3 team is a *supplier team.* Such teams meet with vendors and outside employees to design mutually beneficial green decisions and solutions.

PRESIDENT'S COMMISSION ON ENVIRONMENTAL QUALITY

On July 23, 1991 the President's Commission on Environmental Quality (PCEQ) was created to look at the possibility of using TQM as a vehicle for preventing pollution. The commission is composed of some of America's most innovative companies. Through its efforts, it has developed 12 demonstration projects that have successfully used TQM to reduce cost and improve profitability through more comprehensive environmental management. Note its following conclusions:

- *Total Quality Management (TQM) and Pollution Prevention are complimentary concepts.* One of the main discoveries has been that successful environmental management depends on a systematic analysis of, or services by, *empowered, cross-functional teams.* Waste reduction is most successful when groups of employees with diverse skills are authorized to identify sources of pollution and make innovative cost-effective recommendations for their reduction and elimination.

- *While successful pollution-prevention efforts do depend on systematic and rigorous analysis, it also relies on flexibility in actual application.* Experience shows that a disciplined approach to environmental management is a prerequisite for success, and that each facility is unique. Therefore, one should not expect one particular sequence to be the most effective approach because the type of business, its culture, and familiarity with TQM varies greatly. For these reasons a flexible approach must be employed. The bottom line is that the number of steps in the pollution-prevention process, their sequence, and the best way to measure them will vary from one site to the next.

- *Pollution prevention can be achieved without large capital investments.* Everyone can benefit from applying TQM to pollution prevention, but the real key to success often depends more on the creativity and energy of the employees involved than on the amount of capital.

- *There is no universal gauge for tracking performance.* There is simply too much diversity of processes, products, and services to have a single uniform standard by which all pollution-prevention programs are measured and compared. However, some form of measurement is essential since credible documented performance data and practical, easily understood information are essential for pollution prevention.

- *Consultation and collaboration with parties interested in pollution prevention is critical in developing credible progress reports.* Early involvement of all parties that have a stake in prevention can be very effective. An understanding of the goals and objectives of various participants is absolutely essential for being able to put information into terms that each can "buy into" and find acceptable. Granted, consensus building is time consuming, but it saves lost time that might occur when you gather data and produce information based on speculation.

- *There are barriers and incentives to pollution prevention.* Reducing cost and enhancing one's public image and competitive opportunities are the driving forces of pollution prevention. Unfortunately, limited resources are the barriers to greater pollution prevention.[6]

CLOSING THOUGHTS

PCEQ companies also found that their improvements were in no small part due to applying quality improvement techniques. Participating companies used a variety of the TQM tools to gather information about the sources of quantity of their waste and emissions. The TQM tool most commonly employed was *Pareto's Chart*, which organizes data in order of magnitude of impact and therefore helps you identify which pollution-prevention areas have the greatest potential for improvement.[1] Benchmarking, brainstorming, flow charting and fishbone charts were also used in pollution problem solving.

Dow Chemical's Louisiana Division Glycol Plant in Plaquemine, Louisiana wanted to implement pollution prevention, so it used the above techniques. International Paper in Jay, Maine, used the TQM process to handle its environmental compliance program. To do this, it used the *Cause and Effect (fishbone) Diagram, Control Charts, Process Flow Charts, Benchmarking* as well as *Pareto Charts.*[1]

What PCEQ demonstrated is that environmental improvement can be taught. It requires employee involvement and specific problem-solving tools. Once people understand the need for environmental improvement, they then must be taught how to look at each step in the design and production process to see if pollution can be eliminated or at least reduced. These same employees will need to know how to measure, analyze, and control their pollution. Each member of the organization needs to be taught "nuts and bolts" problem-solving tools and this is the subject of the next chapter.

ENDNOTES

1. *Total Quality Management: A Framework for Pollution Prevention*, Quality Environmental Management Subcommittee, President's Commission on Environmental Quality. Washington, D.C., January 1993. pp. 5–73.

2. Quad/Graphics: Taking Better Care of our World. Annual Report of Quad/Graphics, 1991, pp. 14–15.

3. "Employees Improve Packaging Through Quality Suggestion Process." *Inter-Comment*, Vol. 21, No. 17, May 1, 1992, pp. 1–2.

4. Verespej, Michael A., "Suggestion Systems Gain New Lustre," *Industry Week*, November 16, 1992, pp. 12–104.

5. *1991 ARCO and the Environment: A Commitment to Quality*, ARCO Brochure, 1991, p. 4.

6. *Partnership to Progress: The Report of the President's Commission on Environmental Quality*. President's Commission on Environmental Quality, Washington, D.C. January 1993.

13

PROBLEM-SOLVING TOOLS FOR CONTINUAL IMPROVEMENT

$\mathbf{C}$reating a desire by employees to reduce waste is obviously essential to any long-term environmental management program, but it is still not enough to ensure long-term success. It is one thing to have a desire to contribute, it is quite another thing to have the skills, abilities and tools to solve those problems. That is what the work of the PCEQ tried to document. Having desire without the know-how to produce results equals "zero." As companies know from the quality movement, it takes training in order to maximize your resources for eliminating waste. A perfect example of this can be seen at Dow's Cumberland, Rhode Island plant.

A high priority at the plant has been to reduce product losses for its SPRAY 'N WASH® STAIN STICK® brand soil and stain remover. Defective STAIN STICK® products had been averaging 2 percent of the total product produced. They were being collected in 30 gallon drums and incinerated. While it was employees who identified opportunities for reducing waste, it

165

was the use of managerial tools like Statistical Process Control (SPC) that were implemented to provide the data. Other tools were then used to prioritize the most severe problem areas.

Through this process the company discovered that canister leakage was the number one problem producing product losses. This problem was virtually eliminated by working with the canister supplier. Other top sources of waste were reduced significantly by working with personnel to implement a procedure that allowed previously discarded material to be reused in the process. Without their problem-solving tools they would not have been able to reduce their losses by 75 percent for the 4.4 oz. STAIN STICK® and by 58 percent for the 2.8 oz. STAIN STICK®. Without tools like SPC they might not have reaped the annual savings of $150,000.

Quality Control tools are not the only problem-solving tools that can be effective in managing waste. At Dow's Eastern Division Polystyrene Films Department in Hebon, Ohio, WRAP studies revealed that much of its waste from processing and packaging was recyclable. A waste reduction team was created that consisted of staff, production engineers, operating technicians, and purchasing personnel. The team needed a way to understand what was going on, so it developed a *process flow chart* that listed all the raw materials, internal and external recycle streams, and process and purchasing materials that were discarded. The use of this process flow chart tool proved invaluable. After evaluating the flow chart, several projects were implemented, including returning damaged pallets to their supplier to be reused or recycled. Loose film resin from plugged equipment was also collected and reused or sold back to other markets. By using this problem-solving tool and with a lot of employee involvement they were able to reduce by 600,000 pounds a year material that was once sent to landfills.

Once you've decided a change is needed and have generated support for change, you'll want to begin the process of continuous improvement. A popular approach for continuous improvement is the so-called Plan, Do, Check, and Act (PDCA) cycle. Popularized in the quality movement, PDCA provides a systematic approach to change for Stage 1, 2 or 3 companies.

The Plan, Do, Check, Action problem-solving method, often called the *Deming circle* or *Shewhart circle* consists of a set of techniques that enhance decision making. The *Plan* part of this approach refers to the need to concisely and precisely describe the problem or opportunities. In this planning stage, symptoms are examined, and someone is identified who is responsible for shepherding the problem until it is resolved. This plan stage also involves prioritizing the most critical problems and measuring the magnitude or severity of those problems.

In the planning stage you are trying to understand the gap between what is expected and what actually happens. In environmental management, anything above zero waste should be considered unacceptable. The planning stage is there so you can create action plans to close that gap. To do this you must identify what you want, define a time for meeting expectations, and create a system to do it.

Do is simply following your action plan by implementing any changes you believe will improve performance. The Do part of this problem-solving approach involves describing the current environmental situation in terms of its most likely cause or causes. In order to do this, the team needs to ask why the problem occurred. The why of an environmental problem *is* its causes. Once causes have been identified, the team should continue to identify, with even more detail, why each of these causes has occurred. The team will need to find out why each of the causes contributed to the development of any secondary problems. It is not unusual to repeat this process of seeking contributing causes to a problem four or five times before root causes are identified.

An illustration of a technique for use in the Do stage of the PDCA cycle is called the *Cause-and-Effect Diagram*, as seen at the end of the chapter. It can help you visually focus on identifying causes of environmental problems. We will look at it closer in a moment.

The *Check* phase of the problem-solving approach occurs once a solution to an environmental problem has been implemented. The objective at this stage is to see if the solutions identified in the Do stage have been effective. If environmental performance has not improved after solutions are implemented, then either we did not correctly identify the true causes of the environmental problem or something else is interfering with them. If your goal is not being met, then it will be necessary to go back to the Do stage and better identify the causes of the environmental problem.

The Check part of the PDCA cycle involves putting into action the plans you've made. It involves collecting data to determine if you are getting closer to your goals. Observe and measure the effects of changes. Use as many objective tools as possible to determine if you are meeting expectations.

The last problem-solving step is the *Act* stage. It is here that successful practices are standardized. Since this problem-solving process is so time consuming, it is important to make sure to work on implementing these successful measures in other areas that are likely to encounter similar problems.

The Act step also involves making changes in your process so you can continually improve. Mark Twain once was asked where good judgment came from. He said from experience. When asked how you got experience, he said from bad judgment! The Act stage is to implement changes learned from bad judgment. The PDCA cycle continues to repeat itself. That is the only way to continually improve.

HOW TO DO IT

Operational tools for helping solve problems can be statistical in nature or not. Some only require addition and subtraction; some require no math at all; some don't even require that you need to read or write. All of them, however, help you organize information so you can better Plan, Do, Check and Act. *Figure 13–1* contains a basic list of these operational problem-solving tools that can be taught to team members so they can better solve environmental problems. A check beside each name indicates in which stage of Plan, Do, Check and Act it is appropriate to use each technique.

BENCHMARKING

Benchmarking involves comparing one of your processes to a "best-in-class" operation. It can be either within or outside your company. Benchmarking should be thought of as a win-win situation because all participants should benefit from each other's experiences. It can take time to do, so it's important to do it right. The following are some suggestions for doing it right.

1. *Define on the front end what is most in need of improvement and rank each characteristic.* Your benchmarking efforts should focus on what your customers most highly prize. For this reason, market research on customer preferences is often necessary.

2. *Try to establish partnerships with outside sources.* Independent researchers and consultants can be of value so your staff can conduct comparisons.

3. *Try to gain cooperation for benchmarking targets by a* **quid pro quo** *or a sharing of information.* Sharing can take several forms, but hiring an independent researcher who gives each company an aggregate set of data is one good approach.

4. *Have a plan for comparison.* It is best to focus your efforts on well-defined customer values or environmental problems. Use cross-functional teams that can see the big picture. Measure and monitor your process. Use all resources available including trade publications and public sources. Use comparisons as well to continually improve.

Some measurements worth evaluating might include total liquid and solid waste generated, percent of training personnel, environmental investments, environmental expenses, energy use, and environmental incidents.

TECHNIQUE	PLAN	DO	CHECK	ACT
Bar Chart	✔	✔	✔	
Benchmarking	✔	✔		
Brainstorming	✔	✔		
Cause-and-Effect Diagrams	✔	✔		
Check Sheets	✔	✔	✔	
Control Chart	✔	✔	✔	
Flip Chart	✔	✔	✔	
Flow Chart		✔		✔
Histogram	✔	✔	✔	
Pareto Chart	✔	✔	✔	
Pie Chart	✔	✔	✔	
Run Chart	✔	✔	✔	
Scatter Diagram	✔	✔	✔	

Figure 13–1

CAUSE-AND-EFFECT DIAGRAM

The *Cause-and-Effect Diagram*, because of its appearance, is also known as the *fishbone diagram*. It is also sometimes referred to as the *Ishikawa Diagram*, named for the Japanese professor who invented it. The diagram as seen in *Figure 13–3* (at the end of the chapter) is designed to help people better analyze the "effects" that "cause" problems. Thus, the objective is to diagram all the possible effects that contribute to any environmental problem. Each response to the question "Why does a problem occur?" is a branch of this fishbone diagram. When using it, you can discover the root causes of an environmental problem.

The Cause-and- Effect Diagram helps to identify possible causes of a problem. The first of this seven-step process involves *stating the problem*. For instance, if you were having trouble meeting your goals for a pollution-prevention project, you could state your problem as "delays in meeting emission standard."

Once you have stated your problem, you then want to *identify possible causes* of the problem. This is often best accomplished by a brainstorming exercise where there are no right or wrong answers. It is at this stage that teams are often called upon to generate a list of possible factors contributing to nonperformance.

After you have generated possible causes, next *define the category of causes*. Traditionally, causes are grouped into one of four categories including machines, manpower, methods and materials. The process of identifying these "4 Ms" and how to do cause screening can be seen in Exercise 1 at the end of this chapter.

The fourth step in Cause-and-Effect Diagrams is the process of actually *drawing the diagram*. As seen in Exercise 1 (at the end of the chapter), it involves drawing a box on the right side of a piece of paper and then making a horizontal line from it. The problem (noted in the first step) should be written in this central box. As seen in Figure 13–3, each category of causes should then be drawn as diagonal lines toward your horizontal line.

Once the diagram is drawn, ask *why* each of your causes or conditions exist. You should make a habit of asking why over and over again until you feel you have gotten to the root cause. For instance, if your initial analysis shows that the cause of an environmental problem is due to poor training, ask why. The reason for poor training may be because the needed training is only offered during the 9-to-5 shift. The reason this is the case might be because people cannot participate due to having to meet production quotas.

Go back once again through this questioning process, only this time in reverse. This time start with the last why (or what you believe to be the root cause) you answered and see if it really does cause the previous why. Continue backtracking until you reach your original why (in this case, poor training). Using the process, you sometimes realize previous cause connections are not logical. In the previous example, production quota requirements do not cause training to occur between 9 and 5.

Lastly, make sure to verify your causes. Potential root causes to problems can be verified by obtaining data through measurement, surveys, observation, or additional analysis.

The Cause-and-Effect Diagram, when used in conjunction with brainstorming, is good for discovering causes of a problem but it is not so good for establishing priorities because it does not show the relative importance of a cause. A Pareto Chart, which we will look at in a moment, can help you set priorities for investigating and correcting causes.

The main power of a Cause-and-Effect Diagram is that it lays out problems before a group so they can be discussed. In order to solve an environmental or similar problem, you will have to collect data so that you can correctly identify the environmental causes.

CHECK SHEET

Once potential causes have been discussed by a group, it will then be necessary to find out the causes. One of the easiest ways to collect hard data is by using a *Check Sheet,* or tally sheet. It can be used whenever you need to collect data by sampling to see the number of times a potential cause does occur within some predetermined time period.

1) Can anyone adopt enviro-management strategies in just manufacturing?

Check Sheets are normally the first step for anyone wanting to solve environmental problems. The power of this tool is its simplicity and ease of use. It also has another very important advantage. In these days of empowerment, Check Sheets are great problem-solving tools because those people closest to the problem are the ones who use it. It is they who will use the Check Sheets to become involved actively in collecting data.

A Check Sheet can be used to first show operational personnel the types of environmental causes that will be observed. Next, those in the area of concern would make a mark or check beside a particular category whenever it was encountered. Check Sheets could be used for each specific area when more information on the true causes of an environmental problem is needed.

It is not always easy to categorize the cause of waste or other environmental problems. Therefore, it is very important for everyone to agree on what will be the operational definition. For instance, one operational definition for a cause that needs to be monitored could be something like "Waste is caused by a lack of cleanliness." The reason you need an operational definition is so everyone understands what they are to look for. Some companies have also found it helpful to display, at least in the inspection areas, the different types of unacceptable environmental by-products.

FLIP CHART

The *Flip Chart* is another simple but potentially powerful tool for improving environmental awareness. Like Check Sheets, they can be used to identify environmental problems and solutions. Flip Charts, along with marking pens, should be conveniently located so they are readily accessible to your people.

Environmental problems should be written down and then discussed every day in a 10- to 15-minute stand-up meeting. The group meeting should consist of people who are directly affected by the environmental problem in question. This would include production people, material people, engineers, managers, and so forth. The purpose of these meetings should not only be to analyze all the ideas posted on the Flip Chart but to also make sure everyone understands each of them. Someone should be assigned to follow up and answer each of the ideas by a certain date. All inquiries should be answered and any action taken should be noted on the Flip Chart.

HISTOGRAM

A *Histogram* or Bar Chart is yet another important diagnostic tool because it provides you with another way to see environmental inefficiencies. It is somewhat like a check list, only much more visual. A Histogram is used whenever you need to discover and display the frequency or distribution of environmental problems. As a graphical tool it shows the distribution or shape of data from a process.

The bars are the causes of an environmental problem and the height represents how frequently the problem has occurred. Thus, a Histogram is simply a graphical way of displaying the number of times a certain event or cause has occurred during some particular time period. It provides you and your team with an excellent tool for finding the most critical causes of an environmental challenge.

To create a Histogram, simply begin collecting data on such things as the number of tons or pounds of waste being created in an area. Next, count the number of times each class of waste occurs, then calculate the range of data. The Histogram shows a picture of the frequency of each occurrence, from the smallest to the largest values. In collecting the data, you will often discover the process is stable and can be predicted. The Histogram can also be used to show your capability limits.

It also can provide you with a method of measuring your environmental program effectiveness. Lockhead has monthly record-keeping requirements for the use of paints and coatings. Over 400 records from over 140 sources are generated each month and submitted to its Environmental Department. Its goal is to file 95 percent of these reports on time to minimize follow-up and increase efficiency. It uses Histograms to track the overall on-time reporting and on-time performance of each organization.[1]

PARETO CHART

Pareto Chart, or *ABC Analysis* is a very popular quality-management tool and one that has great potential in the environmental area. In many ways it resembles the vertical bar chart, but it has a theory behind it—and that is unique. Its roots go all the way back to the 15th century. The theory behind the chart is often referred to as "the critical few, the trivial many." In theory, Pareto says that while a large number of causes may contribute to some problem (environmental or otherwise), only a few critical ones cause most.

The Pareto Chart is a vertical bar chart. As a graphic tool it helps you organize data so you can identify and focus on major problems. It is used to display the relative importance of all of the causes to some environmental problem. By doing so, management is able to rank the relative importance of contributing causes (all causes are not equal, many are trivial). Most of these critical few (usually about 20 percent) will be the source of 80 percent of your problem. It is this critical 20 percent that should be the focus of management.

A Pareto Chart uses data collected on a situation or process, ranks it in order and helps you focus attention on ways to improve performance. Frequently, a Pareto Chart is constructed after operational personnel have recorded the frequency, in percentage, of each event that has occurred. Next, you would want to plot a Pareto Chart by first listing each cause based on its frequency of occurrence. If a cause of some problem occurred most often, it would be listed on the left, and less frequent causes would be listed in descending order. In most cases, as seen in *Figure 13–2,* you will find one or few causes account for the majority of the problems.

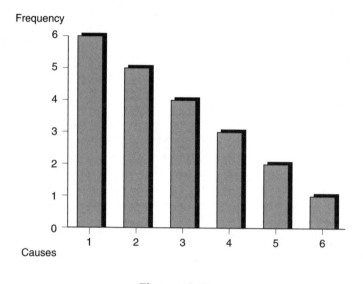

Figure 13–2

Pareto Charts can be used to rank the frequency of causes of particular problems. Arrange your data in descending order from left to right. To construct a Pareto Chart, first identify the number one environmental problem. It might be something like "reducing the number of environmental violations in an area." Next, classify the types of violations occurring (e.g., hazardous waste, air, asbestos, and so on), then determine how often each occurs. Create your Pareto Chart by classifying violations beginning on the left with the most frequent occurrence. Continue until all causes, from the largest to smallest, are graphed on the vertical axis. The result is a graphical picture that helps you prioritize and decide where to focus your pollution efforts so you can get the most improvement for your time and money.

RUN CHART/CONTROL CHART

A *Run Chart* is another tool for collecting data. You would use a Run Chart whenever you needed to do a simple display of trends that were occurring over some time period. These charts are often used in quality, inventory or sales areas. The objective is to identify meaningful trends or changes in the average performance. According to statistical theory, we can expect that there would be an equal number of points or measurements falling both above or below the mean. Any changes in one's average performance should be investigated. The Run Chart is similar to 100 percent inspection since particular environmental causes or characteristics you are interested in are measured over time. While some of the previous tools we have looked at are optional, run diagrams are not. In order to find long-term causes, you must look for patterns that occur over time or excessive or unusual points.

Control Charts are similar to Run Charts. They are statistical tools that help you determine how much variability in a process is inherent (called common causes) and how much of the variability is due to unique events (chance causes). Control Charts can be used to define expected performance, and can also help you understand the variability occurring in a normal system. Normal upper and lower limits of performance are determined mathematically. Such environmental Control Charts, as with quality Control Charts, would be used whenever you needed to know if a production or pollution process was in control or out of control. It is a good feedback and motivational tool for operators to use because it helps them monitor and correct their own processes before the environmental impact becomes too serious.

Control Charts are one way to help you analyze pollution problems. They help you decide if the variability you are experiencing in your process is due to normal or unusual causes. To create one you would statistically calculate the normal variability occurring in your process. By creating Control Charts you are defining your maximum acceptable level of performance (for example, pounds per day lost in sewer, and so forth). These charts also help you identify your normal level of performance during typical operating procedures.

After such a chart is established, you then continue to collect pollution data to determine if you are falling within previously determined control limits. If at any point a value goes above or below these limits, it is then out of control. There is almost always some unusual or special cause for it. The reason for this unusual change can then be identified and eliminated.

There are other things Control Charts can do for you even when there is no unusual problem to solve. By tracking your normal variation in pollution control, you can make changes that hopefully will change and improve process efficiencies. When this occurs the size of the variation will decrease and efficiency can be improved.

SCATTER DIAGRAM

A *Scatter Diagram* can be used to study the potential relationship between one variable (environmental problem) and other variables. It helps you test cause-and-effect relationships. It will not prove that one variable causes another variable, but it does show that when one problem exists, other situations (like poor training, motivation, and so on) will also exist.

FLOW CHART

A *Flow Chart* often follows a Pareto analysis to define the process and decide where to make changes that will improve the production process. Flow Charts are much like a picture or diagram of how your operation flows. It will schematically show movement of people, information, equipment, and so forth. If there is movement, the Flow Chart will show it. Sometimes these charts are used in conjunction with the cause-and-effect diagrams, but not always. The Flow Chart graphs each step in a production process. A Flow Chart shows how communication materials or other things move and what should happen at each step in the process. They are utilized for a wide range of uses. CSR Limited is one company that uses them to help its managers find ways to improve its environmental efficiencies.

Solving problems sometimes involves finding where the problem is in the process. Therefore, a Flow Chart often follows a Pareto Chart where you chart the step-by-step sequence of the flow of decisions involving an environmental issue. While you are charting the *actual* flow be sure to also chart the *ideal* way it should flow. By using experts in the field you can compare the actual to the ideal to more easily pinpoint flows in the process.

CLOSING THOUGHTS

To summarize, the first step in any problem-solving effort begins by *identifying the problem*. This is often harder than it appears because environmental problems can be complex. Multiple problems lead to disappointed efforts. Environmental data is either scientific data (concentration of pollutants, waste, and so on) or management data (laws, policies, regulations, and customer requirements). Stage 1 companies typically concentrate on compliance data that shows how well they meet minimum standards. Higher-stage companies focus more on their short- and long-term customer needs.

An essential part of a good solution is a good definition. Once you have defined the problem adequately, it is half-solved. Definitions also help you determine what data should be collected and how it will be processed. If you have a precise definition, root causes can be identified more easily.

After you have identified the problem, you will then want to *analyze possible causes*. Constructing a cause-and-effect diagram here often helps identify possible causes by category and level. First, you would note the environmental problem (on the right side box). Then you would list possible causes to the left of the problem. These causes are usually due to some process, procedures, or personnel problems.

Once you feel, through brainstorming and construction of the cause-and-effect diagram, that you have a good idea of the potential effects that cause a particular environmental problem (violations, spills, complaints), you can then begin *collecting data*. Decide which data you want to track; the time, dates, location, cause, and action taken are the usual types of information. Make sure you prepare instructions on how to collect and report the data. Be sure to include typical definitions, categories, and possible causes and trial cause-and-effect diagrams that serve as a map.

Make sure to maintain a database that makes it easy to manipulate and process. In order to have an empowered Stage 1 company, you must have well-defined categories of environmental compliance activities. After some time has passed, and some data has been collected, make sure your team reviews the information. Ask yourself, is the right data being collected, is it being collected correctly, is enough data being collected, and finally is the data meeting your objective?[2] After reviewing the data you may decide to revise the database or the ways you are collecting the information.

Once you are happy with the data, the last step is to present your data and determine the cause of your problem. Pareto Charts, Histograms, along with other tools we have already looked at can be very effective. You can present data by location or type of problem. Causes of problems can be sorted into different categories. By using the tools we have already looked at, you can identify and determine the root cause of a problem.

As can be seen, such a problem-solving approach does take time, but teaching everyone how to use the tools is critical to Stage 1, 2 or 3 efforts. Whether it's customer complaints or compliance problems, people need tools to make good decisions.

EXERCISE 1
BASIC CAUSE-AND-EFFECT ANALYSIS

1. State the problem as precisely as possible.

2. State the major groupings for the possible causes: The beginning team may want to use the 4 M's here (manpower, machinery, methods, materials). These are sometimes referred to as process, procedures, personnel, and place.

3. Brainstorm the various causes: Respondents should state under which of the major groupings their idea falls.

4. Conduct cause screening.

5. Rank the most probable causes.

6. Test the most likely cause.

Figure 13–3

BASIC CAUSE-AND-EFFECT ANALYSIS

Basic cause-and-effect analysis is primarily a problem-solving technique. The problem is the effect and the various possible causes are listed on the diagram under specific headings.

When problem-solving teams are first beginning to work with this concept it is a good idea to use the 4 M's (machinery, manpower, methods, and materials) as major headings. The brainstorming procedure is used to identify possible causes of the effect or problem. Participants should identify the major grouping to which their particular cause belongs.

As with all brainstorming activities, the exercise is continued until all ideas have been recorded. The diagram on the bottom of the page displays a typical basic cause-and-effect diagram format.

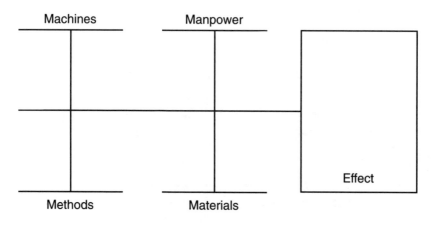

Figure 13–4

CAUSE SCREENING

1. Each item is examined by asking, "How can this suggested cause result in our problem?"

   If no reasonable/logical relationship can be established, the item can be removed from the list by unanimous agreement. If a reasonable/logical relationship can be established, the cause is kept on the chart.

2. The next question is, "How likely is this cause to occur?"

   The responses are labeled according to the thinking of the team.

   V = Very likely
   S = Somewhat likely
   N = Not likely

   V, S, or N is recorded beside the cause based upon majority vote.

3. The third question to ask is, "How easy will this be to check out or verify?"

   V = Very likely
   S = Somewhat likely
   N = Not likely

   V, S, or N is recorded by majority vote.

4. The final step is to thoroughly test the causes.

ENDNOTES

1. Pierle, Michael A., *Environmental Stewardship: A Case History in Environmental Quality Management*, remarks at CMA Chemical Industries Conference. New York, October 29, 1991, p. 4.

2. *Total Quality Management: A Framework for Pollution Prevention*, Quality Environmental Management Subcommittee, President's Commission on Environmental Quality. Washington, D. C., January 1993.

3. Friendly, Alfred, Jr. (Ed.), *Partnerships to Progress: The Report of the President's Commission on Environmental Quality*, President's Commission on Environmental Quality. Washington, D. C., 1993.

14

WHERE DO WE GO FROM HERE?

$\mathbf{A}$ coordinated and systematic approach to pollution management has been presented. It is not necessary to be a Stage 3 company to have successful pollution-management efforts, but for any approach to be successful you need to fit all the pieces together. Sometimes it seems we have a long way to go and it begins with recognition. In order to have an effective Stage 1 effort, senior management must at least recognize the risk of poor environmental efforts. Even this simple concept is foreign to many senior-level people. In fact, according to a survey, only about seven percent of senior managers say they are "very comfortable" with their understanding of the company's environmental risk, or that they feel they have adequate risk-management strategies in place to resolve their environmental problems.[1] The *first* and most important thing senior management needs to recognize is the risk the company faces.

LEGAL RISKS

The CEO and senior management may not be aware of the risk, but there is one group that recognizes both risk and opportunity. Lawyers are very good about assessing the liabilities of current practices. The government has taken the position that corporate management can, in certain situations, be held criminally liable. As individuals you can be held criminally liable for environmental violations even if you did not personally participate in, or direct each of the actions, that led to criminal liability.[2] Clearly, corporate personnel had better start understanding corporate and personal liability or there will be a price to pay.

It is a fact that if a violation of the law is discovered while you are collecting data, you must contact the appropriate agency. The Clean Water Act, the Resource Conservation and Recovery Act (RCRA), along with other laws have self-reporting requirements. In the context of RCRA, the government tries to hold corporate officers and CEOs criminally accountable for both the action of their subordinates and employees. This applies even when top executives did not have actual knowledge of their employees' illegal conduct. In other words, you do not have to be bad to do bad.[2] Senior managers should know the so-called black heart associated with criminal activities is not necessary to sustain criminal convictions.

While only seven percent of senior managers feel "very comfortable," clearly some are now understanding their risk. In the fiscal year ending September 30, 1991, the EPA announced that it had obtained $14.1 million in criminal fines and defendants convicted of environmental crimes had served a total of 550 months in prison. There were 125 indictments and 72 convictions during 1991. Federal sentencing guidelines for corporations became effective November 1, 1991. These guidelines greatly restrict a judge's discretion with multimillion-dollar fines as high as $300 million.[2]

Under these conditions, it seems absurd for any manager not to be aware of his or her environmental liability. At the minimum, Stage 1 managers need to make sure they have good audit programs in place. They should regularly conduct a comprehensive audit of their compliance with all environmental requirements. If the audit uncovers illegal activities of employees, investigations should proceed. Assuming you already have a good compliance program, you would then probably find that you have had good clear policies, employees had received the proper training, and there has been a hot line for reporting suspected violations.

If violations did occur, the appropriate governmental agency must be contacted. It is everyone's responsibility to work with the government to develop satisfactory remediation measures. You would assume the company would discipline employees involved in the violations, including lax supervisors. This also involves disclosing to the government the names of employees responsible for violations and providing the necessary documentation.

SOURCE REDUCTION IDEAS

Making sure every "i" is dotted and every "t" is crossed is a good Stage 1 perspective. It will not make you any money, or lower your costs relative to your competitor, but it will keep you out of trouble. Better environmental management can be a revenue generator if you are willing to put all the pieces together. The money is there, both from the marketing and operations end. Consumers have indicated that they are willing to pay 20 percent more for high quality automobiles, 67 percent for premium televisions, and 72 percent more for sofas.[3]

As we have seen in earlier chapters, consumers are also willing to pay for more environmentally friendly products. But here is the real plus: Better environmental management does not have to be something that "costs." We saw many cases where employee involvement and continuous improvement led to profitable ventures. If you focus on compliance and failure cost you cannot create revenue generators out of environmental initiatives. Prevention cost can create a more competitive situation for you, but what many fail to understand is that it is also possible to generate revenue out of better-run operations. One way to make money is to create products and services that satisfy our customers' green needs. In addition, when you reduce waste inefficiencies you get greener operations with lower cycle times and better yields. INFORM is a nonprofit environmental research and education organization that tries to identify practical ways to protect natural resources. It has done several studies with the chemical industry that support the notion that going green is the right operational thing to do. It recently studied 29 chemical plants and discovered some interesting facts. One of the first of many startling revolutions was that *68* of the 70 waste source reduction activities it studied showed an *increase in yield*. Think about that, when INFORM was able to identify a change in yield in 68 out of 70 times, it meant an *increase* in yield. One activity had no effect and one decreased the yield.[4] In its studies it found 35 percent had yield increases between 10 to 40 percent, 25 percent had increases from 1 to 10 percent, and 40 percent had yield increases of one percent or less. From a monetary standpoint, 15 percent of the *source reduction activities* saved $1 million or more annually, almost half had savings of $45,000 to $1 million annually, and one-quarter had savings between $6,000 to $45,000.

The good news continues. INFORM also found out that one-quarter of the source reduction activities for which capital information was available showed that there was no capital investment for implementation. Just one-half required investments of less than $100,000 and on average investments were recouped in 18 months. Of the source reduction activities mentioned, about two-thirds required less than six months to implement, and another 30 percent required 6 months to three years. What may also be a surprise to many is the payback period for recouping their initial investment, which averaged eight months for nonproduction function, and five months for research and development activities.[4]

From the standpoint of techniques for source reduction, INFORM found that in its study, 64 percent of the activities were operational changes, while 27 percent were equipment changes. In order to make these changes successful, it found that plants had one of three individual program features. These included cost accounting, employee involvement, and leadership from both environmental and other departments. Plants with some type of employee involvement had an average of *twice* as many source reduction activities. Senior management roles can also be seen in this study. What they found was that leadership from both the environmental department and from the plant manager or other nonenvironmental departments reported twice as many source reduction activities as plants with only leadership from environmental or nonenvironmental departments.[4]

All these profits occurred without applying some of even the most fundamental of management principles! INFORM discovered that only 10 of the 25 plants studied reported that they had established environmental *goals*. This meant that only 10 had specific targets for reducing waste or reporting releases. Moreover, the concept of environmental goals had only recently been seen as a tool for implementing source reduction, so its impact was marginal. At this stage, INFORM noted it may be too early to see what effect the concept of environmental goals would have on the number of source reduction activities. For instance, those companies with goals may have used them to identify reduction activities, but may not have had a chance to implement them. They did note that plants with these goals did have accounting systems in place and this may have aided them in identifying and quantifying reduction goals.[4]

ELIMINATING THE SOURCE OF POLLUTION

In conclusion, what INFORM found was that among other things, source reduction continues to rapidly reduce cost and increase production efficiency. That's the stuff that Stage 3 is made of. Generally, the cost for implementing source reduction activities is low (one-quarter required, no capital) and investments of less than $100,000 required in just under half of these source reduction activities. Furthermore, the chemical company tended to recoup their initial investment rapidly (in less than 6 months, in two-thirds of its cases). Where data was provided, product yield increased in 97 percent of the cases, and implementing times were short. Finally, full cost accounting, employee training and incentive programs, as well as a high level of leadership from both the operations and environmental side produced more source reduction ideas.

Clearly, the message for anyone thinking of implementing Stage 3 is that the focus of pollution management must change from recycling to source reduction. The study is extensive, but it was after all, only one study and it involves chemical companies. Perhaps not all companies will have the same experience, but the early indications are that there are real opportunities to increase productivity when you *eliminate* sources of waste. Just as clearly, it shows that it will be a transition to teach people that there is more to pollution control than recycling. It is also obvious that many people will need to be trained in problem solving, and be integrated into the decision-making process.

Reducing the need for waste management will produce cost savings, improved product yield, and quality. Despite the potential, corporations spend very little time or effort on permanent pollution solutions. The prevailing attitude is to focus on "end-of-pipe" Stage 1 controls. After the fact recycling efforts can be of some value but revenue generators come from eliminating pollution at the source. In order to generate revenue for pollution management you must first capture your people's hearts and minds. Employees must want to be a part of the solution, and they must know how to solve problems. The reasons are simple; most of the answers come from our people.

The INFORM studies show that low technology and efficiency improving techniques accounted for *87 percent* of the source reduction activities. Process changes involved refinements or alterations in the (chemical) process itself (such as its temperature or pressure). Some of the changes were operational in nature, like improving material handling and equipment waste. Equipment changes, modifications and additions can occur at every stage of the manufacturing process. The surprising fact is that in its studies, only 13 percent of source reduction activities involved the more innovative techniques like product changes (e.g., redesigning the end product so you create less waste) or chemical substitution.[5]

CREATING THE NEED FOR CHANGE

When managers in the INFORM study were asked why they implemented source reduction activities, 41 percent said the problems and costs
associated with waste disposal was the main reason. Thirty-six percent
mentioned environmental regulations. While cost, regulatory, and even
market forces are forcing firms to rethink pollution management practices, the pace remains slow. Federal regulations are forcing disclosure,
bans on disposal of many hazardous wastes and escalating waste disposal costs are strong mandates for change—but changes still occur slowly.
"Green" products and services are the exception rather than the rule.

The New Jersey Department of Environmental Protection (NJDEP)
has studied the issue of slow conversion to a more preventive mode and
found the cause to be two-fold. The first is organizational in nature and
the second involves the nature of capital. On the organizational side, as
we have already seen, there are often weak signals being sent from top
management. Where is the clear and strong signal that adopting an environment perspective is not a choice, but a mandate? Failure to assign
environmental managers with adequate standing or authority over capital investments and insufficient information flow to product design and
operations staff to build a broad constituency for prevention prospects
are additional reasons.[6] In such cases, opportunities for pollution prevention go unrecognized. The environmental perspective must be a part
of design, procurement, production and marketing decisions. Such obsta-
cles block financially promising prevention work from becoming part of
the firm's capital allocation process. The integrated approach recommended by Stage 3 would resolve many of these issues, but a second
point by NJDEP is more fundamental.

The second reason found for the slow pace of change is the inability of
pollution prevention investments to compete with other potential uses of
limited capital because such projects are at a big disadvantage. The disadvantage for environmentally related projects is that management's standard project evaluation techniques shortchange them. It also faces other
external and internal economic barriers including the inaccessibility to
capital. Some of these external barriers include lenders and investors.

Rather than focus on what they cannot control, NJDEP has concentrated on internal economic barriers because pollution prevention projects must compete with other projects for scarce capital resources.
Which projects get funded are based on financial analysis and other qualitative analyses as well as management judgment. In the past economic
return on investment for environmentally related projects tended to show
up in diverse and indirect ways. Since the time horizon for such envi-

ronmental projects was assumed to occur over a longer time frame, conventional project analysis often underestimated or omitted the benefits altogether. This is the case in the capital budgeting process where such things as avoiding liability, reduced staff time for monitoring and paperwork, and enlarged market share because of your "green" image were not considered relevant. As a result, environmental projects suffered from a systematic bias in capital allocation decisions. The result has been continuing under investment in them.[6]

The NJDEP developed an alternative to conventional project analysis by extending the cost/benefit inventory and time horizon, and by using long-term profitability indicators so a more comprehensive investment could be made. The hope has been to "level the playing field" so environmental projects can more fairly compete. NJDEP is trying to address inequities in the capital budgeting area and has called the approach Total Cost Assessment (TCA).

To see if it could come up with a more equitable costing model, it selected 10 firms of varying sizes and product lines. The goal has been to create a more expansive cost inventory and time horizon, and calculate longer-term project financial indicators so a sharper picture of a project's profitability could be seen. The hope is that TCA can serve as a valuable tool for translating judgments into concrete dollar values used during the capital budget process. TCA does give you more precise estimates of the real economic return on projects.

ACCOUNTING FOR INTERNAL COSTS

A company's project must pass a so-called "hurdle rate," which means a manufacturer looking for some threshold of acceptable profitability. Environmental projects compete with other investment alternatives within and outside the environmental area. A critical dimension of this capital allocation project process is looking at how a firm defines and estimates project cost and benefit. Normally, when looking at proposed projects, estimators will want to account for all *internal* costs. Most of the time project estimators leave out the so-called *external* costs because they do not directly affect a project's financial profile.

Some would argue these external costs are just as real because they consume important assets like clean air and clean water, but it is a fact that standard cost accounting procedures exclude them. Therefore, it is only cost that directly affects buyers and sellers of goods and services as well as debtors, creditors, and owners that really matter. For this reason, we will concentrate our discussion on these specific internal costs.

With rising disposal cost, some environmental projects compete quite well even under the crudest of cost accounting systems. In order for these projects to reach corporate hurdle rates (which vary from industry to industry) you need to include indirect or hidden regulatory and liability costs that are involved in your current production process. Likewise, you will need to use a longer time frame and account for any indirect benefits of alternative production processes. TCA makes the point that without these considerations it will be impossible for environmental projects to have the level playing field needed to compete. This is not to imply that if you use its new system that all or most environmentally oriented projects will be able to successfully compete on purely economic terms. It does mean you will discover a wider variety of benefits over a longer time frame than you normally would. It also means that the cost of existing environmental practices will not be excluded from the calculation. With today's cost accounting, these costs are omitted routinely, thus biasing decision making.

From a business point of view, even a Stage 1 company should challenge cost assumptions. The NJDEP instituted its study because the New Jersey State Assembly passed a wide-ranging law called the Pollution Prevention Act (P.L. 1991, Chap 235, approved August 1, 1991). The act wants a 50 percent reduction in generating nonproduct hazardous waste over five years. The act requires a "comprehensive financial analysis" if cost associated with use generation, release or discharge of hazardous substances are occurring because of current production processes. The NJDEP will be required to review the project cost accounting methods utilized by firms in determining cost and benefits of *both* approved and disapproved projects. The spirit of the law is to clearly challenge conventional project analysis methods so a broader spectrum of direct and indirect costs as well as long- and short-term costs are considered.

NJDEP believes prevention projects benefit from these procedures, rather than the normal end-of-pipe solutions that are often chosen. Having a broader view of cost and allowing for liability contingencies often means prevention projects are viewed more favorably. It also helps managers make better choices between two or more prevention-oriented projects. NJDEP also thinks such an analysis will help support projects with more profitability potential, like those involving process redesign and substitution of materials.

DEVELOPING A COMPREHENSIVE FINANCIAL ANALYSIS

Capital budgeting is the process of analyzing alternative investments and deciding which, if any, projects will be included in your company's investment budget. Such capital budgets provide you with information on planning expenditures for fixed assets that might be aimed for five or ten years in the future. The capital budgeting process involves identifying financial resources available or required. Capital budgeting decisions are a combination of objective financial analysis and subjective managerial judgment.

A *project financial analysis* is the heart and soul of this capital budgeting process. It is here that capital cost, operating cost, savings, and financial or profitability indicators are developed and evaluated. A company's cost accounting system is used to track, as well as allocate, production cost to a process or product. Such a system is supposed to provide a neutral unbiased source of cost information, but it has advantages and drawbacks. You can more clearly see where costs are occurring and where cost savings are possible. It also helps highlight the advantages of prevention over after-the-fact solutions because it shows where pollution originates and what it costs. It allows you the chance to evaluate project cash flows, profitability, and lets you more easily compare potential projects.

Capital cost (purchased equipment, etc.) and operating cost (raw materials, labor, supplies) are reported in your income statements and balance sheets. All these costs are of interest to investors, creditors, and owners. Inclusion of *all* these costs are therefore essential for you to get an accurate picture of the firm. However, deciding what to include is not a black or white issue because firms have considerable discretion about which costs to include. Decisions about if and when certain costs become part of the project analysis are critical to determining whether a project is potentially profitable or not.

In the past, pollution projects have not fared well because there is a systematic bias in project financial analysis that places them at a competitive disadvantage. The mere fact that many environmental costs are uncertain is one such bias. Many managers do not know what these costs are, how large they will ultimately be, or when they will occur. Such uncertainty exists because of the inherent complexity associated with use, moving, and exposure to hazardous substances. Lastly, uncertainty exists because of rapidly changing regulations and judicial decisions. New regulations require monitoring, training, and paperwork. In some cases, contingent cost must be prepared where certain costs *may* materialize *if* certain things happen, such as exceeding permissible limits. There are already federal guidelines for inclusion of such contingencies whenever there is probable loss, but generally, it is only for probable "major losses."

The Securities and Exchange Commission (SEC) requires disclosure of things that might affect future expenditures on environmental controls so there is clearly a mandate to disclose them. Ignoring these costs when analyzing projects can also help you avoid misallocation of scarce capital. If you misallocate these capitals, you shift investment dollars toward projects that can generate future liability (which should be a big concern for Stage 1 companies). Prevention projects help identify this liability and hopefully resolve it before it becomes a reality.

PRIORITIZING POLLUTION EFFECTS

Projects are generally classified as one of three types: (1) market expansion projects, (2) revenue generating and cost reduction projects, and (3) cost minimization projects. Market expansion projects are usually a first priority with companies because they add directly to the growth of the firm. Examples include projects that create new markets or expand existing ones. Generally, they require relatively large capital investments and with new products it also means relatively high risk.

Revenue generating and cost reduction projects improve competitiveness by increasing yield and lowering relative cost. These types of projects would involve purchasing new equipment that lowers labor cost, upgrades quality, or reduces pollution. Investments here are seen as a way of enhancing market position of products you already sell.

Cost minimization projects are normally for maintenance, compliance, or for replacement. In the past, managers have seen these as a "must do" and this is where environmental projects have been placed. Managers see them as being required by laws and regulations, but of having little or no relevance to either adding new markets, or enhancing revenue. Hopefully, after reading thus far, you are convinced that environmental projects can increase market share and revenue, while lowering cost.

In the past, managers have assumed environmental projects were necessary "losers" and that return-on-investment would be negative. Comparing operating cost of several options was about the best you could expect from simple short-term analysis. The object here, and in Stage 1, is to find the least costly option for complying with environmental standards.

Environmental projects tend to be either after the fact (end-of-pipe) or preventative in nature. There is little favoritism toward prevention, even though this would seem the most logical route. The reason is simple. Simplified cost analysis tends to favor the so-called end-of-pipe options because prevention methods like material substitution, product reformulation, and process modification are complex in nature. In turn, their yield is indirect and occurs over a longer period of time.

Clearly, it is a mistake to think that every environmental investment is a net loser. As off-site waste management price increases, and as growing consumer demand shows that green products and processes make good business sense we must rethink our assumptions. Reducing current and future liabilities as well as seeking cost-effective pollution solutions should also be of increasing concern. Therefore, it does not seem wise at all to assume environmental projects are economic losers. As we have seen it is possible to frame them within a market expansion and revenue generation context.

In order to frame them within a revenue generator or market expansion, you must make a more comprehensive analysis of your cost and benefits. However, better identifying your true cost, and/or expanding your time frame will not always result in favoring prevention over end-of-pipe solutions. But, the relative return for your investment will be closer to reality than through conventional accounting procedures.

ALLOCATING COST AND BENEFITS STAGES

Some things must change to move environmental projects from Stage 1 to 2 and 3. There must be a more precise allocation of cost and benefits to processes and products, instead of to overhead accounts. You must calculate a wider range of project cost and savings and accept a longer time frame for calculating financial indicators (usually five or more years, rather than the usual three to five year horizon).

In general, conventional cost analysis includes only capital costs directly associated with the investment. NJDEP's approach has been to consider a broader range of cost and savings. The four categories were:[6]

(1) Direct Costs
- Capital expenditures
  - buildings
  - equipment
  - utility connections
  - equipment installations
  - project engineering

- Operation and maintenance expenses/revenue
  - raw materials
  - labor
  - waste disposal
  - utilities, energy, water, sewage
  - value of recovered material

(2) Indirect Hidden Costs
  • Compliance costs
    • permitting
    • reporting
    • monitoring
    • manifesting
  • Insurance
  • On-site waste management
  • Operation of on-site pollution-control equipment

Hidden costs are only hidden in the sense that they are normally allocated to overhead rather than their source, or are omitted altogether.

(3) Liability Costs
  • Penalties
  • Personal injury and property damage

Liability cost occurs due to penalties and fines for noncompliance as well as from legal claims, or settlements for remedial action that may be due to personal injury and property damage. Pollution prevention eliminates, or at least reduces, the source of these hazards and the source of potential legal actions. Still, it is true that liability costs are difficult to estimate and to pinpoint on the life cycle of a product. By estimating future liability you introduce uncertainty which senior management may not want to do, or find difficult to accept as part of a project's justification. In this case, NJDEP notes some companies use a narrative that accompanies a profitability calculation. The narrative calculates an estimate of liability reductions or refers to a penalty or settlement that may be avoided. Without making reference to some dollar amount, you may still make reference to reduced liability because of some pollution prevention project.

Liability estimation is part of doing business, but it is controversial because the SEC requires companies to report liabilities to stockholders and secure assets to cover the cost. Such estimates could be damaging if the information ever made it to the public in legal hearings. Therefore, it is wise to exercise caution in assigning quantitative estimate of liability.[6]

The fourth and last category in this study can be identified as:

(4) Less Tangible Benefits
  • Increased revenue from better product quality
  • Increased revenue from a better product and company image
  • Reduced wealth maintenance cost from improved employee health
  • Increased productivity from improved employee relations[6]

Again, these costs are difficult to estimate, but are essential to a true cost picture. Even a qualitative rather than quantitative analysis can prove to be eye-opening.

ASSESSING TRUE COST

In assessing the value of a project, decision makers want to know all negative and positive cash flows over the life of a project, and to have an understanding of the time value of money (you have to discount future cash flows). For many finance types, the so-called Net Present Value (NPV) method among others, meets these criteria. Under NPV, the present value of inflows and outflows of cash is calculated and discounted. A positive NPV means a project is worth doing—the opposite is true for a negative one. The more positive, the better. When NPV is applied to long-term projects, where significant cash flow occurs in later years, it is very sensitive to levels of discount rates. Projects with most of their cash flow in early years will not have their NPV lowered much by discount rates. On the other hand, NPV of projects where cash flows come later will have significantly lower NPVs, thereby making it a less attractive investment. As such, NPVs are a short-term incentive.

Payback is the simplest technique for evaluating capital projects. It's "quick and dirty," and has to do with the expected number of years it takes to recover the original project investment. Regular payback methods do not account for cost of capital or for cash flows beyond payback year.

A *cost accounting system* is used to track and allocate production cost to a product or process line. From an investment point of view, a good cost accounting system should allocate *all* costs to the processes responsible for creating them. It seems financial officers are always trying to decide whether to allocate costs to overhead or product or process accounts. To this end, waste disposal costs are often placed in overhead accounts. It is also not unusual for disposal costs to be allocated to administrative, research and development, and manufacturing use of floor space rather than the quantity and type of waste these areas generated! Clearly, this practice greatly impedes financial analysis of waste generation.

AN ALTERNATIVE APPROACH TO POLLUTION COSTING

NJDEP continues to look at several alternative methods to project analysis. For a system to be useful, it felt it should help you include a complete set of cost and savings, but still be flexible enough to be useful for different-sized firms and projects as well as different types of projects. It wanted a simple method that took very little time to learn and use. It felt one that required only rudimentary computer skills and financial terminology would work best, so it looked at several methods.

One was the so called "GE Method" or Financial Analysis of Waste Management Alternatives developed by GE. Another was the Pollution Prevention Benefits Manual developed by the U.S. EPA or "EPA Method."

The GE method has a workbook and software tools for identifying and ranking waste minimization options. You quantify direct cost and future liability cost (potential liabilities for remedial action and cost related to personal and property damage). Its workbook has waste-flow diagrams, a detailed checklist and ways to estimate direct capital and operating costs associated with on- and off-site waste management. Future liabilities in connection with current and alternative approaches are also examined. The GE workbook provides step-by-step instruction for identifying both direct and future liability cost and is a good start for Stage 1 companies because it generally is applicable to regulatory situations.

It is a flexible system and is good for someone who is beginning to develop a Stage 1 strategy of waste and cost minimization and wants some guidance. GE financial software is programmed on Lotus, so it is familiar to many small business managers. The drawback of the GE method is that it does not encourage more comprehensive pollution-prevention methods involving material substitutions and process changes.[6] Such considerations will be necessary if you plan to move to a Stage 2 or Stage 3 company.

The EPA method also has a manual and worksheets and is designed to assist you in making a cost comparison of one or more pollution-prevention projects. It developed a *hierarchy of cost,* including: *usual cost* (equipment, labor and materials), *hidden cost* (compliance and permits), *liability cost* (penalties, fines and future liabilities) and *less tangible cost* (consumer response and employee relations). Usual and hidden costs are a more conventional part of financial analysis while things like less tangible costs have rarely been included in any analysis. The EPA manual contains numerous cost equations for estimating potential future liability cost and helps you calculate three financial indicators: *analyzed savings, internal rate of return,* and *net present value.*

The following summarizes these types of cost:

Usual Cost
- Depreciable capital cost
    - equipment
    - materials
    - utility connections
    - site preparation
    - installation
    - engineering and procurement

Expenses

- start-up cost
- permitting cost
- salvage cost
- working capital
- initial chemicals
- insurance costs
- raw material cost
- utilities cost
- catalysts and chemicals
- operating and material supplies cost
- disposal cost
- operating and material labor cost

Operating Revenue

- Sales of primary products
- Sales of marketable by-products

Hidden cost

- Federal regulations and relevant state regulatory programs
- Pollution technology with associated costs
- Cost for regulatory activities including costs for
    - (a) notification
    - (b) reporting
    - (c) monitoring/testing
    - (d) record keeping
    - (e) training
    - (f) modeling planning/ studies
    - (g) inspection
    - (h) labeling
    - (i) preparedness/protective equipment
    - (j) medical surveillance
    - (k) insurance and special taxes

Liability cost (cost equations help you calculate)

- soil and waste removal and treatment cost
- ground-water removal and treatment cost
- surface sealing
- personal injury
- economic loss
- real property damage
- natural resource damage

The EPA manual uses a wide range of costs, including the less tangible, that help you consider the full range of cost, thereby encouraging quantitative analysis. It also helps you do a step-by-step analysis and, if necessary, helps you calculate less certain and more subtle costs. Its big drawback is that the EPA System has no software. Since some of the equations involve long algorithms, you might have difficulty using these equations without some software.[7]

The EPA also developed something called the *Waste Minimization Opportunity Assessment Manual* (EPA/625/7–88/003) which is a series of data collection sheets and profitability worksheets for calculating several financial indicators. This cost analysis tool is simple yet comprehensive, and does include computer software.

CLOSING THOUGHTS

The point of this discussion is two-fold. In order to move from one stage to another requires more than desire. It requires overhauling how we think of waste and pollution. We have got quite a long way to go when you remember the fact that senior managers do not even understand the environmental risk they face. Moreover, at present, most managers are not integrating their approach to pollution control or management. That is what the SEM "pollution wheel" is all about. They have some of the pieces, but not all of them. In order to minimize the cost of pollution, you have got to have all of the pieces. Even at Stage 1 it will require rethinking how we arrive at cost and what the true costs of pollution are. Earlier we discussed life-cycle costing and here we have looked at more comprehensive approaches to capital projects. In order to make good decisions, you have got to have good information about the true cost of pollution and potential benefits of pollution prevention.

Expanding your definition of what costs are involved in pollution practices is a matter of survival. Ignoring them leads to poor choices and puts both individuals and the firm at risk. There is no one best method for calculating risks and costs, but to remain with the old short-sighted and short-term approach is to flirt with disaster. Restructuring your cost accounting system should be the highest priority for anyone looking to the future.

Some companies intuitively understand that the future involves green products, services, and operations. While a Stage 1 company simply wants to "stay out of the paper," a Stage 3 company recognizes the opportunities. The Home Depot has recognized the green opportunity, ARCO's reformulated gas also shows this recognition. Ben and Jerry's use of brazilian nuts in their ice cream isn't just a humanitarian gesture. When Proctor & Gamble made more environmentally friendly packaging for their fabric softener, sales went up 20 percent. Melitta's unbleached coffee filters gave them a 50 percent market share. Polaroid created a revenue generator when it eliminated mercury in its batteries and created a new market—recyclable batteries. Green, though, is more than just sales.

From the operations side, Dow's WRAP program has been an early forerunner of companies that recognize that waste reduction can be a competitive advantage. If you are less wasteful and more efficient, you win. It requires being in it for the long haul. It requires raising the level of pollution to that equal with other corporate concerns. You have to identify all process losses and their sources. You have to prioritize your efforts to allocate resources. In short, simply recycling will not do it.

What we learned earlier was that pollution management cannot only be a cost-competitive advantage, it can also be a revenue generator. Studies like those of INFORM show better pollution management can be a revenue generator, not just a way to cut cost. It is possible if we "integrate green" within the day-to-day strategic decision making, but it means changing the way decisions are made. There must be an obsessive focus on source reduction or incorporating green considerations into the strategic, financial design, operations, and employee perspective. It is a journey that ultimately will transform the organization where profits and pollution elimination are considered complimentary. But it cannot happen without *employee integration*. It takes more than simply getting together a few waste reduction teams. If you want a Stage 3 firm you have to get everyone thinking not only about recycling, but about how to close the loop, to eliminate waste and incorporate green choices.

The path is before us: Whether we choose Stage 1, 2 or 3 will depend on what resources are available, what our customers want and what our competition is doing. Being able to turn green into green will depend on understanding who we are, what we do, and what we want to accomplish. Filling out the green survey is a good place to start, but it is just a start. Improving cost-accounting procedures, employee training, incentive programs, and creating a higher level of environmental leadership are the next steps.

ENDNOTES

1. Breeden, Kay, "Changing Corporate Culture" in *Corporate Quality/Environmental Management II Conference*, Global Environmental Management Initiative, Arlington, Virginia, March 16–18, 1992.

2. Friedman, Frank B, "The Perils of Self-Assessment or No Good Deed Goes Unpunished," in *Corporate Quality Environmental Management II: Measurements and Communications Conference*, Arlington, Virginia, March 16–18, 1992, p. 169.

3. Thompson, Fred L., "Statistical Measures for Management Oversight to Achieve Continuous Improvement at Monsanto Chemical Company," in *Corporate Quality Environmental Management II: Measurements and Communications Conference*, Arlington, Virginia, March 16–18, 1992, p. 11.

4. Dorfman, Mark H., Warren R. Muir, Catherine G. Miller, *Environmental Dividends: Cutting More Chemical Waste*, INFORM Report, New York, 1991, pp. 16–86.

5. Dorfman, Mark H., Warren R. Muir, Catherine G. Miller, *Environmental Dividends: Cutting More Chemical Waste*, Executive Summary, 1991, pp. 1–5.

6. White, Allen L., Monica Becker, James Goldstein, "Alternative Approaches to the Financial Evaluation of Industrial Pollution Prevention Investments," New Jersey Department of Environmental Protection, Division of Science and Research Project No. P32250. November, 1991, pp. 1–125.

7. You can get a copy of the EPA manual by contacting the EPA Office of Pollution Prevention, Washington, D.C.

Appendix

A

SUMMARY OF FTC ENVIRONMENTAL MARKETING GUIDELINES

BACKGROUND

The Federal Trade Commission's Guides for the *Use of Environmental Marketing Claims* are based on a review of data obtained during FTC law-enforcement investigations, from the two days of hearings the FTC held in July of 1991, and from more than 100 written comments received from the public. *Like all FTC guides, they are administrative interpretations of laws administered by the FTC. Thus, while they are not themselves legally enforceable, they provide guidance to marketers in conforming to legal requirements.* The guides apply to advertising, labeling, and other forms of marketing to consumers. They do not preempt state or local laws or regulations.

The Commission will seek public comment on whether to modify the guides after three years. In the meantime, interested parties may petition the Commission to amend the guides.

Basically, the guides describe *various claims, note those that should be avoided because they are likely to be misleading, and illustrate the kinds of qualifying statements* that may have to be added to other claims to avoid consumer deception. The claims are followed by examples that illustrate the points. The guides outline principles that apply to all environmental claims, and address the use of eight commonly-used environmental marketing claims.

GENERAL CONCERNS

As for any advertising claim, the FTC guides specify that any time marketers make objective environmental claims—whether explicit or implied—they must be substantiated by competent and reliable evidence. In the case of environmental claims, the evidence will often have to be competent and reliable scientific evidence.

The guides outline four other general concerns that apply to all environmental claims:

1. Qualifications and disclosures should be sufficiently clear and prominent to prevent deception.

2. Environmental claims should make clear whether they apply to the product, the package, or a component of either. Claims need not be qualified with regard to minor, incidental components of the product or package.

3. Environmental claims should not overstate the environmental attribute or benefit. Marketers should avoid implying a significant environmental benefit where the benefit is, in fact, negligible.

4. A claim comparing the environmental attributes of one product with those of another product should make the basis for the comparison sufficiently clear and this should be substantiated.

The guides then discuss particular environmental marketing claims. In most cases, each discussion is followed in the guides by a series of examples to illustrate how the principles apply to specific claims.

General environmental benefit claims. In general, unqualified general environmental claims are difficult to interpret, and may have a wide range of meanings for consumers. Every express and material implied claim conveyed to consumers about an objective quality should be substantiated. Unless they can be substantiated, broad environmental claims should be avoided or qualified.

Degradable, Biodegradable, and Photodegradable. In general, unqualified degradability claims should be substantiated by evidence that the product will completely break down and return to nature—that is, decompose into elements found in nature within a reasonably short period of time after consumers dispose of it in the customary way. Such claims should be qualified to the extent necessary to avoid consumer deception about: (a) the product or package's ability to degrade in the environment where it is customarily disposed; and (b) the extent and rate of degradation.

Compostable. In general, unqualified compostable claims should be substantiated by evidence that all the materials in the product or package will break down into, or otherwise become part of, usable compost (e.g., soil-conditioning material, mulch) in a safe and timely manner in an appropriate composting program or facility, or in a home compost pile or device. Compostable claims should be qualified to the extent necessary to avoid consumer deception: (1) if municipal composting facilities are not available to a substantial majority of consumers or communities where the product is sold; (2) if the claim misleads consumers about the environmental benefit provided when the product is disposed of in a landfill; or (3) if consumers misunderstand the claim to mean that the package can be composted safely in their home compost pile or device, when in fact it cannot.

Recyclable. In general, a product or package should not be marketed as recyclable unless it can be collected, separated, or otherwise recovered from the solid waste stream for use in the form of raw materials in the manufacture or assembly of a new product or package. Unqualified recyclable claims may be made if the entire product or package, excluding incidental components, is recyclable.

Claims about products with both recyclable and nonrecyclable components should be qualified adequately. If incidental components significantly limit the ability to recycle product, the claim would be deceptive. If, because of its size or shape, a product is not accepted in recycling programs, it should not be marketed as recyclable. Qualification may be necessary to avoid consumer deception about the limited availability of recycling programs and collection sites if recycling collection sites are not available to a substantial majority of consumers or communities.

Recycled Content. In general, claims of recycled content should only be made for materials that have been recovered or diverted from the solid waste stream, either during the manufacturing process (pre-consumer) or after consumer waste (post-consumer). An advertiser should be able to substantiate that pre-consumer content would otherwise have entered the solid waste stream.

Distinctions made between pre- and post-consumer content should be substantiated. Unqualified claims may be made if the entire product or package, excluding minor, incidental components, is made from recycled material. Products or packages only partially made of recycled material should be qualified to indicate the amount, by weight, in the finished product or package.

Source Reduction. In general, claims that a product or package has been reduced or is lower in weight, volume, or toxicity should be qualified to the extent necessary to avoid consumer deception about the amount of reduction and the basis for any comparison asserted.

Refillable. In general, an unqualified refillable claim should not be asserted unless a system is provided for: (1) the collection and return of the package for refill; or (2) the later refill of the package by consumers with product subsequently sold in another package. The claim should not be made if it is up to consumers to find ways to refill the package.

Ozone Safe and Ozone Friendly. In general, a product should not be advertised as "ozone safe," "ozone friendly," or as not containing CFCs if the product contains any ozone-depleting chemical. Claims about the reduction of a product's ozone-depletion potential may be made if substantiated adequately.

GUIDES FOR THE USE OF ENVIRONMENTAL MARKETING CLAIMS

THE APPLICATION OF SECTION 5 OF *THE FEDERAL TRADE COMMISSION ACT TO ENVIRONMENTAL ADVERTISING AND MARKETING PRACTICES*

Federal Trade Commission
July 1992

TABLE OF CONTENTS

A. STATEMENT OF PURPOSE:

These guides represent administrative interpretations of laws administered by the Federal Trade Commission for the guidance of the public in conducting its affairs in conformity with legal requirements. These guides specifically address the application of Section 5 of the FTC Act to environmental advertising and marketing practices. They provide the basis for voluntary compliance with such laws by members of industry. Conduct inconsistent with the positions articulated in these guides may result in corrective action by the Commission under Section 5 if, after investigation, the Commission has reason to believe that the behavior falls within the scope of conduct declared unlawful by the statute.

B. SCOPE OF GUIDES:

These guides apply to environmental claims included in labeling, advertising, promotional materials and all other forms of marketing, whether asserted directly or by implication, through words, symbols, emblems, logos, depictions, product brand names, or through any other means. The guides apply to any claim about the environmental attributes of a product or package in connection with the sale, offering for sale, or marketing of such product or package for personal, family or household use, or for commercial, institutional, or industrial use.

Because the guides are not legislative rules under Section 18 of the FTC Act, they are not themselves enforceable regulations, nor do they have the force and effect of law. The guides themselves do not preempt regulation of other federal agencies or of state and local bodies governing the use of environmental marketing claims. Compliance with federal, state or local law and regulations concerning such claims, however, will not necessarily preclude Commission law enforcement action under Section 5.

C. STRUCTURE OF THE GUIDES:

The guides are composed of general principles and specific guidance on the use of environmental claims. These general principles and specific guidance are followed by examples that address a single deception concern. A given claim may raise issues that are addressed under more than one example and in more than one section of the guides.

In many of the examples, one or more options are presented for qualifying a claim. These options are intended to provide a "safe harbor" for marketers who want certainty about how to make environmental claims. They do not represent the only permissible approaches to qualifying a claim. The examples do not illustrate all possible acceptable claims or disclosures that would be permissible under Section 5. In addition, some of the illustrative disclosures may be appropriate for use on labels but not in print or broadcast advertisements and vice versa. In some instances, the guides indicate within the example in what context or contexts a particular type of disclosure should be considered.

D. REVIEW PROCEDURE:

Three years after the date of adoption of these guides, the Commission will seek public comment on whether and how the guides need to be modified in light of ensuing developments.

Parties may petition the Commission to alter or amend these guides in light of substantial new evidence regarding consumer interpretation of a claim or regarding substantiation of a claim. Following review of such a petition, the Commission will take such action as it deems appropriate.

E. INTERPRETATION AND SUBSTANTIATION OF ENVIRONMENTAL MARKETING CLAIMS:

Section 5 of the FTC Act makes unlawful deceptive acts and practices in or affecting commerce. The Commission's criteria for determining *whether an express or implied claim has been made are enunciated in the Commission's Policy Statement on Deception.** In addition, any party making an express or implied claim that presents an objective assertion about the environmental attribute of a product or package must, at the time the claim is made, possess and rely upon a reasonable basis substantiating the claim. A reasonable basis consists of competent and reliable evidence. In the context of environmental marketing claims, such substantiation will often require competent and reliable scientific evidence. For any test, analysis, research, study or other evidence to be "competent and reliable" for purposes of these guides, it must be conducted and evaluated in an objective manner by persons qualified to do so, using procedures accepted in the profession, to yield accurate and reliable results. Further guidance on the reasonable basis standard is set

---

* [Und]Cliffdale Associates, Inc. [und], 103 F.T.C. 110, at 176, 176 n.7, n.8, Appendix, [und]reprinting[und] letter dated Oct. 14, 1983, from the Commission to the Honorable John D. Dingell, Chairman, Committee on Energy and Commerce, U.S. House of Representatives (1984) ("Deception Statement").

forth in the Commission's *1983 Policy Statement on the Advertising Substantiation Doctrine*. 49 Fed. Reg. 30,999 (1984); *appended to Thompson Medical Co.*, 104 F.T.C. 648 (1984). These guides, therefore, attempt to preview Commission policy in a relatively new context—that of environmental claims.

F. GENERAL PRINCIPLES:

The following general principles apply to all environmental marketing claims, including, but not limited to, those described in Part G below. In addition, Part G contains specific guidance applicable to certain environmental marketing claims. Claims should comport with all relevant provisions of these guides, not simply the provision that seems most directly applicable.

1. Qualifications and Disclosures: The Commission traditionally has held that in order to be effective, any qualifications or disclosures such as those described in these guides should be sufficiently clear and prominent to prevent deception. Clarity of language, relative type size and proximity to the claim being qualified, and an absence of contrary claims that could undercut effectiveness, will maximize the likelihood that the qualifications and disclosures are appropriately clear and prominent.

2. Distinction Between Benefits of Product and Package: An environmental marketing claim should be presented in a way that makes clear whether the environmental attribute or benefit being asserted refers to the product, the product's packaging or to a portion or component of the product or packaging. In general, if the environmental attribute or benefit applies to all but minor, incidental components of a product or package, the claim need not be qualified to identify that fact. There may be exceptions to this general principle. For example, if an unqualified "recyclable" claim is made and the presence of the incidental component significantly limits ability to recycle the product, then the claim would be deceptive.

> *Example 1:* A box of aluminum foil is labeled with the claim "recyclable," without further elaboration. Unless the type of product, surrounding language, or other context of the phrase establishes whether the claim refers to the foil or the box, the claim is deceptive if any part of either the box or the foil, other than minor, incidental components, cannot be recycled.

Example 2: A soft drink bottle is labeled "recycled." The bottle is made entirely from recycled materials, but the bottle cap is not. Because reasonable consumers are likely to consider the bottle cap to be a minor, incidental component of the package, the claim is not deceptive. Similarly, it would not be deceptive to label a shopping bag "recycled" where the bag is made entirely of recycled material but the easily detachable handle, an incidental component, is not.

3. Overstatement of Environmental Attribute: An environmental marketing claim should not be presented in a manner that overstates the environmental attribute or benefit, expressly or by implication. Marketers should avoid implications of significant environmental benefits if the benefit is in fact negligible.

Example 1: A package is labeled, "50 percent more recycled content than before." The manufacturer has increased the recycled content of its package from 2 percent recycled material to 3 percent recycled material. Although the claim is technically true, it is likely to convey the false impression that the advertiser has increased the use of recycled material significantly.

Example 2: A trash bag is labeled "recyclable" without qualification. Because trash bags will ordinarily not be separated out from other trash at the landfill or incinerator for recycling, they are highly unlikely to be used again for any purpose. Even if the bag is technically capable of being recycled, the claim is deceptive since it asserts an environmental benefit where no significant or meaningful benefit exists.

Example 3: A paper grocery sack is labeled "reusable." The sack can be brought back to the store and reused for carrying groceries but will fall apart after two or three reuses, on average. Because reasonable consumers are unlikely to assume that a paper grocery sack is durable, the unqualified claim does not overstate the environmental benefit conveyed to consumers. The claim is not deceptive and does not need to be qualified to indicate the limited reuse of the sack.

4. Comparative Claims: Environmental marketing claims that include a comparative statement should be presented in a manner that makes the basis for the comparison sufficiently clear to avoid consumer deception. In addition, the advertiser should be able to substantiate the comparison.

Example 1: An advertiser notes that its shampoo bottle contains "20 percent more recycled content." The claim in this context is ambiguous. Depending on contextual factors, it could be a comparison either to the advertiser's immediately preceding product or to a competitor's product. The advertiser should clarify the claim to make the basis for comparison clear, for example, by saying "20 percent more recycled content than our previous package." Otherwise, the advertiser should be prepared to substantiate whatever comparison is conveyed to reasonable consumers.

Example 2: An advertiser claims that "our plastic diaper liner has the most recycled content." The advertised diaper does have more recycled content, calculated as a percentage of weight, than any other on the market, although it is still well under 100 percent recycled. Provided the recycled content and the comparative difference between the product and those of competitors are significant and provided the specific comparison can be substantiated, the claim is not deceptive.

Example 3: An ad claims that the advertiser's packaging creates "less waste than the leading national brand." The advertiser's source reduction was implemented sometime ago and is supported by a calculation comparing the relative solid waste contributions of the two packages. The advertiser should be able to substantiate that the comparison remains accurate.

G. ENVIRONMENTAL MARKETING CLAIMS:

Guidance about the use of environmental marketing claims is set forth in the following. Each guide is followed by several examples that illustrate, but do not provide an exhaustive list of, claims that do and do not comport with the guides. In each case, the general principles set forth in Part F above should also be followed.*

1. General Environmental Benefit Claims: It is deceptive to misrepresent, directly or by implication, that a product or package offers a general environmental benefit. Unqualified general claims of environmental benefit are difficult to interpret, and depending on their context, may convey a wide

---

* These guides do not address claims based on a "life cycle" theory of environmental benefit. Such analyses are still in their infancy and thus the Commission lacks sufficient information on which to base guidance at this time.

range of meanings to consumers. In many cases, such claims may convey that the product or package has specific and far-reaching environmental benefits. As explained in the Commission's Ad Substantiation Statement, every express and material implied claim that the general assertion conveys to reasonable consumers about an objective quality, feature, or attribute of a product must be substantiated. Unless this substantiation duty can be met, broad environmental claims should either be avoided or qualified, as necessary, to prevent deception about the specific nature of the environmental benefit being asserted.

Example 1: A brand name like "Eco-Safe" would be deceptive if, in the context of the product so named, it leads consumers to believe that the product has environmental benefits that cannot be substantiated by the manufacturer. The claim would not be deceptive if "Eco-Safe" were followed by clear and prominent qualifying language limiting the safety representation to a particular product attribute for which it could be substantiated, and provided that no other deceptive implications were created by the context.

Example 2: A product wrapper is printed with the claim "environmentally friendly." Textual comments on the wrapper explain that the wrapper is "environmentally friendly because it is not chlorine bleached, a process that has been shown to create harmful substances." The wrapper is, in fact, not bleached with chlorine. However, the production of the wrapper now creates and releases to the environment significant quantities of other harmful substances. Since consumers are likely to interpret the "environmentally friendly" claim, in combination with the textual explanation to mean that no significant harmful substances are currently released to the environment, the "environmentally friendly" claim would be deceptive.

Example 3: A pump spray product is labeled "environmentally safe." Most of the product's active ingredients consist of volatile organic compounds (VOCs) that may cause smog by contributing to ground-level ozone formation. The claim is deceptive because, absent further qualification, it is likely to convey to consumers that use of the product will not result in air pollution or other harm to the environment.

2. *Degradable/Biodegradable/Photodegradable:* It is deceptive to misrepresent, directly or by implication, that a product or package is degradable, biodegradable, or photodegradable. An unqualified claim that a product or package is degradable, biodegradable or photodegradable should be substantiated by competent and reliable scientific evidence that the entire product or package will completely break down and return to nature—decompose into elements found in nature within a reasonably short period of time after customary disposal.

Claims of degradability, biodegradability, or photodegradability should be qualified to the extent necessary to avoid consumer deception about: (a) the product or package's ability to degrade in the environment where it is customarily disposed; and (b) the rate and extent of degradation.

Example 1: A trash bag is marketed as "degradable," with no qualification or other disclosure. The marketer relies on soil burial tests to show that the product will decompose in the presence of water and oxygen. The trash bags are customarily disposed of in incineration facilities or at sanitary landfills that are managed in a way that inhibits degradation by minimizing moisture and oxygen. Degradation will be irrelevant for those trash bags that are incinerated and, for those disposed of in landfills, the marketer does not possess adequate substantiation that the bags will degrade in a reasonably short period of time in a landfill. The claim is therefore deceptive.

Example 2: A commercial agricultural plastic mulch film is advertised as "photodegradable" and qualifies with the phrase, "will break down into small pieces if left uncovered in sunlight." The claim is supported by competent and reliable scientific evidence that the product will break down in a reasonably short period of time after being exposed to sunlight and into sufficiently small pieces to become part of the soil. The qualified claim is not deceptive. Because the claim is qualified to indicate the limited extent of breakdown, the advertiser need not meet the elements for an unqualified photodegradable claim—in other words, that the product will not only break down, but also will decompose into elements found in nature.

Example 3: A soap or shampoo product is advertised as "biodegradable," with no qualification or other disclosure. The manufacturer has competent and reliable scientific evidence demonstrating that the product, which is customarily disposed of in sewage system, will break down and decompose into elements found in nature in a short period of time. The claim is not deceptive.

3. Compostable: It is deceptive to misrepresent, directly or by implication, that a product or package is compostable. An unqualified claim that a product or package is compostable should be substantiated by competent and reliable scientific evidence that all the materials in the product or package will break down into, or otherwise become part of, usable compost (for example, soil-conditioning material, mulch) in a safe and timely manner in an appropriate composting program or facility, or in a home compost pile or device.

Claims of compostability should be qualified to the extent necessary to avoid consumer deception. An unqualified claim may be deceptive: (1) if municipal composting facilities are not available to a substantial majority of consumers or communities where the package is sold; (2) if the claim misleads consumers about the environmental benefit provided when the product is disposed of in a landfill; or (3) if consumers misunderstand the claim to mean that the package can be composted safely in their home compost pile or device, when in fact it cannot.

Example 1: A manufacturer indicates that its unbleached coffee filter is compostable. The unqualified claim is not deceptive provided the manufacturer can substantiate that the filter can be converted safely to usable compost in a timely manner in a home compost pile or device, as well as in an appropriate composting program or facility.

Example 2: A lawn and leaf bag is labeled as "Compostable in California Municipal Yard Waste Composting Facilities." The bag contains toxic ingredients that are released into the compost material as the bag breaks down. The claim is deceptive if the presence of these toxic ingredients prevents the compost from being usable.

Example 3: A manufacturer indicates that its paper plate is suitable for home composting. If the manufacturer possesses substantiation for claiming that the paper plate can be converted safely to usable compost in a home compost pile or device, this claim is not deceptive even if no municipal composting facilities exist.

Example 4: A manufacturer makes an unqualified claim that its package is compostable. Although municipal composting facilities exist where the product is sold, the package will not break down into usable compost in a home compost pile or device. To avoid deception, the manufacturer should disclose that the package is not suitable for home composting.

Example 5: A nationally marketed lawn and leaf bag is labeled "compostable." Also printed on the bag is a disclosure that the bag is not designed for use in home compost piles. The bags are, in fact, composted in municipal yard waste composting programs in many communities around the country, but such programs are not available to a substantial majority of consumers where the bag is sold. The claim is deceptive since reasonable consumers living in areas not served by municipal yard waste programs may understand the reference to mean that composting facilities accepting the bags are available in their area. To avoid deception, the claim should be qualified to indicate the limited availability of such programs, for example, by stating, "Appropriate facilities may not exist in your area." Other examples of adequate qualification of the claim include providing the approximate percentage of communities or the population for which such programs are available.

Example 6: A manufacturer sells a disposable diaper that bears the legend, "This diaper can be composted where municipal solid waste composting facilities exist. There are currently [X number of] municipal solid waste composting facilities across the country." The claim is not deceptive, assuming that composting facilities are available as claimed and the manufacturer can substantiate that the diaper can be converted safely to usable compost in municipal solid waste composting facilities.

Example 7: A manufacturer markets yard waste bags only to consumers residing in particular geographic areas served by county yard waste composting programs. The bag meets specifications for these programs and is labeled, "Compostable Yard Waste Bag for County Composting Programs." The claim is not deceptive. Because the bags are compostable where they are sold, no qualification is required to indicate the limited availability of composting facilities.

4. Recyclable: It is deceptive to misrepresent, directly or by implication, that a product or package is recyclable. A product or package should not be marketed as recyclable unless it can be collected, separated or otherwise recovered from the solid waste stream for use in the form of raw materials in the manufacture or assembly of a new package or product. Unqualified claims of recyclability for a product or package may be made if the entire product or package, excluding minor incidental components, is recyclable. For products or packages that are made of both recyclable and non-recyclable components, the recyclable claim should be qualified adequately to avoid consumer deception about which portions or components of the product or package are recyclable.

Claims of recyclability should be qualified to the extent necessary to avoid consumer deception about any limited availability of recycling programs and collection sites. If an incidental component significantly limits the ability to recycle the product, the claim would be deceptive. A product or package that is made from recyclable material, but, because of its shape, size or some other attribute, is not accepted in recycling programs for such material, should not be marketed as recyclable.

Example 1: A packaged product is labeled with an unqualified claim, "recyclable." It is unclear from the type of product and other context whether the claim refers to the product or its package. The unqualified claim is likely to convey to reasonable consumers that all of both the product and its packaging that remain after normal use of the product, except for minor, incidental components, can be recycled. Unless each such message can be substantiated, the claim should be qualified to indicate which portions are recyclable.

Example 2: A plastic package is labeled on the bottom with the Society of the Plastics Industry (SPI) code, consisting of a design of arrows in a triangular shape containing a number and abbreviation identifying the component plastic resin. Without more, the use of the SPI symbol (or similar industry codes) on the bottom of the package, or in a similarly inconspicuous location, does not constitute a claim of recyclability.

Example 3: A container can be burned in incinerator facilities to produce heat and power. It cannot, however, be recycled into new products or packaging. Any claim that the container is recyclable would be deceptive.

Example 4: A nationally marketed bottle bears the unqualified statement that it is "recyclable." Collection sites for recycling the material in question are not available to a substantial majority of consumers or communities, although collection sites are established in a significant percentage of communities or available to a significant percentage of the population. The unqualified claim is deceptive since, unless evidence shows otherwise, reasonable consumers living in communities not served by programs may conclude that recycling programs for the material are available in their area. To avoid deception, the claim should be qualified to indicate that limited availability of programs, for example, by stating, "Check to see if recycling facilities exist in your area." Other examples of adequate qualifications of the claim include providing the approximate percentage of communities or the population to whom programs are available.

Example 5: A soda bottle is marketed nationally and labeled, "recyclable where facilities exist." Recycling programs for material of this type and size are available in a significant percentage of communities or to a significant percentage of the population, but are not available to a substantial majority of consumers. The claim is deceptive since, unless evidence shows otherwise, reasonable consumers living in communities not served by programs may understand this phrase to mean that programs are available in their area. To avoid deception, the claim should be further qualified to indicate the limited availability of programs, for example, by using any of the approaches set forth in Example 4 above.

Example 6: A plastic detergent bottle is marketed as follows: "recyclable in the few communities with facilities for colored HDPE bottles." Collection sites for recycling the container have been established in a half-dozen major metropolitan areas. This disclosure illustrates one approach to qualifying a claim adequately to prevent deception about the limited availability of recycling programs where collection facilities are not established in a significant percentage of communities or available to a significant percentage of the population. Other examples of adequate qualification of the claim include providing the number of communities with programs, or the percentage of communities or the population to which programs are available.

Example 7: A label claims that the package "includes some recyclable material." The package is composed of four layers of different materials, bonded together. One of the layers is made from the recyclable material, but the others are not. While programs for recycling this type of material are available to a substantial majority of consumers, only a few of those programs have the capability to separate out the recyclable layer. Even though it is technologically possible to separate the layers, the claim is not adequately qualified to avoid consumer deception. An appropriately qualified claim would be, "includes material recyclable in the few communities that collect multilayer products." Other examples of adequate qualification of the claim include providing the number of communities with programs, or the percentage of communities or the population to which programs are available.

Example 8: A product is marketed as having a "recyclable" container. The product is distributed and advertised in Missouri only. Collection sites for recycling the container are available to a substantial majority of Missouri residents, but are not yet available nationally. Because programs are generally available where the product is marketed, the unqualified claim does not deceive consumers about the limited availability of recycling programs.

5. Recycled Content: A recycled content claim may be made only for materials that have been recovered or otherwise diverted from the solid waste stream, either during the manufacturing process (pre-consumer), or after consumer use (post-consumer). To the extent the source of recycled content includes pre-consumer material, the manufacturer or advertiser must have substantiation for concluding that the pre-consumer material would otherwise have entered the solid waste stream. In asserting a recycled content claim, distinctions may be made between pre-consumer and post-consumer materials. Where such distinctions are asserted, any express or implied claim about the specific pre-consumer or post-consumer content of a product or package must be substantiated.

It is deceptive to misrepresent, directly or by implication, that a product or package is made of recycled material. Unqualified claims of recycled content may be made only if the entire product or package, excluding minor, incidental components, is made from recycled material. For products or packages that are only partially made of recycled material, a recycled claim should be qualified adequately to avoid consumer deception about the amount, by weight of recycled content in the finished product or package.

Example 1: A manufacturer routinely collects spilled raw material and scraps from trimming finished products. After a minimal amount of reprocessing, the manufacturer combines the spills and scraps with virgin material for use in further production of the same product. A claim that the product contains recycled material is deceptive since the spills and scraps to which the claim refers are normally reused by industry with the original manufacturing process, and would not normally have entered the waste stream.

Example 2: A manufacturer purchases material from a firm that collects discarded material from other manufacturers and resells it. All of the material has been diverted from the solid waste stream and is not normally reused by industry within the original manufacturing process. The manufacturer includes the weight of this material in its calculations of the recycled content of its products. A claim of recycled content based on this calculation is not deceptive because, absent the purchase and reuse of this material, it would have entered the waste stream.

Example 3: A greeting card is composed 30 percent by weight of paper collected from consumers after use of a paper product, and 20 percent by weight of paper that was generated after completion of the paper-making process, diverted from the solid waste stream, and otherwise would not normally have been reused in the original manufacturing process. The marketer of the card may claim either that the product "contains 50 percent recycled material," or may identify the specific pre-consumer and/or post-consumer content by stating, for example, that the product "contains 50 percent total recycled material, 30 percent of which is post-consumer material."

Example 4: A package with 20 percent recycled content by weight is labeled as containing "20 percent recycled paper." Some of the recycled content was composed of material collected from consumers after use of the original product. The rest was composed of overrun newspaper stock never sold to customers. The claim is not deceptive.

Example 5: A product in a multicomponent package, such as a paperboard box in a shrink-wrapped plastic cover, indicates that it has recycled packaging. The paperboard box is made entirely of recycled material, but the plastic cover is not. The claim is deceptive since, without qualification, it suggests that both components are recycled. A claim limited to the paperboard box would not be deceptive.

Example 6: A package is made from layers of foil, plastic, and paper laminated together, although the layers are indistinguishable to consumers. The label claims that "one of the three layers of this package is made of recycled plastic." The plastic layer is made entirely of recycled plastic. The claim is not deceptive provided the recycled plastic layer constitutes a significant component of the entire package.

Example 7: A paper product is labeled as containing "100 percent recycled fiber." The claim is not deceptive if the advertiser can substantiate the conclusion that 100 percent by weight of the fiber in the finished product is recycled.

Example 8: A frozen dinner is marketed in a package composed of a cardboard box over a plastic tray. The package bears the legend, "package made from 30 percent recycled material." Each packaging component amounts to one-half the weight of the total package. The box is 20 percent recycled content by weight, while the plastic tray is 40 percent recycled content by weight. The claim is not deceptive, since the average amount of recycled material is 30 percent.

Example 9: A paper greeting card is labeled as containing 50 percent by weight recycled content. The seller purchases paper stock from several sources and the amount of recycled material in the stock provided by each source varies. Because the 50 percent figure is based on the annual weighted average of recycled material purchased from the sources after accounting for fiber loss during the production process, the claim is permissible.

6. Source Reduction: It is deceptive to misrepresent, directly or by implication, that a product or package has been reduced or is lower in weight, volume, or toxicity. Source-reduction claims should be qualified to the extent necessary to avoid consumer deception about the amount of the source reduction and about the basis for any comparison asserted.

Example 1: An ad claims that solid waste created by disposal of the advertiser's packaging is "now 10 percent less than our previous package." The claim is not deceptive if the advertiser has substantiation that shows that disposal of the current package contributes 10 percent less waste by weight or volume to the solid waste stream when compared with the immediately preceding version of the package.

Example 2: An advertiser notes that disposal of its product generates "10 percent less waste." The claim is ambiguous. Depending on contextual factors, it could be a comparison either to the immediately preceding product or to a competitor's product. The "10 percent less waste" reference is deceptive unless the seller clarifies which comparison is intended and substantiates that comparison, or substantiates both possible interpretations of the claim.

7. Refillable: It is deceptive to misrepresent, directly or by implication, that a package is refillable. An unqualified refillable claim should not be asserted unless a system is provided for: (1) the collection and return of the package for refill; or (2) the later refill of the package by consumers with product subsequently sold in another package. A package should not be marketed with an unqualified refillable claim if it is up to the consumer to find new ways to refill the package.

Example 1: A container is labeled "refillable x times." The manufacturer has the capability to refill returned containers and can show that the container will withstand being refilled at least x times. The manufacturer, however, has established no collection program. The unqualified claim is deceptive because there is no means for collection and return of the container to the manufacturer for refill.

Example 2: A bottle of fabric softener states that it is in a "handy refillable container." The manufacturer also sells a large-sized container that indicates that the consumer is expected to use it to refill the smaller container. The manufacturer sells the large-sized container in the same market areas where it sells the small container. The claim is not deceptive because there is a means for consumers to refill the smaller container from larger containers of the same product.

8. *Ozone Safe and Ozone Friendly:* It is deceptive to misrepresent, directly or by implication, that a product is safe for or "friendly" to the ozone layer. A claim that a product does not harm the ozone layer is deceptive if the product contains an ozone-depleting substance.

Example 1: A product is labeled "ozone friendly." The claim is deceptive if the product contains any ozone-depleting substance, including those substances listed as Class I or Class II chemicals in Title VI of the Clean Air Act Amendments of 1990, Pub. L. No. 101-549, or others subsequently designated by EPA as ozone-depleting substances. Class I chemicals currently listed in Title VI are chlorofluorocarbons (CFCs), halons, carbon tetrachloride and 1,1,1-trichloroethane. Class II chemicals currently listed in Title VI are hydrochlorofluorocarbons (HCFCs).

Example 2: The seller of an aerosol product makes an unqualified claim that its product "Contains no CFCs." Although the product does not contain CFCs, it does contain HCFC–22, another ozone depleting ingredient. Because the claim "Contains no CFCs" may imply to reasonable consumers that the product does not harm the ozone layer, the claim is deceptive.

Example 3: A product is labeled "This product is 95 percent less damaging to the ozone layer than past formulations that contained CFCs." The manufacturer has substituted HCFCs for CFC–12, and can substantiate that this substitution will result in 95 percent less ozone depletion. The qualified comparative claim is not likely to be deceptive.

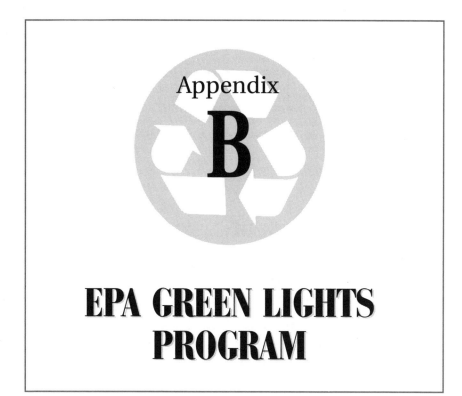

Appendix B

EPA GREEN LIGHTS PROGRAM

United States Environmental Protection Agency
Air and Radiation 6202J
EPA 430–F–92–013, August 1992

A BRIGHT INVESTMENT IN THE ENVIRONMENT

The *U.S. Environmental Protection Agency's (EPA's) Green Lights Program*
is a breath of fresh air for the nation's environmental health and economic
growth. Green Lights, a voluntary program that encourages the widespread
use of energy-efficient lighting, is proving that environment and industry
can work together to create a cost-efficient and environmentally aware
America.

As part of this unique partnership, Green Lights participants—including
corporations, environmental groups, electric utilities, and state, city, and

local governments—have come together to promote the widespread use of efficient lighting systems that reduce pollution. By investing in these technologies, Green Lights participants realize average returns of 25 percent, with average savings in lighting electricity bills of 50 percent or more. Through the use of these technologies, partners are reducing emissions of pollutants associated with global warming, acid rain, and smog.

As the first of similar market-driven, nonregulatory "green" programs sponsored by EPA, Green Lights is revolutionizing the way America cleans up the environment.

ENERGY-EFFICIENT LIGHTING PREVENTS POLLUTION

Increased energy efficiency is the cornerstone of the EPA's new pollution-prevention strategy. Green Lights encourages voluntary reductions in energy use through revolutionary lighting technologies.

The process by which energy-efficient lighting reduces pollution is simple. Lighting accounts for 20–25 percent of electricity used annually in the United States. Lighting for industry, businesses, offices, and warehouses represents 80–90 percent of total lighting electricity use.

Generating electricity involves the burning of fossil fuels or running a nuclear reactor or hydroelectric plant. These processes often result in various types of pollution, including acid mine drainage, oil spills, natural gas leakage, toxic waste, and air pollutants.

Energy-efficient lighting can reduce lighting electricity demand by over 50 percent, thereby enabling the power plant to burn less fuel. It is estimated that every kilowatt-hour of electricity avoided prevents the emission of 1.5 pounds of carbon dioxide, 5.8 grams of sulfur dioxide, and 2.5 grams of nitrogen oxides. It also reduces other types of pollution resulting from mining and transporting power plant fuels and disposing of power plant wastes.

If energy-efficient lighting were used everywhere profitable, the nation's demand for electricity could be cut by more than 10 percent. This would result in reductions of annual carbon dioxide emissions of 202 million metric tons (4 percent of the national total)—the equivalent of the exhaust emitted from 44 million cars. Reductions in annual emissions of sulfur dioxide would total 1.3 million metric tons (7 percent of the national total), and reductions in annual emissions of nitrogen oxides would amount to 600,000 metric tons (4 percent of the national total). By the year 2000, Green Lights is expected to save 226.4 billion kWh, resulting in total electricity demand savings of 39.8 million kilowatts.

Tackling the Barriers to Innovation

One goal of Green Lights is to encourage widespread use of lighting technologies that use less energy. In doing so, Green Lights endeavors to reduce air pollution while redirecting dollars toward profitable investment. Indeed, if energy-efficient lighting technologies are used nationwide, they will reduce electricity bills by $16 billion per year.

Although the market is encouraging the use of energy-efficient lighting technologies, Green Lights is designed to tackle the barriers that impede the widespread use of these technologies.

Common Problems	The Green Lights Solution
Lighting Is a Low Priority—Few organizations focus on the opportunity to invest in their own lighting systems.	*Green Lights* participants see lighting as an investment—a source of profits. Signing the MOU makes lighting an organizational priority.
Lack of Information and Expertise —Lighting information travels slowly outside the world of the lighting industry.	*Green Lights* provides informational tools to help lighting investors make an informed upgrade decision.
Difficult Financing—Investments in energy-efficient lighting require up-front capital.	*Green Lights* has developed a registry of financing resources available free of charge to all Green Lights participants.
Restricted Markets—Low demand for energy-efficient lighting technologies results in lack of consumer understanding about potential cost savings and enhanced lighting. Prices remain high due to small production runs.	*Green Lights* promotes energy-efficient lighting technologies as cost-effective and high-quality products to consumers, and informs manufacturers about benefits of investing in new technologies.
Split Incentives Between Landlord and Tenant—To realize savings from a lighting upgrade, each tenant must renegotiate the lease with the landlord. The landlord rarely installs energy-efficient lighting in new construction, since utility charges are passed on to tenant.	*Green Lights* is developing a standard lease language that removes the split incentive barrier between landlord and tenant.

EPA'S GREEN LIGHTS PROGRAM SUMMARY

The Environmental Protection Agency's Green Lights Program was official-ly launched on January 16, 1991. The program's goal has been to prevent pollution by encouraging major U.S. institutions—businesses, governments, and other organizations—to use energy-efficient lighting. Because lighting is such a large consumer of electricity (about 25 percent of the national total) and so wasteful (more than half the electricity used for lighting is wasted by inefficient technology and design practices), the Green Lights Program offers a substantial opportunity to prevent pollution, and to do so at *profit*. Lighting upgrades reduce electric bills and maintenance costs and increase lighting quality; typically, investments in energy-efficient lighting yield 20 to 30 percent rates of return (IRR) per year.

EPA promotes energy-efficient lighting by asking major institutions to sign a Memorandum of Understanding (MOU) with the Agency; in this MOU, the signatory commits to install energy-efficient lighting in 90 per-cent of its space nationwide over a 5-year period, but only where it is *prof-itable* and where lighting *quality* is maintained or improved. The EPA, in turn, offers program participants a portfolio of technical support services to assist them in upgrading their buildings (see below). Sample MOUs are available upon request.

Every kilowatt-hour of electricity not used prevents the emission of 1.5 pounds of carbon dioxide (the most important greenhouse gas), 5.8 grams of sulfur dioxide (a principal component of acid rain), and 2.5 grams of nitro-gen oxides (precursor to both acid rain and smog), as well as the pollution attendant upon mining and transporting power-plant fuels and disposing of power-plant wastes.

If energy-efficient lighting were used wherever profitable, the nation's demand for electricity could be cut by more than 10 percent, leading to 4 to 7 percent reductions in the emissions of carbon dioxide, sulfur dioxide, and nitrogen oxides. In terms of carbon dioxide, energy-efficient lighting offers the same pollution-prevention opportunity as taking 42 million cars off the road, the equivalent of one-third of the U.S. fleet.

EPA's Commitments

When the EPA signs the *Memorandum of Understanding,* it agrees to pro-vide Decision Support System—a state-of-the-art computer software pro-gram that allows Green Lights corporations to survey lighting systems in their facilities, assess their options, and select the best energy-efficient light-ing upgrades.

Training Workshops—programs, scheduled nationwide, that feature comprehensive training on the Decision Support System as well as lighting fundamentals, technology, project management, and Green Lights reporting.

National Lighting Product Information Program—an independent lighting information program that provides an objective source of name-brand product information.

Financing Registries—computer databases containing information on utility-sponsored financial assistance (for example, auditing and technical support, lighting design services, free installation, rebates, and loans), energy-service company programs, and government grants and low-interest loans.

Lighting Services Group—offers technical support, problem solving, and training for Green Lights participants installing energy-efficient lighting.

Corporate Communications—advertising and marketing materials designed to recognize participants for their commitment to the program and to keep them informed.

Ally Programs—individual programs designed for manufacturers, lighting management companies, and utilities to ensure that the lighting industry is involved in the program and aware of the environmental and economic benefits of Green Lights.

Partner's Commitments

When a Green Lights Partner signs the *Memorandum of Understanding,* it agrees to

- Appoint an implementation manager to coordinate the program.
- Survey the lighting in all of its U.S. facilities.
- Consider a full range of lighting options to reduce energy use.
- Upgrade 90 percent of the square footage of its facilities with the options that maximize energy savings to the extent that the upgrade is profitable and does not compromise lighting quality. There are no technology prescriptions.
- Complete upgrades within 5 years of signing the agreement.
- Annually document the improvements it makes.
- Design all new facilities to meet most current building efficiency standards.
- Educate its employees about the benefits of energy-efficient lighting.

When companies sign the Green Lights *Memorandum of Understanding*, they agree to upgrade their facilities with energy-efficient lighting. In return, the EPA commits to provide a wide variety of products and services designed to make the job easier. Over the program's first year, the EPA has delivered on every one of its commitments.

WHY GREEN LIGHTS?

An often-asked question runs, "If energy-efficient lighting is so profitable, and is so good for the environment, and delivers such superior lighting quality, why does the Federal Government have to get involved?" The answer lies in the haze between the ideals of economics and the reality of lighting today. Energy-efficient lighting technologies, design practices, and maintenance systems evolve over decades (if not centuries, if one considers the evolution from the open fire to the candle to the oil lamp to Edison's light bulb), and market penetration is often slow. The energy-efficient lighting technologies and design principals available today were introduced 5 to 10 years ago but have been rarely used, typically capturing between 1 and 5 percent of the market. There are six principal barriers, and Green Lights is attacking all of them:

Problem—Low Priority: Lighting is not a high priority for the vast majority of U.S. institutions. Typically the province of facility management, lighting is viewed as an overhead item. Because of this, most facilities are equipped with the lowest first-cost (rather than the lowest life-cycle cost) lighting systems, and profitable opportunities to upgrade the system are ignored or passed over in favor of higher visibility projects. As a result, institutions pay needless overhead every year, reducing their own competitiveness and that of the country. Wasteful electricity use becomes a particularly senseless source of pollution.

Solution: By signing the Green Lights *Memorandum of Understanding*, a corporation's senior management makes clear that energy-efficient lighting is now one of the business' high priorities. Authority is granted, budgets are approved, procedures are streamlined, and staff are assigned to make the upgrades happen.

Problem—Information and Expertise: Lighting is more complex than screwing in a light bulb, and the technologies and design strategies are diverse and sometimes complex. To arrive at an energy-efficient lighting solution for a particular space requires accurate, comparable information about dozens of lighting technologies, design ability, and an investor's eye for long-term profit. Unfortunately, information is often scarce or suspect, design is frequently overlooked in favor of "cookie-cutter" solutions, and few institutions focus on lighting as a profit (rather than cost) center.

Solution: Green Lights has created the institutions and tools to help overcome these barriers.

On November 4, 1991, Green Lights released its Lighting Decision Support System, the most sophisticated lighting survey and economic analysis software available. The system allows a building surveyor to rapidly inventory the current lighting system and choose from the more than thousand different upgrade options to find the system that will be most energy-efficient. The financial analysis is done on a life-cycle basis and allows the user to capture all relevant streams of costs and benefits, including taxes and depreciation, operation and maintenance expenses, and the potential benefits of improved lighting quality. The software is offered to Green Lights participants free of charge at a series of training workshops held twice a month around the country.

A second institution created by Green Lights is the National Lighting Product Information Program (NLPIP), based at Rensselaer Polytechnic Institute's Lighting Research Center. NLPIP produces name-brand reports on lighting hardware, covering dozens of manufacturers and models. All data are gathered using standardized procedures and allow direct comparison among competing products for *all* relevant performance characteristics. These reports are sent free of charge to all Green Lights participants.

Green Lights is also working with several lighting professional societies to build a national certification program for lighting professionals. This will permit individuals with true expertise in lighting to demonstrate their skills and distinguish themselves in the marketplace.

Problem—Financing: In existing buildings, the lighting system is usually working, and any improvements are viewed traditionally as an expense, despite the fact that they are actually an investment that is frequently more profitable, and lower risk, than any other investment the company might make. Even where lighting investments are demonstrably more lucrative than other investments, companies will sometimes have different "hurdle rates" for different kinds of investments—a low one for core business investments, and a higher one (paradoxically) for lower-risk cost-cutting investments. Smaller businesses and governmental agencies frequently have no capital to spare for any cost-cutting investment and accept paying a higher operating overhead year after year.

Solution: Green Lights has developed a unique registry of financing resources. First offered in February 1991, it has since been updated twice. The registry provides detailed information on more than 200 utility programs that offer lighting rebates and free installations to their customers. It also provides a directory of more than 75 companies that can finance lighting efficiency upgrades using leasing, shared savings, guaranteed savings, and other financing techniques. The registry is provided free of charge to all Green Lights participants.

Problem—Restricted Market: Because energy-efficient lighting has captured only a tiny fraction of the overall lighting market, unit prices have often been high compared with the "garden variety" of products they replace. When new technology is introduced, R&D costs and new factories have to be amortized, and the unit marketing costs for low-volume products further raises the price. Distributors are often reluctant to reserve valuable shelf space for slower-moving products. Innovators are slow to introduce new technology. As a result, energy-efficient lighting hardware has remained expensive, further slowing its penetration in the marketplace.

Solution: Green Lights. The program is catalyzing a rapidly increasing demand for energy-efficient lighting products, with visible impacts on shipment volumes and prices. New competitors are entering the market, bringing innovative technologies and further price and service competition. Green Lights and other lighting efficiency programs are projected to increase the market share of energy-efficient lighting products from its current 5 percent to around 40 percent by 1995. Prices of some products have already been falling (by as much as 25 percent in the last 12 months) and are expected to continue declining as shipment volumes increase.

Problem—Split Incentives: There is often no incentive to upgrade lighting systems. For example, a typical lease in a master-metered building requires the tenant to pay a fixed rent, which includes a pro-rata share of the building's utility charges. If the tenant wants to upgrade the lighting system and reduce his or her electricity consumption, the lease would need renegotiation to allow pass-through of the savings. In addition, without direct metering, it is difficult to validate the exact amount of savings due to the tenant. Conversely, with all the utility charges passed through the tenants, the landlord rarely sees it in his or her interest to install more efficient lighting systems when the building is first built. Instead, the lowest first-cost system is chosen.

Solution: Green Lights has initiated a project to develop standard lease language that will remove the split incentive barrier, and the program will encourage participants to use the model language in lease negotiations. The program is also working to accelerate the adoption of submetering by encouraging Partners to submeter their lighting upgrades.

Problem—Market Fragmentation: Buyers and sellers of lighting equipment and services often have trouble communicating. Most lighting manufacturers produce and market only one kind of product: lamps, ballasts, fixtures, and so on. Lighting purchasers need *systems* composed of many different products and need "system thinking" from their vendors. Vendors, in turn, are frustrated by the low priority assigned to lighting by most major businesses and by their lack of understanding of the importance of good lighting.

Solution: The Green Lights Allies programs. Green Lights Allies are members of the lighting manufacturing and service industries as well as electric utilities who join Green Lights on terms very similar to those of the Green Lights Partners. However, in addition to committing to upgrade their facilities, Green Lights Allies also commit to help the EPA and the Green Lights Partners successfully implement the program. Allies have delivered on this commitment in a variety of ways: recruiting new Partners, providing data to the National Lighting Product Information Program, helping to design the Decision Support System, and advertising their membership in an allegiance to the principals of the Green Lights Program. While Green Lights does not endorse the products or services of the Green Lights Allies, the existence of the program has enhanced communication throughout the lighting industry on the subjects of energy efficiency, environmental protection, and lighting quality.

PROGRAM HIGHLIGHTS

Recruitment

Green Lights is a voluntary program. As such, the program must *persuade* lighting users that energy-efficient lighting is good for the environment, good for the bottom line, and a good opportunity to work in cooperation with the EPA. The program office has used a variety of marketing tools to recruit new members to Green Lights.

Conferences: Green Lights has conducted three large marketing conferences in 1991 (Washington in January; Portland, Oregon in May; and Atlanta in July), attended by representatives of 600 corporations.

Direct Visits: Green Lights staff has visited dozens of corporate and governmental headquarters, a process that accelerated with the inauguration of a full-time travelling sales campaign in October 1991.

Telemarketing: Starting in July 1991, the program office built a telemarketing system, complete with the latest telemarketing software, to assist in selling the program to the 8,000 contacts stored in the program's marketing database.

Mass Communication: Green Lights is increasingly using advertising and news coverage to reach a broader audience. More than a hundred Green Lights news stories have appeared in dozens of media outlets, and Green Lights advertising (sponsored by the program office or by program participants) is increasingly visible in the popular, business, and trade press. Green Lights advertising has appeared in the Portland *Oregonian*, the *Atlanta Constitution* and *Journal*, *Atlanta* magazine, *Business Week*, and *Discover*.

The typical organization takes approximately 4 months to decide to join Green Lights, with some taking up to a year. The process starts with an EPA presentation, a piece of direct mail, an article in a newspaper, or an advertisement in a magazine. Several rounds of visits, telephone contact, and technical support follow, sometimes including a lighting survey of a major facility to validate the savings opportunities available to the potential Partner. It is normal for several different groups within the organization to get involved: facilities management, environmental compliance, energy, finance, strategic planning, public affairs, and so on. Each department may require direct contact with the EPA to ensure that all of its questions and concerns are addressed. The final step is the signing of the *Memorandum of Understanding* by a senior officer and the initiation of the lighting upgrade program.

SCORECARD

On January 31, 1991, Green Lights had 40 participants. As of February 18, 1992, 402 institutions had signed memoranda with the EPA to join Green Lights. This number includes 168 Corporate Partners, 9 Government Partners, 144 Manufacturer Allies, 48 Lighting Management Company Allies, and 27 Electric Utility Allies. In addition, 6 trade and professional organizations have endorsed the program. The program participants collectively own or lease 2 billion square feet of facility space, about 2.5 percent of the national total. This is equivalent to all of the leasable office space of the metropolitan areas of New York City, Los Angeles, Chicago, San Francisco, Washington, D.C., Philadelphia, and Dallas.

IMPLEMENTATION

Green Lights participants have five years to complete their lighting upgrades. The typical plan for most companies has been to use the first year or two to survey buildings, develop expertise, train staff, and acquire budgets. The first two years also include, in most cases, some lighting upgrades; this helps with the training process and allows staff to develop procedures for budgeting, procurement, installation, contracting, reporting, and so on. Years three and four will be the time of major upgrades by Green Lights participants; several are planning national procurements for firms that will supply upgrade materials and installation labor for all facilities.

Green Lights staff and contractors assist participants in implementing the program. The program offers two-day training courses twice a month across the country:

Washington, D.C.	11/91	Chicago	4/92
Ashland, KY	12/91	Oklahoma City	4/92
Los Angeles	12/91	Boston	4/92
New York City	1/92	Raleigh, NC	5/92
New Orleans	1/92	San Francisco	5/92
Nashville	2/92	Boulder	6/92
Washington, D.C.	2/92	New York City	6/92
Tampa, FL	3/92	Seattle	7/92
Washington, D.C.	3/92	Kansas City	7/92

The training courses feature an intensive introduction to energy-efficient lighting, instruction on the use of the Decision Support System software, and ideas on how to be an effective project manager. Green Lights staff and contractors have also conducted more specialized meetings at participants' buildings, either to help perform a lighting survey or to help the company organize its resources to implement Green Lights. The program also operates two hotlines: The Customer Service Center answers general questions about the program and mails out program materials (approximately 2000 envelopes per month), while the Lighting Services Group operates a hotline for Partners with technical questions. Participants also receive a monthly newsletter, the Green Lights *Update*. Finally, the Green Lights Electronic Bulletin Board will come on-line March 2, 1992.

IMPLEMENTATION SCORECARD

Because program participants report their progress on an anniversary basis, the signatory "classes" of January and February 1991 recently reported their upgrade status. Several nonanniversary participants also have submitted interim reports on their progress to date. All told, as of February 23, 1992, 181 buildings were in the officially-reported "upgrade pipeline," covering 77 million square feet of facility space (equivalent to the office and warehouse space of the Baltimore metropolitan area). Forty-nine buildings have been fully upgraded, with a typical reduction in lighting electricity use of 40 to 70 percent.

ALLY PROGRAM HIGHLIGHTS

- Manufacturers Prolights, American Energy Management, and Sylvania Lighting recruited Domino's Pizza, Brach Co., and Westin Hotels, respectively, as Partners. And, at least seven LMC Allies recruited one or more Partners—the biggest being the Melville Corporation, recruited by Mira Lighting and Electric Service.

- Lamp and ballast manufacturers as well as Lighting Management Company Allies provided information for the publication *Survey and Forecast of Marketplace Supply and Demand for Energy-Efficient Lighting Products*.

- Ballast manufacturers cooperated with the Lighting Research Center to produce the first NLPIP *Specifier Report* on ballasts. Reflector and power-reducer manufacturers are now working on future *Specifier Reports*.

- Several Lighting Management Company Allies provided case studies and gave comments on the *Green Lights Lighting Upgrade Manual*.

- Manufacturers and Lighting Management Company Allies sit on the Decision Support System user advisory group. Allies beta-tested the system, and in September, 40 Allies came to a prescreening of the system to review the software and help develop a list of prices for the database.

- Portland General Electric and the EPA sponsored a Green Lights workshop in Portland, Oregon, in May. More than 300 participants representing 200 corporations attended the marketing event. Twenty manufacturers exhibited their technology and services at the Green Lights conference in Atlanta in July, helping to make the event a big success.

- Magnetek developed its own Green Lights brochure and launched its Green Zone program to promote energy-efficient lighting, targeting Green Lights Partners. Other companies (for example, Sylvania Lighting) developed brochures promoting the environmental benefits of energy-efficient lighting, and Lithonia Lighting incorporated Green Lights into their LEEP (Lithonia Energy-Efficiency Program), using the Green Lights logo extensively and distributing Green Lights *Light Briefs*.

- Fifteen LMC Allies advertised their participation in a Green Lights "Special Report" in the September *Building Operating Management* magazine. IllumElex promoted the Green Lights program through its "Business Spotlights" in national newspapers. And O & A Electric Cooperative featured a special Green Lights section in its summer marketing publication "Along Our Highlines."

FIRST-YEAR SUCCESS STORIES

Johnson & Johnson: Charter Member Upgrades 20 Facilities

Johnson & Johnson has been one of the charter members of Green Lights. Under the leadership of Harry Kauffman, Johnson & Johnson's corporate energy manager, the company has comprehensively surveyed more than 1.9 million square feet of corporate space located in New Jersey, Georgia, Massachusetts, California, Pennsylvania, Ohio, and Connecticut. The facilities run the gamut of use: office and administration buildings, manufacturing facilities, warehouses, and research laboratories. Even a parking lot is included.

Lighting upgrades are underway or complete at 20 facilities. These upgrades are responsible for more than $338,000 in annual savings, and internal rates of return (IRRs) range between a low of 17 percent and a high of 120 percent. Just as important is the pollution prevented. The upgrades at these 20 facilities have meant that more than 4.6 million kilowatt-hours per year of electricity use has been avoided.

This is good news for the environment, for it translates into important pollution prevention. Saving more than 4.6 million kilowatt-hours per year means that 7.3 million pounds of carbon dioxide, more than 55,000 pounds of sulfur dioxide, and more than 27,000 pounds of nitrogen oxides are not released into the air. The greenhouse effect, acid rain, and smog are alleviated by serious energy efficiency efforts such as those of Johnson & Johnson.

Johnson & Johnson has been involved in the installation of energy-efficient designs and technologies since the early 1980s. Its efforts over the last year have included installing the latest in lighting technology: occupancy sensors, T8 fluorescent lamps, electronic ballasts, compact fluorescent lamps, dimming devices, and high pressure sodium lamps.

Amoco Corporation: 6,000 Sensors Save $316,413 per Year

The Amoco Corporation, a Green Lights Charter Partner, recently replaced 6,000 light switches with 6,000 occupancy sensors in its

Naperville, Illinois, office and laboratory buildings. Comprising more than 1.2 million square feet, the buildings have been upgraded with the sensors early this year, effecting $316,413 in savings annually and avoiding almost 4.5 million kilowatt-hours per year.

Preston Trucking: Partner Receives Maryland Energy Award

Preston Trucking received the State of Maryland's first Energy Achievement Award from Governor William Donald Schaefer on October 29, 1991. Preston's successful energy conservation program, led by Construction Manager Steve Gay, reduces energy use, establishes an energy education program for company associates, and contributes to an improved environment. The new lighting system at Preston uses 40 percent less energy and will save the company more than $20,000 per year.

Preston changed more than 2,500 40-watt lamps to 32-watt T8 lamps; upgraded 950 fixtures with electronic ballasts; and converted the loading dock's mercury vapor lighting system to high-pressure sodium. The company saves approximately 300,000 kilowatt-hours annually.

Elkhart General Hospital: Upgrade Saves More Than $100,000

Elkhart General Hospital in Elkhart, Indiana, became a Green Lights Partner in June 1991. A relatively small institution, yet with all of the high electricity use associated with hospitals, Elkhart had completed about a third of its upgrade work by the end of August 1991 and was projecting more than $100,000 in annual energy savings. The upgrade included the installation of T8 lamps. compact fluorescents, electronic ballasts, occupancy sensors and timed switches, and reduced light levels where appropriate. Additionally, the reduced heat load has solved some air conditioning problems and there has been a dramatic drop in maintenance costs: an annual maintenance savings of $20,000 is projected.

The Boeing Company: Energy Use in Upgraded Buildings Drops 50 percent

Boeing has upgraded an incredible 4 million square feet since becoming a Green Lights Charter Partner in January 1991. Led by Larry Friedman, energy conservation manager for Boeing Support Services, the company has saved 14 million kilowatt-hours and almost $500,000 already. The energy savings translate into reductions in power plant emissions of 26 million pounds of carbon dioxide, 110,000 pounds of sulfur dioxide, and 70,000 pounds of nitrogen oxides. That's a lot of pollution taken out of our air—and Boeing is just getting started. It has 64 million square feet to go, and it's working on it.

Charter Partners Report Progress

A large number of Green Lights partners who have been in the program for a year are just completing the survey phase of their effort. A combined total of more than 16 million square feet has been surveyed by Browning-Ferris Industries, Yellow Freight Corporation, Whirlpool Corporation, Union Camp Corporation, Joseph E. Seagram & Sons, Texaco, Hasbro, Inc., Gerber Products, and American Standard, Inc.

Other companies are further along. The Oliver Carr Company in Washington, D.C. has upgraded more than 1.3 million square feet through delamping, reballasting, and reflector installation, for an estimated annual savings of $480,000. The LoneStar Steel Company in Texas has upgraded more than 400,000 square feet by replacing mercury vapor lamps with high-pressure sodium lamps and through general delamping. Officials plan to install occupancy sensors and to reduce daily lighting hours in remote facilities from 24 to 3. Wolverine World Wide, Inc., in Michigan has upgraded its exit signs by replacing incandescent lamps with fluorescent. Workers also are installing reflectors in many fixtures.

Warner-Lambert in Morris Plains, New Jersey, has installed almost 3,500 T8 fluorescent lamps, which will yield an annual savings of $190,000. Phillips Petroleum has replaced approximately 16,000 40-watt lamps with 34-watt lamps for an annual savings of $17,000; almost 500 incandescent lamps have been replaced with compact fluorescent lamps, yielding annual savings of $7,000. Additionally, lighting management systems have been installed at 38 locations. American Express in New York has completed 85 percent of a 1.6 million square-foot installation. Annual savings of almost $285,000 will be realized through the use of T8 lamps, reduction in lighting hours, and occupancy sensors.

The Polaroid Corporation in Waltham, Massachusetts has surveyed almost 1.3 million of its square feet and begun upgrades. In general, T8 fluorescent lamps are being installed with electronic ballasts; compact fluorescents are replacing incandescents; mercury vapor lamps are giving way to high-pressure sodium lamps; and some occupancy sensors are being installed.

SELECTED GREEN LIGHTS MATERIALS
(*Available only to program participants)

Green Lights produces several information and promotional products.

Video: A general overview of the program as well as a section on the program's more technical aspects.

Brochure: A general overview of the program.

Light Briefs: Technical product-description flyers for the layperson; these cover such topics as electronic ballasts, energy-efficient lamps, occupancy sensors, reflectors, disposal of lighting products, and financing options.

Financing Database: Diskette containing a database of funding sources from utilities, energy-service companies, and government sources.

Update Newsletters: Monthly newsletters distributed to all program participants, designed to provide the latest information on all aspects of the program.

Slide Show: A 46-slide presentation with annotations; describes the Green Lights program in detail.

Camera-ready Logos: Color and black-and-white versions of the Green Lights logo, distributed for participants' use in their own printed materials.

Buttons: Imprinted with the color Green Lights logo.

Window Decals: Stickers imprinted with the color logo.

U.S. EPA GREEN LIGHTS PROGRAM
Prospective Partner Information Form

In order to continue with the next step in participating in Green Lights, please complete the information below, and fax or mail this form to:

U.S. EPA
Green Lights Program 6202J
401 M Street, SW
Washington, D.C. 20460
Fax: (202) 775-6680

Please call the Green Lights Hotline at (202) 775-6650 with questions.

NAME _____

TITLE _____

OFFICIAL ORGANIZATION NAME _____

ADDRESS _____

CITY, STATE, ZIP _____

TELEPHONE _____ FAX _____

- Type of business or government organization:

- Approximate number of employees:

- Approximate number of facilities:

- Approximate square footage of all U.S. facilities:

- Location of corporate headquarters:

- How did you hear about Green Lights?:

Do you have questions about Green Lights? Please describe below:

MOST FREQUENTLY ASKED QUESTIONS ABOUT THE EPA GREEN LIGHTS PROGRAM

1) **Q:** While considering the MOU, may we speak with current participants in the program?

    A: Yes, prospective Partners may call the Green Lights Hotline at (202) 775–6650. We can put you in touch with any participants with whom you are interested in speaking.

2) **Q:** If we are already in our local utility's program, why should we join Green Lights?

    A: Most utilities are running programs that will run complementary to ours and Green Lights is designed to work well with utility rebate programs. Green Lights will provide your organization with national as well as regional recognition for its pollution-prevention efforts.

3) **Q:** We are a highly decentralized organization. Can't we just sign up a couple of our divisions or subsidiaries?

    A: The EPA encourages corporations to join Green Lights as a whole. However, subsidiaries and divisions that have control over their facilities, budget, and have their own management structure and president, may become Partners independent of their parent corporation.

4) **Q:** How will the EPA ensure that participants do the upgrades?

    A: Participants report on an annual basis to EPA. EPA expects Green Lights participants to complete the surveys and upgrades in the agreed timeframe, but recognizes that unforeseen events might prevent an organization from fulfilling its entire obligation to Green Lights.

    The Green Lights MOU is an entirely voluntary, good-faith agreement. Both the EPA and the Partner organization may terminate the agreement at any time, for any reason.

5) **Q:** What if we just upgraded our lighting? Are we also responsible for facilities under construction?

    A: EPA wants to recognize those corporations that have already successfully upgraded their facilities. If your organization can document the recent upgrade to demonstrate that it meets the Green Lights standard, then you are not obligated to survey the space until 5 years hence. [If the space does not appear to meet the Green Lights standard, the EPA asks you to treat it like normal, owned space by surveying the upgrading where profitable.]

In working with current participants, however, the EPA has learned that lighting upgrades often don't capture all the available energy savings, and that further investment will yield even greater profitability on the overall project.

New construction is subject to Green Lights standards as well. Partners agree to design all their new facilities in accordance with lighting energy standards as outlined and defined in the MOU.

6)   **Q:**   Is this program a major administrative burden on organizations?

      A: Some participants have found it necessary to add or redirect staff to manage the Green Lights implementation effort. This only enhances the success of the upgrades. Of course, the Green Lights profitability calculations account for these administrative costs.

7)   **Q:**   What if my organization cannot and does not want to finance the lighting upgrades "on budget"? Are there financing alternatives?

      A: Green Lights provides an updated Financing Directory that includes all known utility rebates and incentives, and sources of "third-party" and "shared-savings" capital where outside firms cover up-front costs of upgrades. We continue to look for ways to make the capital investment more attractive and easier.

8)   **Q:**   Do Partners have to document their progress?

      A: The MOU requires Partners to document their progress annually on reporting forms provided by the EPA. However, Partners are strongly encouraged to document and report their progress on an ongoing basis as the upgrades are completed.

9)   **Q:**   Why is the Hurdle Rate Prime + 6 percent?

      A: The hurdle rate is a floor to ensure profitability. Partners maximize energy savings while maintaining at least prime rate + 6 percentage points internal rate of return. Actually, many Green Lights participants have experienced 30 percent average returns through upgrades.

Prime + 6 percent is justified further by the low-risk nature of the lighting upgrade project.

10) Q: In the past, our lighting upgrades have been unsuccessful. Should we expect the same type of equipment failure when we join Green Lights?

A: No, there have been vast improvements in lighting technology in the past decade that have helped to maximize the technology risk of a lighting upgrade investment. The EPA also provides Partners with access to the National Lighting Information Program (NLPIP), which is an objective source of name-brand product information.

11) Q: What happens if we merge with, or are bought out by another company?

A: If your organization purchases another company, then that company would also be included in the commitment to Green Lights. However, if your organization is "bought out," your new parent company is not obligated to join Green Lights automatically. Ideally, your company would set an example in environmental leadership for its new parent company that would encourage the parent to join Green Lights.

12) Q: What about our leased space?

A: Participants do not need to survey/upgrade space held under a short-term lease agreement (fewer than 5 years.) Long-term leased space (over 5 years) should be treated like wholly-owned space, with the following considerations:

If the utility costs are paid separately by your organization, survey and upgrade the facility with the cooperation of the landlord.

If the landlord doesn't cooperate, provide the EPA with an opportunity to communicate the benefits of participation in Green Lights.

If utility costs are rolled into the monthly rental payment, participants are not required to survey or upgrade the space unless the landlord passes the energy savings on to your organization.

If a participant's facilities are primarily or entirely leased space, you must upgrade, at a minimum, 25 percent of the square footage, regardless of the length of the lease.

13) **Q:** What kind of public recognition does the EPA provide to Partners?

A: EPA encourages and places news stories in major newspapers on the collective behalf of Program participants. Similarly, the EPA places Green Lights public service advertisements and special supplements in trade publications, environmental magazines, and business magazines. Finally, by distributing ready-to-use Green Lights materials, the EPA encourages participants to publicize the Program on their own.

GREEN LIGHTS
FAX-A-QUESTION

FAX: (202) 775–6680

Do you have a question about EPA's Green Lights? Write or type your question in the space below, fax it to the Green Lights number above, and we will fax you an answer.

_____

_____

_____

_____

_____

_____

_____

_____

_____

_____

_____

_____

Your Name: _____ Phone: _____

Organization: _____

Address: _____

City, State, Zip: _____

Fax: _____ Date: _____

INDEX